FANTASTIC!
He Loves Me

by
Fr. Patrick A. Martin

Why am I blind?
Why can't I go to school?
Why am I different?
I can't be a priest?
What can I do with my life?
Is there anything in life for me?

Ave Maria Place
"Speaking God's Love to a Broken World"
P.O. Box 16
Stafford Springs, CT 06076
(860) 684-7409

Published by
Ave Maria Place
P.O. Box 16
Stafford Springs, CT 06076
Telephone (860) 684-7409
Email: amhouse@snet.net

Library of Congress Catalog Card Number 97-74574

Printed in the United States of America
First English Printing - April, 1984: 10,000
Second English Printing - February, 1986: 10,000
Third English Printing - April, 1990: 10,000
Fourth English Printing - November, 1994: 10,000
Fifth English Printing - September, 1997: 10,000
Sixth English Printing - November, 2000: 10,000

First Chinese Edition - April, 1994: 1,500
For information contact: Fr. Joseph Huang, S.J., Faculty of Theology, Fujen Catholic University Press, Hsinchuang, Taipei Hsien (242), Taiwan, Republic of China.

"FANTASTIC! He Loves Me" is also available on recorded cassettes from Ave Maria Place.

Cover design compliments of Bert Fafard, Boston, MA, USA
Cover photo compliments of Rene Louvat, Burlington, Ontario, Canada

Table of Contents

Page

FOREWORD
ACKNOWLEDGEMENTS
Chapter
1	"There is no hope..."	1
2	"I see an airplane..."	7
3	"What are you going to do...?"	17
4	"You could have gotten killed out there..."	25
5	"Take as much time as you need..."	35
6	"Run, Brother, run...!"	43
7	"Are you still there...?	51
8	"Patrick, you have to call your mother..."	57
9	"You've got nothing to lose..."	61
10	"You know what you were hired for..."	68
11	"Couldn't you do both...?"	77
12	"Free...free to say 'yes'..."	94
13	"We love you..."	98
14	"Why didn't you ask us...?"	112
15	"A new nation I will give you..."	122
16	"He was born this way that the works of God might show through him..."	133
17	"Dear Brother..."	139
18	"He loves me..."	155
19	"Who needs Mary...?"	171
20	"A wild canary..."	179

Letters from the Spirit of the Handicapped:
See pages IX, 56, 120, 147, 189 and 196.

to
my dear mother
Amanda

and

to
our dear mother
Mary

Foreword

Father Patrick Martin is an apostle, in touch with God – on fire with the Good News – in love with people.

For him the handicap of blindness is a gift of God that makes him an extraordinary person of very special vision.

His faith and ministry are a source of hope and consolation to all the handicapped that he serves in the Lord's name and welcomes as very special brothers and sisters.

I am happy that this courageous story is now in print. I am sure that it will lead all who read it to a deeper understanding of how God has "gifted" His handicapped people.

God bless all who made this story possible and may God continue to bless Father Pat and the great work he does for His people.

Daniel P. Reilly

Bishop of Norwich

More thanks are owed for the completion of this book than are possible to give in an encyclopedia of books! Those who helped me, with their undying love, their example and their own stories, to "live this story" are owed a debt of thanks that will last through eternity — my mother, who was the first to read my manuscript, and without whose loving encouragement, and "staying up all night" reading, this story would never have been published, my father, my brothers and sisters; the nurses and doctors who cared for me and believed in the possibility of my life; the Brothers of Christian Instruction and more specifically, Brother Francis Blouin; Howard Haycraft of Wilson Library Foundation and Fr. James Kortendick and Dr. Elizabeth Stone and all at the Catholic University of America Library School who were so instrumental in my calling to the handicapped; Charlotte Harrison and the entire staff of the New York Public Library's branch for the blind and physically handicapped; the Hoppers of Stuyvesant Town, New York City, and all the families and friends of the handicapped who became my family and friends; all the FANTASTIC couples, priests, brothers and sisters of the Marriage Encounter Movement which turned my life around and helped me to believe in the gift of "me"; Mrs. Mary Y. Parr, my "New York City Momma" and the director of the Library School at St. John's University, and all the staffs of the library schools and various agencies that I have been so privileged to work with these past dozen years as an "apostle of the handicapped"; the priests, sisters, lay faculty and students of the seminary program in the Theology Department at St. John's University, New York, who prepared me academically and spiritually for the dream of serving the handicapped as a priest; and, of course, the Most Reverend Daniel P. Reilly, Bishop of the Diocese of Norwich, who seems at times to believe in my calling to serve my handicapped brothers and sisters more than I do, and who made the calling to serve them as a priest *a dream come true;* the priests, religious brothers and sisters, and all the people of the Diocese of Norwich who have made their diocese "my home"; all the volunteers, staff, and loving benefactors who have given so much over the years, each in his/her own beautiful way, to nurture and guide the Office of Ministry of the Handicapped to what it is today; and finally, and probably most importantly, my brother and sister handicapped persons all over the United States and Canada who have accepted and loved me as their brother, who have dared to need me to be their brother, and who, in a very real way, have called me to be their priest! *Thank You! Thank You! Thank You!*

And, more specifically with regard to this book I want to say a very deep, sincere thank you to all those who for the past fifteen years have been challenging me to sit down and write "my story". There was my college journalism teacher, Mr. Jack DeLong of Canton, Ohio, who "bribed" me into writing it as my "final feature story" for the course; there was Mrs. Eaton, Personnel Office, Manhattan Borough, The New York Public Library, who all but *demanded* one day that it be written for the *New York Daily News* "so it can help others"! And then there was Father Joe Nevill of the Fordham Charismatic Prayer Community who said so forcefully one night after the "Brother Francis Story", "Pat, you've got to write a book; God's gifts to us must be shared with others!" Mrs. Alice Long, of Jamaica, New York City, whose sister-in-law, Carol, had given me my first Chalice, offered to type the book if I ever got it done on cassettes; when Don Zirkel of the *Brooklyn Tablet*, the diocesan newspaper, had interviewed me for several hours the next day, she had typed the cassettes, hoping — in vain — that something would be published from it. My volunteer secretary at the Hickory Street office in Norwich, Mrs. Arlene Neunier, practically begged me to work on the book that summer that "the hernia disappeared"; the Buechlers of Groton, the Croteaus at the Cape, and the countless other families who gave me a room at times "to work on the book"; Fr. Ellis Zimmer and the FANTASTIC Franciscans and staff at Monte Alverno Retreat House, in Appleton, Wisconsin, who gave me room and board and a week of spiritual renewal in the fall of 1980 so that I might then profitably begin work on the volume you now hold in your hands, and the countless numbers of people — friends and strangers — who have read and proofread its various chapters these past two years as they've rolled out of my typewriter, are all owed more thanks than I could ever add up!

And, a very special thanks has to go to Father George Murtagh and all the FANTASTIC staff and people of St. Ambrose's Parish in Bristol, Vermont, who have given me haven these past ten days so I might finally *finish the book!*

My thanks, also must go to Don James, "The Spirit of the Handicapped" for editing this book for me.

A final word of thanks must go, very appropriately, to a "broken person" who in the midst of her own personal and family brokenness heard "my story" from the pulpit of her Church one Sunday morning in early December, 1979. She immediately wrote and asked to buy four copies of "my story" as gifts for her family that Christmas"...that's presuming it's published," she said in her letter, "and just in case it isn't may I be so bold as to ask *why not?* and *is there anything I can do to help get it published?*" She certainly did help — taking all the piles of manuscript starts that I had collected for fifteen years and combining them, line by line, into one volume, then interviewing me day after day for long hours at a time over the period of a full year seeking to put "the whole story" together, and then producing the outline from which this volume has been prepared! She even recorded the outline "so I could read it!" At Monte Alverno in 1980, as I began to listen to the outline tape I smiled as I noted that she had added a few words at the beginning. "Dear Father Pat," her note began,

"Remember the story about the little canary who perched on St. Francis's window sill? He sang and carried on with such enthusiasm that St. Francis completely forgot about his worries! When the bird had flown away St. Francis knew that he had experienced what all men should see and hear, that is, that he should sing and praise his Lord with such abandon that whoever would hear him would forget himself completely, if even for a short time. It meant to him a brief glimpse of the freedom of Paradise, and it meant being as available as is a bird on everyone's window sill! I pray that your work on this book may accomplish just that, that you may give your readers a short time in which to forget themselves while you sing and praise the Lord with your story!"

She "signed" the note on tape saying only "Jeanne"! "Jeanne, thank you". And my prayer, Jeanne, is simply that because of all your work and all the work of those who came before you on this book, may *Your Prayer* be answered!

THANK YOU!!!!

It is now April of 1983. As this now edited manuscript is presented to the publishers another very necessary "thank you" is obvious. Our "Spirit of the Handicapped" and his writer-friend, Donald P. James, Sr. of Norwich, Connecticut, gave me the final push that I needed to ready the manuscript for me, but also left the beautiful "letters from our Spirit" to go to press along with the manuscript. "Thank you" just seems too small for such a precious gift.

As of this date, April 5, 1983, the 17-year-old battle to get "my story" into print is finally over! I surrender these pages into the hands of a very dear friend, Mrs. Elizabeth Beebe of Cheboygan, Michigan, who has offered so graciously to prepare the final copy for publication. Thank you "Mamma" Beebe...and thank you all.

Father Pat

Dear Brother,

Have you, during the past few years ever had the crawly feeling that someone or something is constantly looking over your shoulder? Have you ever gotten all goose-bumps because you feel that there is someone in the room with you, watching your every move and listening to your every word? And, no matter how quick you look or no matter how hard you listen, you are never able to see or hear that someone or something. Do you ever feel that your very thoughts are being transmitted or perhaps stolen from you, before you can even put them into words...someone or something has moved in and picked them right out of space?

Relax, Patrick, it is only me and I have been doing it for quite some time. Ever since I first had the good fortune, or was it bad...whatever, ever since I first met you, I have studied you from all angles. I have always wanted to know much more about you...more than I hear people talk about. I have always wondered about where you came from when you entered my existance. I have thought, why is he the way that he is? Why is he blind...why does he walk like a sailor on shoreleave after many months at sea? Why do you work so incessantly at your vocation? Why do you consider that your handicap is a blessing...a gift?

Oh, Patrick, I have had so many questions...and I have never summoned up the courage to ask for the answers. My friend, who shares most of my thoughts, tells me that it is none of my business, keep my nose out of your affairs. He says that I should not ask a lot of questions, that I should accept you just as you are, on any given day or at any given time, all that other stuff does not matter. Easy for him to say, he knows much more than I do about you. But, he can't keep me from wondering, can he?

I really figured that I would never get all of the answers I want...until one day recently, I was alone in the barn at Wauregan. That was the day I stumbled onto your manuscript...your story from childhood until the present time. What a gold mine of information about you, I hope you don't mind my reading it. And, Patrick, would you care if I wrote a few lines now and again, telling you of your story's effects on me and how I think it may affect those who are fortunate enough to read it? Good or bad, Patrick, you know me.

I am sure that you won't care, although my friend reiterates that it is your story, your life, your business and your affairs...but they are all mine too, Patrick, after all when I made your dream mine, I took on all the rest too, didn't I?

So I shall read your story, make my judgement of it and share my comments with you...is that alright? If it isn't, I'll proceed anyway, you know that I am rather headstrong and inclined to have my own way about things like this. My friend will suffer and fume at me, but I know that he will transmit my words to paper as he has done in the past...and you can do with them what you will.

With the peace and love of the great I AM,

The Spirit of the Handicapped

"There is no hope..."

I don't know his name. I can't even remember his face, probably because I really couldn't see it. He was a minister from one of the churches in Caribou, Maine, where I was in the hospital. He had come to see a girl across the hall from me and he stopped in to see me too. He had something in his hand but I couldn't make out what it was until he brought it very close, a plastic jack-o-lantern with a light inside!

It was a Halloween night, October 31st, 1953, and it's the first night that I can recall in my whole life even though I was nine and a half years old at the time! The meningitis that had plunged me into the hospital more than three months earlier stole my memory as it attempted to take my life. I never realized that memory loss until months, years? later; that little act of kindness from a stranger somewhat immortalized the day that I now look back to as the first date I can "remember" in my whole life – my "birthday?"

"Your son is very sick" the family doctor had told my parents as he examined me on July 25th, 1953, a hot summer day that just happened to be their 31st Wedding Anniversary. "He has tuberculosis. Don't ask us where he got it or how he got it. Just rush him to the hospital in Caribou, and...don't ask us for a cure. There really is no hope."

With that, they tell me, I was bundled up and rushed to Carey Memorial Hospital in the neighboring town since our own home town, Limestone, had no hospital. I was placed in a private room with full-time nursing care, but with no hope whatever of survival. I know absolutely nothing of that time in my life – or anything before it – except what people have told me. They say I complained of severe headaches...and total darkness in my bright hospital room. My brothers and sisters tell me how they all had to undergo tests immediately to be sure that the tuberculosis that now threatened my life wasn't also doing its havoc elsewhere. No traces of it were found, however, and the doctors just shook their heads whenever questions were asked of them. "No, we just don't know...we just don't know..." And for months they continued to shake their heads and wonder...why had I gotten sick? Why was I still alive? What was I holding onto? Why hadn't I died yet?

Carey Memorial Hospital was about a half-hour drive from my home in Limestone, Maine, in the heart of Maine's "potato country", Aroostook County. My Dad, a self-taught carpenter/cabinet maker, with several of my older brothers, had built the house the family now lived in a few years before I was born. The white frame house on Van Buren Street sat on a quarter-acre lot about a half mile from the center of town and about a mile from church and school. After working full, long days Dad would come home to supper, I'm told, and then he and a couple of my brothers would go down to the "new house" and work on it late into the night by lantern light. They built a simple, two-story home with 4 bedrooms upstairs, kitchen, dining room and living room downstairs. Open porches were built on three sides of the house and a garage was later attached on one side. Cement foundation walls enclosed a large cellar which, together with the garage, served as Dad's shop. Nine cords of wood and a few barrels of coal could be snugly packed into the cellar as the year's fuel.

I was the third or fourth child to be born in that house, but the seventeenth child in the family. Eventually we were twenty-two children in all, eleven boys and eleven girls; I was the baby of the boys. Seven of my brothers and sister died in the infancy stages of their lives of childhood diseases we rarely speak of today. One brother was married and already had a child of his own when he died of kidney trouble while in the Army. I don't really remember any of those who died since it all happened before 1953. At the time of my hospitalization there were eleven of us kids still at home. The open porches around the house had gradually all been closed in making available the needed extra rooms.

The symptoms of the on-coming meningitis in the summer of 1953 are as lost to my memory as all the other childhood experiences prior to that year's Halloween night. Several of my brothers and sisters tell me that they seemed to notice something when I didn't want to come out and play those latter days of July. "Mom," they'd say, "Patrick just sits on the steps and does nothing." My older brother, Gerard, says he knew something was up, though. He had a job mowing the grass in the church cemetery. While helping him I began to cry of a bad headache, he says, so he brought me home. The doctor's visit...the trip to the hospital...treatments...pain...they're all gone for me, but not for the rest. Every once in a while a word or a comment tells me of a deep love and a deep concern that they all had that soon their son, their little brother, might...die.

A good many years before my illness a salesman had come to the house one day displaying a beautiful three-foot high crucifix. Mom fell in love with it immediately but knew we couldn't afford it so she let it go. That night Daddy came home from the potato storage house where he was working and he handed her a package wrapped in brown meat wrapping paper. Every now and then he would buy a piece of meat, etc. on his way home so Mom wasn't too surprised when he handed her the meat-wrapped package this time. She cried, though, when she unveiled the same beautiful crucifix she had turned down earlier that day! That crucifix had the prize spot on our living room wall, and, I'm told, that spot became a rather important and much-frequented spot those five months while I lay in the hospital. If it wasn't Mom and Dad or either one of them, then it was one or several of my brothers and sisters who knelt in front of it and prayed for me. Aunts and uncles, cousins, friends...all were asked to stop and say a prayer for me.

Caribou was about a half hour from home. Mom couldn't drive and Daddy had to keep up his work. How they ever got to the hospital as often as they did only the Good Lord knows! Mom loves to tell how she'd "grab every ride she could to get there". And she always seemed to be there. Day after day, week after week, month after month...the reports were all the same..."he's no better...a little worse...the end should be soon...what's he holding on to?..." But they kept coming, hoping. And they'd return to the crucifix and redouble their prayers.

School started up again in August of 1953 and my seat in the fourth grade classroom was left empty. Schools in Aroostook County began in mid-August each year because of the potato-harvesting season which came in late September or early October and lasted for several weeks. School would then shut down to permit the students to aid in the harvesting. When harvest time began in 1953 Mom was still finding rides to the hospital and the news was still pretty much the same: "he'll go any day now." Everyone waited whenever she or another visitor returned; any news? but no, it was always still the same, or a little bit worse today. And prayers went on...A child's immaturity doesn't permit the recognition of sacrificial love but my eyes fill up tonight as I write these pages some twenty-seven years later.

Some time in November of that year a bit of a change for the better seemed noticeable – or was it wished? Hope was guarded, very guarded at first. Was it perhaps but the final flutter before the flame would go out? The flutter continued. Mom came home with guarded but *good* news. Prayers continued. By Thanksgiving Day things really seemed to be looking up. A bed was even prepared at home for my return. But, no, that couln't be just yet, the doctors cautioned. They weren't exactly sure *why I was getting better* or if the trend would continue! I was well enough, though, to want to go home and well enough to miss everyone at home. I loved it those Sunday afternoons when Mom and Daddy would bring those who

3

were too young to come into the hospital. Daddy would lift them as high as he could outside my window. That made me want to go home even more. And I was getting well enough, too, to hate all the medicine and needles! I dreaded that early-morning penicillin shot but I think I hated the one every night even more! But the shots and the medicines and tests went on and on, and the doctor wouldn't even talk about "going home"!

By early December "they" were letting me out of bed almost every day. I couldn't walk but they'd sit me up in the big chair in my room and it felt so good just to be out of bed! How much they at home must have prized each one of these "giant steps forward"! I remember the day when Daddy — who, in addition to being carpenter, cabinet-maker, plumber, electrician, and everything else we needed him to be, was also our barber — brought his clippers and gave me my first hospital haircut. Boy, did it feel neat! It was just a few days after that haircut when Mom came into the hospital with my Aunt Maggie for what was by now a routine visit. As she walked into my room, however, she was sure "it was the end". There was blood on my sheets but the bed was empty. "I went half crazy," she told me years later. As the nurse calmed and reassured her, she told her how I had fallen backwards while being helped back into bed that afternoon, how I had hit my head on the corner of the hospital room dresser, but that I was alright and would soon be back in my room. As the nurse finished her explanation I was wheeled in with a white headband, a lot of screams, but no other serious repercussions.

December was fast rolling by that year and I really began to panic that "they" wouldn't let me go home for Christmas, but my fears were soon put to rest when my doctor announced that yes, the weekend before Christmas I could go home! I don't think I slept at all Saturday night. My Aunt Phoebe and Uncle Ken brought Mom and Dad with their car to pick me up Sunday afternoon. They packed all my stuff, and believe me, after the spoiling I got in the hospital there was a truck-load of it! The car was packed. It was a warm, sunny December afternoon, quite unusual for northern Maine in that there was absolutely no snow on the ground. The doctor still had not arrived to discharge me so we waited. He still didn't come. Finally, the nurse went out to call him. What was taking him so long? I wished he'd hurry up. I was already to go, all dressed in *real* clothes — no johnny, real underwear, shoes and socks, grey pants, white shirt...The nurse walked in...it wasn't good news, I just knew it! The doctor thought it was too damp outside, she said. He said I should wait to go home tomorrow. He'd come in *first thing in the morning,* she promised for him, give me my physical, discharge me, and then I could go home. That was a promise. I didn't want promises. I wanted to go home! I cried. I wanted to go home! After spending much time trying to console a broken-hearted child, Mom and Daddy and Uncle Ken and Aunt Phoebe left. The nurse took me down to the kitchen "to find some ice cream" and I wondered if I'd ever be able to go home. Somehow, I must have fallen asleep that night. I remember that I insisted on sleeping in my underwear – no johnnies for me! The morning nurse woke me up for that shot and thought she'd cheer me up with the weather report. It was really beautiful out, she said. We'll have a white Christmas after all! I panicked beyond all telling. Now, with snow on the ground, I'll never get out of here! If it was too damp yesterday and there wasn't any snow, today's got to be even worse! The doctor kept the promise he had made through the previous afternoon's nurse. He showed up early that morning, gave me my physical, and told me I could go home! I couldn't believe my ears! I didn't know whether to laugh or cry. I think I did both – at the same time!

A lot of people were there for good-byes when discharge moment actually arrived. There was the nurse who had been like a mother to me those five months, and her husband; there was the policeman who had given blood several times for me; the whole hospital administration and staff; the doctors and nurses...They were as excited as I was happy. They couldn't believe this day actually had arrived; they had been so sure it never would. Dad and my brother Philip, had driven over to pick me up in our red International pick-up. They rolled me up in a woolen blanket and carried me out amid all the "good-bye's" and "Merry Christmas's". A snowflake hit my nose as I was carried out...I hadn't been outdoors in so long! I don't remember who carried me out, Dad or Phil, but they sat me up between them and off we drove in the snowstorm! I was going home!

Only bits and pieces of those first days back home come back to memory now. They were exciting days...a huge snow storm outside...my brothers out shoveling...I wasn't allowed to go outside at all that winter...a price tag for going home that had seemed "well worth it" while I was still in the hospital...I slept in the living room because I couldn't climb the steps to get upstairs...a nurse came every day for my penicillin shot, *but just once a day now!*...a lot of relatives and friends of the family kept coming in those days to see me...Mom and Daddy sounded so pleased as they'd "show me off"...A fear lurked somewhere in the back of my head that I had been allowed to come home only for Christmas and I'd have to go back to the hospital right after...Even to my child's mind there's no

5

doubt that the biggest Christmas gift that year was *my being home!*

2

"I see an airplane..."

On leaving Carey Memorial Hospital after just three days short of a five-month stay there, I could not walk at all and I could barely see anything in front of me. During that long battle with the meningitis I am sure that the possibility and then the actuality of these resulting "handicaps" affected my family an awful lot more than me at first. It was they who had been plagued with that awful fear that I might never leave that hospital alive. It was they who for months had listened to my complaints about the darkness of my bright hospital room and had wondered if I would ever see again if I did survive the battle. It was they who "knew" that I couldn't walk when I left the hospital on December 22, 1953.

As for me, I don't think I ever "knew" I was handicapped, I don't think I ever "knew" I *couldn't* walk until the day I *wanted to walk!* How well I still recall that "tinker toy" experience of that first Christmas morning back home. We had risen early that morning and excitedly opened all our presents from Santa Claus. After awhile the house had been put back in order, somewhat at least, and everyone had gone to church. Only Mom or one of my sisters had stayed home to watch me. That was some Christmas. Two big cans of those much longed for "tinker toys" had been found *for me* under the Christmas tree that morning! I was in heaven! After all, I was home from the hospital with Mom and Daddy and my brothers and sisters and I had a whole pile of tinker toys! What more could I want? I was seated at a table in the living room attempting to build something in my tinker-toy heaven. Mom or my sister was busy in the kitchen preparing the things for Christmas dinner. I heard it roll. One of those absolutely essential red sticks of the tinker toy world went rolling off the table and onto the linoleum-covered living room floor. I wasn't about to lose a precious piece already and I certainly didn't want somebody else to come home and step on it, so off my chair I went and onto the floor to find it. I felt around and found the stick with no trouble at all, and...oh, wow, I couldn't get back up! I was shocked! I mean, I was almost ten years old! Why *couldn't I get up? Would I* **ever** be able to get up...and walk...by myself?

I don't really recall what happened next, if someone from the kitchen helped me up, if I hollered for help, if they came home from church and found me...but I've never forgotten the shock of discovering that I absolutely *couldn't* get up. The fun and excitement of being home, of Christmas day in a big family, of new games and toys...didn't leave me too much time to dwell on the discovery, however. It was quickly pushed into the background by all the excitement. Each night as I lay on my cot in the living room I'd get all excited all over again as I'd realize "I'm *really* home!"

When I first came home from the hospital, Mom would prepare my meal on a tray and someone would set it up in front of me wherever I might happen to be at the time. That didn't last too long, however. A place was soon made for me at the family table in the dining room and I found myself being helped along to my place each meal time. And thus began my "home therapy" program. Going to and from meals was as much fun as eating them. One or several of the family would hold me up and encourage my feet to take the right steps. As I seemed to get a little stronger as time passed the "therapy" was stepped up. My youngest sister had gotten a red and white tricycle for Christmas and Daddy soon had me sitting on that, pushing the peddles and holding on for dear life, while he or someone else held me from behind. I was sort of big as a ten-year-old for the tricycle; it skinned the knees a bit but seemed to accomplish what they were after so the "therapy" continued. It wasn't too long before I was able to "graduate" to the upstairs sleeping quarters. Beds were rearranged to make a place for me and that added steps to my therapy program. At night and in the morning when we were alone several of my brothers and sisters would do their own part of the program. A couple would hold me up and a couple would stand in front of me. How many steps could I take before they'd have to reach out and catch me?

Our family doctor made quite frequent visits to the house those days and weeks after my return home. He had given up on me ever recovering at all and so Mom and Daddy had hired another doctor while I was in the hospital. Now he began making regular visits to our house. One evening, after I had been home for a few weeks or a month, he stopped in to see me again. He, sitting in one corner of the living room, Dad in the other, "let's try, Patrick," Dad said, and, feebly but definitely, I walked from one to the other. The doctor's amazement was unbounded. He'd scratch his head and watch in silence while his face, I'm told, expressed volumes!

Discovering my "blindness' was very much like the discovery of my inability to walk those days after my return home. I had enough vision, upon my leaving the hospital, that I could see obstacles in front of me and if they were held close enough I might even be able to make out what they were. Touch, smell, and hearing I used quite naturally to compensate without really realizing I was doing so. *I never remembered what it was like to see "normally" so it would be* difficult to say I missed it terribly, if at all, until I experienced a need for more vision than I had. The day I realized that there were things I could not do because of my "poor eyesight"; the day I became aware that my "poor eyesight" might close doors in life to me; the day my "poor eyesight" caused an accident or embarrassing situation...those were the days when I began to be aware that I was "handicapped." And I grew to fear and hate the whole situation!

Staying indoors and staying at home those first few days and weeks of 1954 weren't heavy burdens, until I began to get well enough and strong enough to want to go out. I soon got bored with the chest full of toys and the various rooms of the house. The daily, and then three-times-weekly, penicillin shots became more and more of a nuisance. We had a regular routine in the family for work and school departures. Mom and Daddy were always up early. Those winter mornings the sound of Dad throwing logs or shoveling coal into the furnace was the best sound of all. You knew after you heard that, that it wouldn't be too long before the heat would find its way up through the floor registers. The boys would get up first, get washed up, have breakfast, take their school books and brown-bag lunch that Mom had all ready for them, and off they'd go. They'd usually leave the house by 6:30 a.m. to get to church, about a mile away, for the daily 7:00 a.m. Mass. All of my brothers had been altar boys, Mass servers, at church, and the Pastor came to rely on the fact that he'd always have a Martin boy there if the scheduled server couldn't show up. From Mass each morning, they'd walk the short hike to school. Daddy would usually leave for work either just before the boys left for church or about the same time. If the weather was really bad he'd try to arrange his leaving to give them a ride to church.

Before leaving for church, one of the boys each morning would run upstairs to wake up the girls for Mom. Now it was their turn for the bathroom and breakfast, and before they left for school on the 8:00 bus they usually had all of the morning dishes and the housework done for Mom. While there were still little ones at home we'd usually be up, washed and dressed before they left for school too. That freed Mom for the laundry, the ironing, the sewing, the baking and cooking, the big cleaning, the canning, jam and jelly making, and the million other tasks that went hand in hand with a large family, not to mention her keeping an eye on those "little ones" still at home!

As winter moved into spring and my walking got better and better, I began to ask more and more, "why can't I go to school, too?" When I couldn't walk it was easier to accept that I couldn't go , but now I *could walk,* so why *couldn't I go?* I didn't count the number of times I bumped into them, the number of times I stepped on their toes or bumped into a door or chair, etc. Those things were just "normal" for me. I never remembered *not* doing them. And besides, I managed to live with them so why couldn't I go to school? It became harder and harder to watch that school bus leaving every morning without me on it.

Mom and Daddy began asking our doctor my question when they saw him each week or so, "Doctor, what about school?" I'd listen intently whenever I was with them and the question was brought up but I never seemed to hear anything that sounded "good". There seemed to be some talk about a school for blind kids. I never let myself think too much about that, though. I knew there was no such school in our town and that would mean going away from home...I just wanted to go to school with my brothers and sisters. Finally, arrangements were made for some doctors to look at me. There were many trips over the next months, sometimes to one doctor, sometimes to whole groups of doctors. Sometimes they'd just want to look at my eyes and sometimes they'd want to look at all of me. They'd make me walk for them, bend down, stand up, on one foot, on the other, look this way, look that way. I loved the trips, usually with Mom and Daddy, but sometimes with Mom alone. One time we even took the train to Bangor, Maine, about two hundred miles from home. I'd get so excited as the eye doctors would try the glasses on me; secretly I'd pray, "Please let this one work!" But every lens he put in was either worse than the one before or at least no better.

As he'd seem to come to the end of his supply I'd pray that maybe he'll find another set with "the right one" in it. But he never did. I'd wait in the waiting room while the specialist talked to Mom and Daddy and I could usually tell by the conversation going home that there wasn't any good news. Then we'd get another letter in the mail; another trip, another doctor to visit. These visits and trips I learned later were arranged by the State. Our family doctor told us it was important to take them and do whatever they asked us because they'd help if any help was possible. So we made trip after trip, sometimes to the same doctor after a few months had passed. But the results were always the same. And more and more the talk I heard was about a school for the blind. In August of 1954, we were asked to make one more trip, this time four hundred miles from home, to Portland, Maine! Mom and Daddy and I drove all the way down in our pick-up truck. There wasn't much talk on the way home so I knew the results were still the same, not good. As best I can recall, it turned out, it was about two weeks after that long trip. It was a warm, late summer evening and some of us were out in the front yard playing. The family doctor had been called for my younger sister who had the summer flu. All of a sudden life stood still for all of us, you might say.

"An airplane! An airplane!" I yelled at the top of my lungs. *"I see an airplane!"* Loring Air Force Base with its huge B-52 jet bombers was just three miles from our house. It was a daily, sometimes hourly routine for the planes to take off and soar right over our house, all but clipping the trees and chimneys as they flew over. All that spring and summer of 1954, whenever the deafening racket of a plane overhead happened, I had searched and searched the sky above to see the plane, but even with people directing my head physically with their hands I had never seen an airplance since my return from the hospital. No one would believe I could see it this night. Mom and Daddy and the doctor practically got caught in the front doorway trying to squeeze out at the same time. They stood there, breathless, and three of them watching and not daring to believe they heard what their ears told them they were indeed hearing. Mom quickly took command of the situation. "Naw," she said. "You don't see an airplane. Where is it now?" hoping, wondering, hoping almost beyond all hope that I had really followed it across the horizon. Sure enough, I pointed excitedly to where the huge bird had travelled. I had never once taken my eyes off the sky. Mom began to cry and quite shameless, Daddy joined her with his own tears, tears of joy.

When the doctor had first arrived at the house he had noticed quite curiously that I was playing cards with one of my sisters on the porch steps. Now he said. "What happened to your cards? Did they take them away from you?"

"No," I said, and I got the deck of cards from my sister and handed it to him. He looked at the cards. "Can you see these?" he asked me. "Yes," I said, not thinking too much of his question. "What's this?" he asked and then proceeded to go through the entire deck of playing cards one at a time. As I named each card correctly, the look of amazement on his face had to be the same as what had been there that night after Christmas when he had watched me walk across the living room floor! Daddy had built a set of shelves for his office and the next night Mom and I went with him to the doctor's office to deliver them. The doctor had quite evidently been thinking all day of his experience of the evening before. "You know", he said to Mom and Daddy after the shelves were in place, "every doctor we've consulted has told us we don't know why he's alive today! Every vision specialist we've sent you to has verified that nothing can be done for his sight! It's very clear, he went on, that something *has been done!* If you had traveled to Lourdes or

Fatima or Ste. Anne De Beaupre or some faith healer somewhere we would have no choice but to admit you've got a miracle on your hands! But you didn't travel," he said, "and so we don't know what to say!" "Doctor," Mom responded in here own quick but calm way, "Can't miracles happen at home, too?" More trips to specialists were arranged. One of them, who had examined my vision before that fateful summer night, now exclaimed to his secretary, "Put this down in the books as a miracle!"

The school question was raised even stronger now that some of my vision had returned. Schools in Aroostook County had re-opened in mid-August and I had now missed an entire year of schooling. And no decision had yet been made as to when and where my educational process would be rebegin! A teacher in the Limestone Public School System had made it known to Mom and Daddy that she'd be willing to take me into her classroom and help me in any way that she could, if she would be allowed to do so by the town and school authorities.

There seems to have been a real fear on the part of some over my re-entry into the public schools because of my still "legal" blindness. My vision had returned sufficiently that I could use "large print" books and materials but the scope or width of my vision was extremely limited. Blindness is defined "legally" in terms of strength (acuity) or field of vision. A person for example, who cannot see at 20 feet with the best possible lens correctives what a "normally" sighted person can see at 200 feet distance is considered legally blind. Someone, on the other hand, who may indeed be able to see at 200 feet distance but has a visual field restricted to less than 20 degrees (as compared to the normal of 180 degrees) would also be considered "legally blind". The hesitation over my re-entry into the hometown schools was because of the still remaining great loss of visual field or "peripheral vision" as it is called. My area of vision was measured to be very much less than twenty degrees. The fact that I could see enough to read only about *one letter* at a time coupled with the fact that all of my reading materials would have to be in "large print" format certainly seemed a great barrier to my going to school in my home town. A decision was finally reached, however, in October of 1954, that with the State of Maine's Division of Eye Care and Special Services providing all needed special materials and the fourth-grade teacher who had offered accepting, I would be permitted to "try it out" in the Limestone Public Schools.

I think my brothers and sisters were more excited, or at least as excited, as I was on my first day back to school. They were so watchful over me on my way to school on the bus, into the building, down the corridor to my classroom. I can still hear my brother who's a year older than I am saying to his friends when I came out for recess, "See, I told you he was coming!"

I *loved* my fourth-grade teacher. She really made me feel good, and at home there at school. It must have been recess time when we arrived at the classroom so she and I stood and talked. "Do you remember your Roman numerals?" she asked. "Roman numerals?" I questioned. "you know," she prodded, "I, II, III..." "Oh yes," I said excitedly as I did indeed recall them. "Why don't you write them on the blackboard here as far as you can go?" she said, handing me a piece of chalk. I was excited as I stood on a chair so I could start at the top of the board and I proceeded to fill the entire front blackboard with the numerals from one to thirty-three! I had written them big enough for me to see!

From my very first day back at school I loved it. That fourth-grade teacher did all in her power, much beyond the call of duty, to help me succeed in school that year. Countless hours she spent copying over exercises in math or English so that I could see them. Much, very much of my previously attained academic learning had to be "recalled" and she took it as her challenge to "catch me up" with the rest of the class. When my textbooks were finally prepared by the State in large print she was always extra sensitive to my need for page numbers, etc. that differed from the regular texts. Homework that might prove impossible because of the visoin would be adapted for me without my even asking! When the State provided my classroom with a large-print typewriter for my use she made it her job to teach me to use it, teaching me to memorize key positions, etc. Due a great deal to her caring and dedication, I am sure, I fell in love with school that year and I succeeded academically without a problem. In fact, I'm told that the difference between my academic performance in the third grade and that of the fourth grade after my hospitalization was so marked that my parents at least jokingly questioned if they had brought "their kid" home from the hospital!

Toward the end of my fourth grade I began to wonder about the next year, a practice that unconsciously became quite habitual for me. Is next year's teacher going to be as understanding and helpful as this year's? Will I have to explain my condition? How? Will she believe me? At times I even wondered if I'd be able to succeed there without the help that I'd received from this year's teacher. Left on my own with a stranger who knew nothing about me, could I really succeed? I mean, this teacher knew me before I got here; she had wanted me to come. Who would my next year's teacher be?

My "central vision", as opposed to the missing "peripheral" or field vision, seems to have continued to improve over that year such that by my fifth grade my reading book, "Days and Deeds," was the only text that was prepared in large print for me. I was able to manage, letter by letter, with the normal print in other subjects. The transition to fifth-grade status was nowhere near the monstrous problem I had imagined it would be. By my sixth grade I needed none of my text books done over in large print and life for me had settled down quite nicely. My visual scope was still as severely restricted as before: I still read only a single letter at a time, followed a line across the page letter by letter, moved my eyes back, hunted for the next line and then began moving across again. I became quite adept at it and, really, I would have to say that at that particular time of my life my visual loss was much more of an inconvenience or an embarrassment at times than it was an outright barrier. Yes, it did mean that sports were out, but in our school they weren't required either. When the family played soft-ball in the cow pasture across the road from our house I was usually allowed to play to help even out the teams. They were always extra considerate, just as a matter of course, when I came up to bat. The pitcher would move up closer and *even aim at my bat!* Somebody was always there to help me run the bases *if I did hit it,* so I managed to be part of it most of the time. When they had enough players for a serious game then the "left-out" feeling might creep in but they usually took care of that for me by having me keep score.

The vision loss did sometimes in those years get me into awkward situations but even these were never major disasters! There was, for example, that proud Sunday morning in the spring of 1954 when I was finally allowed to go to church for the first time since my hospitalization! The family had grown quite accustomed to my knowing where steps and other obstacles were at home, so no one thought to point out the foot-high ropes protecting the lawns from walkers because of the spring-time muddiness. Everyone was excited as we all walked from the pick-up toward the church. I guess Mom and Daddy were telling some of our friends that it was my first time at church, when it happened...with my new grey pants I was kneeling *in the mud!* I hadn't seen the rope! Or, then, there was the time at home that Daddy had finished some work on the side of the house; someone was carrying away a left-over eight- or ten-foot long board; I saw the one carrying the board but didn't see the end of that board several feet away that wacked me across the head as he turned! I can still see Daddy sitting on the steps and roaring with laughter after he saw that I hadn't really been hurt, except in my pride. Again, that summer I was helping Daddy in the garden behind the house. He sent me for some tool. As I took off running he hollered after me, "Watch out for that rake!" "I see it, " I hollered back, and I had indeed seen the handle of the rake. What I did *not* see was the end of the rake that I stepped on! Well, when that rake handle came up and slapped me on the side of the head I wanted to laugh and cry at the same time!

There were some times during those years that my blindness began to hurt. "Hey, stuck up," a good friend of the family said one day, "I tooted the horn at you and waved and you acted like you didn't even know me!" That still bothers me even today at times when I am unable to recognize people who want/need to be recognized. I will never forget the morning I passed my own dear mother on the sidewalk in Norwich, Connecticut. I knew someone was there but couldn't really tell you who it was as I hurried by so I said simply "Good morning," and continued on my way. "Good morning," she responded in her own FANTASTIC humorous way! I was dumbfounded as I heard *her* voice come back at me. We still laugh over that "Good morning!"

Our home in Limestone was about a mile or so from school and so the small ones in the family always took the school bus to and from school. With older and younger brothers and sisters growing up together "imitation" was a way of life and that imitation produced a few very definite family "traditions". For example, as younger kids we carried our lunch to school every day in "dinner pails" as we called our lunch boxes, but when one reached that certain (unspecified but definitely known) age, he was permitted to "graduate" to a brown bag which was foldable when empty and thereby less cumbersome to hold onto! Another of those "family traditions" was the privilege of walking home from school instead of waiting for the school bus. Because the bus made so many stops and varied its route to be fair to all of its users, it sometimes meant our arriving home as much as an hour and a half or so after school had finished for the day. A good walker could make it in about 15 or 20 minutes! Walking home from school was one of the "grown up" privileges I really yearned for and was granted in due time. I began getting up early in the morning to walk to Mass with my brothers and even *alone* if they weren't there for one reason or another. I even became a Mass server again. That wasn't too difficult because I was able to memorize the altar boy's responses and the ceremonial movements and gestures of the Mass. I loved the grown-up feeling of leaving every morning as I had so often watched my older brothers do; how I had wondered if I'd ever be able to do that. Being free to leave school as soon as the bell rang and even beat the first bus home was really neat! I loved it. Now I was able to run errands for Mom, too. One day as I was walking

15

home from school I thought I recognized the green pick-up as it passed me, and sure enough, Dad was home when I got there just a couple minutes later. "He's gonna get himself killed one of these days" I heard him say to Mom as I came walking in. I knew by the way the conversation died that they were talking about me. My balance never returned completely after the meningitis so I weave quite naturally as I walk. I wondered – and feared – how long it would be before my "grown up" privilege would be taken away from me bacause of that weaving and/or the blindness. Every time I walked after that I treasured the privilege even more, and how careful I tried to be! I'd try to "walk a staight line" but always got extremely frustrated when after two or three steps I'd fall out of line! The conversation was never mentioned to me and the privilege was never taken away and how greatly I loved my Mom and Dad at that time for that gift!

3

"What are you going to do?"

One of the advantages (disadvantages?) of growing up one of the younger children in a large family is that you could look at the various stages of life that lay ahead of you before you had to enter them. I remember well seeing my older brother gradually grow more and more disinterested in our toys down in the cellar. One day as I played in my own world I wondered if I too would one day lose interest in these things that now filled the happiest moments of my days. I remember thinking to myself on that occasion, "If that's what 'growing up' is all about, then I don't want to grow up!"

Watching my older brothers and sisters graduate from high school and go off to work and/or married life made me both excited and quite frightened as I contemplated myself in their shoes. The glamor of graduation was most certainly exciting. Academically I knew I could do that. But then what? My blindness must have been quite a burden unconsciously at least at that time, because I recall vividly my musings about the avenues of life that I was sure would be closed to me! Looking at my brothers and sisters who were married, I'd wonder, "What girl would ever want to marry a blind guy? And even if she did, what could I ever do to support a family, let alone myself?" I knew I couldn't be a bus driver, a truck driver, or an airplane pilot. I had helped Daddy enough in the shop and had been clumsy enough at it to know that carpentry and cabinet making were out. Several of my brothers had gone to high school seminaries to see if they would like to be priests. That was one thing I was sure I could do, but our pastor stopped that dream cold in my eighth grade when he said to my parents one day, "You know, I'd pay Pat's way through the Seminary if they would accept him and he wanted to go; but he can't go because of the blindness."

In the spring of my eighth grade the State sent a counselor to my school to help me prepare my high school program. After talking with the principal of the junior high and myself he suggested that I plan to take a "college prep" program in high school. That would prepare me best, he suggested, for whatever I might wish to do after high school. And so, in the fall of 1959, at his suggestion, I entered the college preparatory program at Limestone High School. I enjoyed my freshman year thoroughly and even managed to get a straight-A report card for the whole year! It was during that freshman year that Mom, who was obviously concerned about my future, asked me one day, "Patrick, what do you want to be when

17

you finish high school?" I was very close to Mom, I guess quite understandably because of the illness, and so I found it very easy to talk with her.

Mom was the daughter of a Limestone farmer, Baptiste Parent, who still lived on the farm where she had been raised, several miles from our home. She had met Dad while he was working for her father and they had been married on July 25, 1922. They had given birth to twenty-two children. They had watched as seven of their children died in childhood years of diseases we hardly speak of anymore, and they had suffered more as they watched another son – twenty-two years old, married, and father of a child – die on Christmas Eve one year. During our growing-up years Mom seemed always to be there. In fact, the only time I remember her working outside the home those years was during the potato-seed cutting time when she and Dad would cut seed together for those few weeks to help the farmers get ready for spring planting. Mom loved to read and I used to love to sit and listen as she'd read to Dad at night after dishes were done. She always belonged to book clubs and read Daddy everything from Mark Twain to the Bible. Since we had no Catholic school in Limestone we attended religious instruction classes on Saturday mornings. Mom always saw to it that our lessons were learned, asking us the questions and hearing our answers over and over again until she was satisfied that we knew them. One of the neat things about walking home from school was that on certain days you could smell Mom's baking a couple houses away! She baked her own bread, rolls, pies, pastries, doughnuts – and she always remembered whose turn it was to get the potato from the doughnut grease. One of the wildest things that we all loved and hated about Mom was that you absolutely *could not surprise her!* Somehow she always could guess what the surprise was! I remember the day I went out shopping for a Mother's Day gift. I didn't know myself what I wanted to get her when I left the house so there's no way that she or anyone else could know. I was determined this year to surprise her. "Is it a recipe cabinet?" she asked laughingly as she hugged me gratefully. I couldn't believe it; she was dead right!

I could talk about Amanda Martin, my mother, forever, but I guess the reason I felt so particularly close to her during those "growing up" years was that she had been so close at all those times of fear and hesitation in my own life. It was quite natural, then, that she would be there now as I looked ahead and wondered what, if anything, was out there for me. "I think I'd like to be a teacher," I said in answer to her question that freshman-year day. We were sitting on the front porch, she in the rocking chair that we always called "Mom's chair" and I in "Dad's."

"Did you ever think about a 'teaching brother'?" she asked. Then she went on to tell me about some brothers that she knew in St. Leonard's, New Brunswick, Canada. The more she talked the more interested I became. She mentioned a place, a boarding school, in southern Maine, where a boy from our town had gone to school. That school was taught by brothers, she told me. The seed was planted.

High school students in our parish received their religious instruction on Monday evenings instead of Saturday mornings when the grade-school students attended classes. One May Monday evening of my freshman year we had a guest speaker, a missionary priest who spoke about the work of his group of priests — and *brothers!* I was immediately intrigued and followed him out to his car afterwards. We sat and talked for quite a while. He asked if I were interested in the priesthood and I said I couldn't because of the blindness, so I was interested in the brotherhood. He said "Oh", took my name and address, and I never heard from him again, even after writing myself. By the beginning of August, after my freshman year, I still had not heard from him. Mom found the address for me of that school in southern Maine that we had talked about earlier. I wrote to the principal and asked him to send me some information about the group of "teaching brothers" that he belonged to. I told him of my interest in becoming such a teaching brother but I decided to tell him nothing of my blindness! Within a week I had a response from the "Vocation Director's Office" of The Brothers of Christian Instruction! The principal of Denis Hall Junior High in Alfred, Maine, had forwarded my letter to him, the Vocation Director wrote, and so he was responding with the information I had requested. I don't really remember what pamphlets and/or brochures he enclosed with his letter but what I do recall vividly was his offer to come up and visit me at my home if I was really interested in the brothers' life! He suggested I read his enclosed literature and then, if I was interested and my parents were willing, I should obtain a letter of recommendation from our pastor. Once he, the Vocation Director, received that letter he would make arrangements for a visit! I was dazed as I finished reading the letter. I read and reread it dozens of times before going to bed that night. I think Mom was perhaps more excited than I was both over the letter and over my reaction to it.

"What do you think Daddy will say?" I asked Mom as we sat and talked about the possibilities that the letter raised. In my childhood years I was quite a lot more reserved with my father than with my mother. He was a self-taught carpenter and cabinet

19

maker who had been brought up in New Brunswick, Canada, where his father had moved to marry his mother. I have no memories whatever of Daddy's parents. He was one of nine children in his family. His relatives from Canada were often at the house during our years in Limestone. Most of them spoke French so we kids weren't too thrilled with having to stay around when they were visiting. Daddy had never learned to read or write in his lifetime; he used to tell us teasingly that when he went to school the teacher wasn't there. But he was somewhat of a "hero" for me growing up. I remember vague stories of how in his early teens he had spent winters in logging camps working as a lumber-jack. Watching him leave for work almost before sun-up and not return till after sundown always amazed me...and then he'd get home, have supper and go down cellar into the shop to work on some chair he was repairing for someone or on a new cedar chest he was putting together. I was always fascinated to watch him build the cedar chests, starting with rough, splinter-full lumber and producing such a beautiful chest with neat little compartments inside and so polished outside it looked like glass!

Sunday afternoons we kids always loved to be with Daddy. We'd come home from church, have our breakfast, hurry up and finish our homework for school, and then he'd be waiting for us with a deck of cards or some trick or stunt that he knew would baffle us. We loved it especially when, after we had played for a while, he'd go over to the cupboard, take out a couple potatoes...and we knew we were in for a treat of "Daddy's potatoes"! When we get together today we still talk about "Daddy's potatoes". He'd slice the potato thin and simply fry the slices in butter on Mom's big black griddle. Salt and pepper made them just "eating ready"! When things were cleaned up then he'd take out his harmonica and play us tune after tune. He had his favorites, like "Red Wing", and they became ours, too. We littler kids loved to watch Daddy match his "informal" education against the formal schooling of our sisters' boy friends or other friends who'd drop in at the house. We could always find a stumper for them and with a paper, a pencil and a ruler he could usually solve any problem they'd give him. And Sundays weren't complete with Daddy without a game of checkers, too. He had a way of making us think we were really beating him and then in one or two jumps he'd gobble up all our checkers and leave us wondering how it all happened!

With a late breakfast on Sunday mornings we usually "combined dinner and supper" late Sunday afternoon. At two o'clock we all usually went back to church for Benediction of the Blessed

Sacrament and the Rosary and by the time we got home dinner-supper was just about ready. Sometimes Daddy would take us all outdoors after supper for a ball game or some more tricks, I'm sure, to get us out of Mom's hair for a while. He used to look at us at the supper table and say, without a hint of a smile, "Eat good! I'm taking you out to the woods tonight!" We'd all laugh. Daddy's "mystery rides" were Sunday fun, too. "Come on, Mum," he'd say, "let's go for a ride." We'd all pile into the back of the pick-up faster than they could get out the front door. Maybe he had to go look at another job he had to do, or maybe he'd want to show Mom one that he had finished or maybe he'd just get us out on some of the back roads to make us think we were lost!

Daddy was the "disciplinarian" at home. If Dad gave us a job to do, clean the cellar, the garage, weed the garden...we got it done! If we gave Mom or each other a hard time, all Mom had to say was "You wait till Daddy gets home!" And we hoped she'd forget when he did come home!

So it was with both love and fear that I wondered how to approach Daddy about having the Brother Vocation Director come up to visit us. "Will you ask him for me?" I said to Mom as we contemplated his possible reaction together. "No," Mom said, "if you're really interested in the Brothers I think you should ask him." That night's supper was a tense time for me. I watched Daddy all the way through, wondering if "this" was the best moment to "bring it up." Mom, knowing my anxiety, came to the rescue. "Pat's got something he wants to ask you," she said proudly to Dad. Daddy turned to me and I blurted out "Can I go away to school this fall?" "Sure," Daddy said; "take the car. It's in the yard." I didn't know whether to laugh or cry; I did both as I told him the dream I had of becoming a "teaching brother." With Mom filling in the details here and there for me, I told him the story of writing to the Brothers and of the Vocation Director's letter that had arrived that day, of his offer to come up and visit – if my parents approved. And then I saw my father's deep love and concern for his "blind son" like I had never been aware of it before. "Will they accept him? Don't they know he's blind?" he said to Mom. How many times those past few years I'd find myself awake at night and overhear them in the next room wondering aloud, "What's going to become of Patrick?" Mom said that she thought the best thing was to let the Brother come and visit and we'd see then. Dad agreed; he said he had no problem at all with my becoming a Brother if they'd accept me. Our pastor was out of town for the week so I asked his assistant, who was dearly loved by all the altar boys of the parish, if he would write the letter of recommendation. He said he knew some of the Brothers; they had had a school in his home town! He wrote the letter and I quickly wrote my own to add to his, inviting the Vocation Director to come and visit! He came a week later. I got a note saying that he would be coming on Wednesday evening. Wednesday was the longest day of my life. The hands on the clock just wouldn't move, it seemed! Daddy came home for supper and had to go out to look at a job so he took Mom and my younger sisters with him. Everyone else just happened to be out too so I stayed home to wait for the Brother's arrival.

I can still see his metalic blue station wagon slowly making the turn into our driveway. He was dressed in black so I knew it *had* to be him. "Yes," I said, "this is the Martins and I'm Patrick." He introduced himself as Brother Cyprian and said he didn't have a bit of trouble finding us. He explained that he had stopped at the church and the priest had praised our family very much and given him directions to our house.

Even now, twenty years later, that night still seems like a dream. Brother Cyprian was so warm and friendly *he* made *me* feel at home! I gave him my straight-A report card from my freshman year at Limestone High School and that seemed to delight him. We talked about my wanting to be a teaching brother and I managed to "beat around the bush" without ever coming out and telling him that I was blind. I think I said something like "there's a vision problem but as you can see from my report card it's really not a problem." He said all I would need is a report from the doctor and from the school principal. I showed him all over the house hoping he'd notice that I didn't trip on the steps, etc. He never asked me to read anything aloud, thank God, and I didn't have to recognize anyone so I managed to do ok – on my own "turf." As my brothers and sisters came in one by one and then my parents entered they all introduced themselves and joined in our conversation. I think the size of the family impressed Brother Cyprian, too. Later that evening, after it got dark outside, he set up a screen in the kitchen and showed us slides on the Brothers of Christian Instruction. He told us they were founded by a priest in France for the education of the poor some time right after the fall of Napoleon, about 1815, and that they were now spread all over: North and South America, England, France, Spain, Italy, Africa and Japan. The brothers lived together in "communities" where they taught, prayed, worked, and shared their meals and recreation together. He explained all of the steps that a young man wishing to become a Brother of Christian Instruction would have to go through and showed us slides about each of these phases of the brother's "formation." Slides and motion pictures aren't exactly my strong points with respect to my visual abilities but I tried my best to "oooh" and "ah" when the rest did that night and to ask some appropriate questions at the "right" times. By the time Brother Cyprian left our home in Limestone that night he had one excited family on his hands! He left me all of the paper work that would have to be completed should I wish to enter the Brothers' prep high school that fall. He made it very clear that they would definitely consider my application if I did send it in. When he left us we all felt like we had known him for a long time. Mom and Daddy and I all looked at each other and it was clear that we all had the same question lurking in the back of our heads. None of us expressed it; we didn't have to. We all knew that the others were feeling it too: will my blindness get in the way?

I didn't sleep that night. My mind raced wildly all night. I went back and forth from being excited about entering the school to being deathly afraid of "what could happen" at the school because of the blindness that no one there really knew anything about. At times I found myself praying desperately that "they'd accept me" and at other times I secretly hoped they wouldn't! At times I found myself telling myself that if they'd only give me a chance I was sure I could live in *their* world perfectly well without them even knowing I was "legally blind" — whatever that was! After all, hadn't I just pulled straight A's this year in school, with no special attention? At other times — like when *I was accepted* and the clothing list arrived and I saw items on it like *tennis shoes, ice skates, gym shorts, baseball glove*...I panicked and wondered what kind of a mess I had gotten myself into!!! I think Mom and Daddy were both acutely aware of the battle raging inside me because they both made it clear to me that I should go and try it out but that if I didn't want to stay I shouldn't hesitate to come home. I wouldn't be "letting them down" by coming home, they wanted me to know.

We filled out all the papers and had the transcript of my grades sent from Limestone High School. I was somewhat afraid of the medical report we had to have filled out. What would our family doctor "tell them"? He was almost hollering at Mom when we went into his office and told him what I wanted to do. "Have you forgotten what he's had?" he snarled at my mother. "Those monks will *kill* him!" he went on. "He should get himself a good desk job or something like that after high school; his strength is gone. Don't forget it." I wanted to punch him in the nose! I don't know if I was angrier because of his attitude towards me or because he was talking to *my mother* that way. Whichever it was, the two reasons worked on each other and I think he could see my anger because he stopped, gave me my examination and filled out the report. I was relieved totally (strangely!) that he did not put any negatives in the medical statement!

The doctor's attitude was like the final straw for me; now I was determined to make it with the Brothers just to "show him!" I know he was a strong motivational force for me because some ten years later when publishing my Master's Degree thesis I sent him one of the very first copies! As I look back at the whole incident now, I can't help but wonder if his remarks weren't precisely calculated to get the results they did...Whatever his intention was, he gave me the last "shove" I needed to head for the world of the "monks" as he called them!

4

"You could have gotten killed out there..."

"Get up! I'm leaving," said Dad at about 10:30 Saturday night before Labor Day, 1960. Daddy hated to drive in traffic and so he preferred to make his long trips at night. Brother Cyprian had sent us maps and directions and we calculated that the trip down would take us seven or eight hours. Being a Sunday, we would have to stop for Mass on the way and that would add another hour or so to the trip. They had decided to drive down, drop me off, see the place, and then drive back home that very day! It was a long trip down, but not long enough for me. I didn't want to see us arrive there. My brother Gerard, who had wanted to become a brother for a long time, came with us for the ride. By eight o'clock in the morning we finally made it to Sanford, Maine, where we stopped for Mass at a parish we found along the way. Mom remarked to Dad as we came out of the church how she felt so good in that town. She felt like she'd even like to live there, she said. Little did any of us know then, but six years later they moved to that town, buying a house right across the street from that same church! Coming out of Mass that Sunday morning, Mom and Daddy were greatly relieved to learn that we were only six miles from "the Brothers' place", as the local people called it. They gave us directions to a restaurant and from there to the Brothers. The closer we got the less I wanted us to get there, but we finally did arrive.

A sign on the right side of the highway took us up a narrow, winding road a mile or so to the top of a hill where we entered what seemed to be a village of sorts. On a huge white rock at the entrance to the "village" was painted the words *"Notre Dame Institute-The Brothers of Christian Instruction"*. We knew we had arrived. The first man we spoke to directed us to the large grey building on the right of the road that ran down through the center of the tiny village. That building, I was soon to learn, would be my home for the next three years of my life. It was called "LaMennais Preparatory School", named after the Brothers' founder, Father Jean-Marie Robert de LaMennais.

We were greeted at the door by a silver-haired, distinguished-looking man who introduced himself as Brother Louis Cote. He was the Director of the Brothers' prep school, he informed us, and he was expecting us! Yes, Brother Cyprian had told him all about his visit with us and they were glad I had decided to come. We asked a few questions. Mom and Dad talked over the financial and travel arrangements for me with him and then he suggested we take a tour of the school. In the study hall (with teacher-size desks!) I found one with my name on it. Somehow it felt good amid the homesickness that was already beginning, to see my name on every list, etc. The dormitory was the second floor of the wood-frame building. It was one neat room, wide open, the whole floor of the building! There were about fifty beds with a wooden locker standing next to each. Every bed was covered with a green spread. We found a bed and locker with my name on it so we left my trunk and suitcase next to it. At both ends of the huge dorm was a shower room and toilets and all along one wall of the dorm was a sight I couldn't believe — there were more sinks there than I had ever seen in my whole life! From the dormitory we went downstairs and saw the library; we met several of the brothers on staff on our tour. Finally we made it to the basement of the building where we found a locker with my name on it. There were pool and ping pong tables in the locker room. Another classroom was revealed in one corner of the basement and a woodworking shop with all sorts of tools in it. Brother Louis then took us across the street to another large grey building facing the one we had just come from. This building we learned, housed the retired brothers, the "working brothers", the dining halls (or refectories, as they were called) for all the various groups on the 300-acre campus, the chapel, and the administrative headquarters for the Brothers of Christian Instruction in the United States. The Brothers were praying in the chapel when we looked in. It was like the scene from some movie...all of the Brothers we had met, including those now in the chapel, were dressed in long black robes (cassocks) that went from shoulders to shoes and buttoned all the way down the front. Each Brother wore a small, four-inch high crucifix on his chest. The slides and pictures Brother Cyprian had shown us had displayed the Brothers' "habit", as it was called, but somehow seeing it now in the naturalness of real life it was quite impressive. Brother Louis explained that the prep school where I would be for the next three years was but one of several "activities" on the Alfred, Maine, campus. The Brothers' property also housed Denis Hall Junior High, the residential school for boys that Mom had seen advertised in our church paper; the "Novitiate" of the Brothers of Christian Instruction was also housed on the property and was the training center for young men taking their first "Official" step into the Brothers community. The "novice brothers" remained in Alfred for one year (usually immediately after high school) and then proceeded to the Brothers' college in Canton, Ohio, for academic preparation as teachers and more spiritual and theological "formation". The "working brothers" (as opposed to the

26

"teachers") ran a large farm on the Alfred property with cows, thousands of chickens in an electric coop, and hundreds of apple trees, a monstrously large garden and garden store, and a bakery.

The tour of the "Notre Dame Institute" campus revealed athletic fields, a gymnasium, a chaplain's residence, tennis courts and even a lakefront all equipped with rowboats, docks, canoes, rafts, picnic tables, fireplaces, etc. As we drove from the lakefront back to the prep school building, I somehow knew this was the end. Mom and Daddy and Gerard would be leaving...without me! We made our good-byes quick and they got in the car, feeling, I'm sure, an awful lot like I was. As I watched our grey and red Ford stationwagon get smaller and smaller and then...disappear around the bend in the road, I wanted to burst into tears. I hated myself for having gotten myself into this mess! Here I was, all alone. They were going home...without me. At least they had each other, I thought. Why couldn't I just stay with them forever. And then a cold, sweaty fear came over me. What if they had an accident on the way home and I never saw them again?

"Pawtrick!?" a voice was calling me. It was Brother Louis. He had a way, right from the beginning, of pronouncing my name that made it more than just a title when he called it. Through all the years I knew him, he always added that special "twist" that made me feel so...loved...just by the way he called my name. Now, he helped me find my way back up to the dormitory to unpack. One by one the Brothers came over, reaching out to a rather evidently homesick newcomer. There was Brother Marcel Crete who had taken us down to see the lakefront. And then little Brother Gabriel, who I don't believe touched the five-foot mark on a measuring tape, came over to bring me on a tour with a few more newcomers. "Leave your things right there," he said jovially; "we don't have any stealers around here!" I was too homesick to eat when it came time for lunch so I told the Brothers I wasn't hungry. They brought me to the dining hall anyway and I sat there along with them through the lunch. Brother Augustine came over to the table with me and coaxed me to at least try the apple pie. I did. I grew to really love him and trust him as "brother." I will never forget him on Thanksgiving Day of that year; if it's possible to hate and love a person at the same time, he was that person! The lake had been frozen over for quite a few days; the ice was tested; and it was decided that we would go skating that afternoon. I was scared. I mean, I weave when I walk, let alone ice skate! But, in keeping with the clothing list, a pair of skates had been packed in my trunk and out they came. I made the mistake of telling Brother Augustine on the way to the lake that I couldn't skate. "Don't worry," he said in his always reassuring way. He helped me get my skates on and then said, "Come on with me. I'll hold you up. Come on. Move your feet like this." Steadying me with his strong arm he gave me enough confidence – foolhardiness? – to move with him. Before long, without my knowing it, we were out in the middle of the lake. Steadying me on my feet he stepped back, let go his grasp on me and said, "See, you're standing all by yourself!" With that he skated away, hollering over his shoulder as he glided so gracefully across the mirror-smooth lake, "See you later!" And yes, I *hated* him and I *loved* him both at the same time! I did manage to learn to skate, somewhat clumsily but really! But, I've jumped ahead of myself.

LaMennais Preparatory School was set up by the Brothers of Christian Instruction as a training center for young men of high school age who felt they might like to become teaching brothers. Boys came to the school from home towns all over the United States and remained enrolled in the school's program as long as they still felt their dream was to become a teaching brother or until advised by the Brothers that they should not pursue the "dream" any further. In the fall of 1960 the school's enrollment was almost fifty young men. The program consisted of academic studies as well as religious studies. A regular "prayer life", consisting of daily Mass, morning, mid-day, and evening prayers said in common, monthly "days of recollection", and an annual three-day "retreat" was also part of the prep-school student's life. The prayer exercises were all introduced to the incoming new students at a regular pace as the school year itself unfolded. In addition to studies and prayer, meals and rest, the prep-school student's day also scheduled mandatory recreation and work periods. The academics were no problem. I loved the afternoon and evening study periods and usually managed to get all my assignments completed in the time alloted. The prayer schedule didn't bother me; daily Mass had been part of my life for a few years and we had been taught to kneel and pray morning and night prayers next to our bed at home. The meals at the prep school I took to well, once the homesickness passed. In fact I gained 47 pounds that year and outgrew every stitch of clothing I had come to school with! Even the dormitory style living didn't bother me that much. I had my own bed and locker; what more could I want coming from a family the size of ours? It was when I saw the mandatory recess lists, however, that I swallowed my heart several times over!!! Brother Augustine came into the study hall after our last class and read out the team lists for *baseball* and, yes, *my name was on that list!* Oh, how well I recall those afternoons. I could make it through the day okay, but I dreaded those recess assignments. One day we'd play intramural baseball; the next day soccer or football...I prayed I'd survive. I'd go up to bat petrified of even accidentally hitting that crazy ball. Most batters want to hit it and some even *pray* to hit it; *I prayed* **not** to hit it. I'd go ice cold whenever I thought of having to run the bases with another batter slugging a ball that was going to whiz right by or right *into me!!!* I learned *fast* that if I swung the bat low enough I'd miss every time! How good those words, *strike three,* sounded. How sweet! The guys were really super. They'd even hold my bat up for me to show me how to do *what I didn't want to do by any means!* I quickly earned the name, "Here come *strike out!*" I didn't mind that. I didn't even mind not being wanted on any team. If participation hadn't been mandatory that would have solved my dilemma nicely! But participation was mandatory and so day after day I found myself praying I'd survive one more recess. Brother Louis and the rest of the staff must have done some close watching those days, weeks...and maybe even some investigating of their own. They never told me and no one else did either but after a few weeks of that mandatory sports nonsense Brother Louis called me into his office one afternoon after all the team lists had been read off and *my name wasn't there.* "Why in hell didn't you tell us you were blind?" he blurted out at me as soon as I was seated in front of his big desk. "You could have gotten killed out there!" I was sure this was the end of the road for me in the brotherhood dream. I murmured something like, "I didn't think you would have accepted me if you had known," and he turned to my files that he had in front of him and said nothing. Then he lifted his head, his face had lost some of its sternness, and he told me that from then on I was not to participate in contact sports during recesses! I think my homesickness left me totally that day!

Each of us students was assigned daily house chores which were usually done right after breakfast before the school day began. In the afternoon we also had a regular "work period" which usually lasted for an hour or so. Our work tasks could take us from the farm to the lake front, from the tennis courts to the library. The discovery of my blindness was very evidently a turning point, I noticed, even in my work-period assignments. Gradually I was assigned more and more to library duties. And here it was that I met two loves of my life: Brother Hervey Brooks and the library! Of all the brothers on staff at the prep school and even later in my years of formation none touched me so deeply and inspired me so strongly to pursue my "impossible dream" of becoming a teaching brother, as Brother Hervey. He wasn't a "sports enthusiast" and that won me over at once! During weekend "organized recesses" he often led a group of us on a hike somewhere or other and we always felt good being with him. His sense of humor and his sensitive spirit drew many of the prep school students close. "Patrick," he said to me one day after the discovery of my blindness, "how would you like to work in the library?" I didn't really know what it involved, I told him, but I'd love to try. During that year he taught me an awful lot about inner workings of a library — classifying books and preparing them for the shelves, preparing their cards for the card catalog, repairing and rebinding broken books, keeping the shelves and the entire collection in order, checking in and checking out books...I really fell in love with the work. The library at the prep school became a heavenly retreat for me. Ultimately it became a "regular" work period assignment for me, with no complaints from me, you may be sure!

The prep-school program was designed and set up by the Brothers to give high school boys a chance to touch the Brother's way of life and see if it might not be for them. The program was also designed, however, from the Brothers' viewpoint as a screening process for young men who indicated an interest in the Brother's way of life. The young man's attendance at the prep school gave him a first-hand chance to evaluate the life for himself and it gave the Brothers a first-hand chance to evaluate him as a possible candidate for their way of life. Once a student had concluded that the brothers' life was not for him or if the Brothers concluded that the way of life was not for him, then the student was usually processed out of the prep school program immediately and re-entered his home school, etc. As a new student, I was quite shocked to notice one day that several boys had left for home. Not too much, if anything, was said, except "they went home," or maybe "they decided this wasn't for them." Realizing that some of those "who left" were "asked" to leave brought a new resident into my heart, a resident that came and stayed for a good many years, *Fear. Will they ask me to leave too, now that they know about my blindness?*

Those first few days after the discovery were nightmarish days — weeks for me. I was sure it was only a matter of time before I would be called in and asked to pack up and go home, that *they* had decided I couldn't really be a teaching brother. Every time I noticed another desk cleared off or another empty bed spot in the dorm, that fear would rush through me again. *Was I next on the list?* The paradox was that now I wanted desperately to stay! The homesickness was gone; I wanted to stay. In fact, I was more convinced than ever that I wanted to be a teaching brother! How many times those days, weeks, months...I would sneak across the street to the chapel and, kneeling at the foot of the life-size crucifix or looking up at the large statue of Mary, I would cry, "Why don't you cure my eyes *all the way* so they'll accept me to become a teaching brother? Every time I had a meeting with Brother Louis (all the students met with him at least once a month) and he seemed "pleased" with me I'd breath a sigh of relief and sleep a little easier that night. How well one meeting comes to mind now, "Pawtrick," he said as I sat down, "I think we're going to make a good monk out of you!" I wrote home to Mom and Daddy that night, crying for joy, and quoted him in my letter! I was so happy.

Weekends and vacations at the prep school, or "Juniorate" as the Brothers called this phase of our training, were FANTASTIC times. Saturday and Sunday mornings we had study periods. Saturday afternoons we usually had longer work periods and then recess or "free afternoon." Sunday afternoons after lunch were usually an organized recess with several choices we could sign up for: "Hike", "Football", etc, depending on the season and the weather. Both Saturday and Sunday afternoons ended with my favorite time, however, "reading period." We were free to read from reading lists that were prepared for each grade level at the school. I found a love for reading during those favorite moments at the juniorate! And I also found a love for "classical music" which was always played in the background during those periods. After a while I even found myself recognizing some of the pieces that were played. Until this time in my life reading was a necessary evil, a burden I had to carry if I wanted to succeed in something! During those reading periods we were not permitted to work on our studies or read textbooks. It was strickly "leisure reading" and I really grew to love it. I dared tackle "big" books like Dickens and others and discovered that I actually enjoyed them! I even found myself carrying a book out to recess at times, to read while I "watched" them play football!

Christmas of 1960 couldn't come fast enough for me; it was to be my very first vacation home from the juniorate. I arranged a ride with several boys from the same northern-Maine area who were attending Denis Hall Jr. High in Alfred. The trip home seemed five times longer than the trip down in September. It's funny, but there are only a couple things that I can recall about that vacation: my brother, Gerard, and I stayed up almost all night when I finally did get home talking about the Brothers and their way of life. A second thing I remember is Mom and Daddy's "mixed emotions" about how well I looked and how much I had grown: yes, it was without doubt, the healthiest I had ever looked since my illness, *but I had to get all new clothes!* Mom dug out the boxes and trunks of stored clothing and found what 'hand-me-downs' she could and the rest we had to go shopping for. A third aspect of that vacation, that I recall vividly, is how eager I was to "get back"! That really baffled me at the time. I remembered how homesick I had once been for home and now I couldn't wait to get back to school. Vacations home from the juniorate were at Christmas, Easter, and the month of August each year. Other holidays were spent at the school with a "holiday schedule" instead of the academic schedule. In June, as soon as school finished, we'd all head to "Camp Boyland", a camp for kids owned and operated by the Brothers about fifty miles from Alfred. We'd spend about two weeks at the camp in Naples, Maine, preparing the facility for summer use by the youngsters who occupied it from late June through early August each summer. Our mornings at the camp were spent on work projects while our afternoons and evenings were free for our enjoying the facility which was situated on a fifteen-mile-long lake! Our month of July, back in Alfred, was spent with somewhat of a "camp schedule," a lot of our time being spent at the lakefront. One thing that was especially great about the summers in Alfred was getting to meet all the Brothers from the other schools who came to spend their summer weeks at the "Mother house" of the United States province of the brothers. They usually joined us for meals and picnics and movies and other recreational activities while devoting most of their days to the various tasks needed to be completed around the busy campus and farm.

My three years at the prep school passed rather quickly and quite peacefully except for that ever-present, gnawing question: *will I be accepted to become a brother in spite of my eyes?* In October of my second year at the juniorate, Daddy came down to do some remodeling work for the Brothers to help pay my tuition at the school. The following winter he came down again and this time he brought my brother, Gerard, to help him. Gerry had been really sick as a child and had been left by the illness with some learning problems. Seven years older that I was, he had been pushed on grade after grade by the schools in our town and then made to quit school when he was sixteen. He had done custodial work in our home town and had simply remained living at home. Ever since I can remember he had a dream of becoming a "working Brother" somewhere. He had come down with Mom and Daddy and I for my very first trip to Alfred in 1960 and I am sure that the dream of his heart was stirred by that trip. He had asked a lot of questions about the working brothers in Alfred when I had come home for my first vacation that Christmas. Now, in early 1962, he came down to help Dad with the remodeling work. Brother Louis was very impressed with him and spoke to the Brothers at the junior high boarding school who had no custodian for their plant. In May, 1962, after my

32

last Easter vacation home, Gerry moved back to Alfred with me. He was hired by the Brothers as custodian for Denis Hall Jr. High School, a position he was to keep for fifteen years.

The first "official" step toward becoming a Brother of Christian Instruction was to become a "Postulant," meaning "one seeking admission." The Postulancy Phase of training usually lasted for six months immediately prior to the candidate's being formally received into the "Novitiate Year" of the Brothers' life. The young man, if accepted to do so by the council of the Brothers, writes an official letter to the Superior General of the Brothers of Christian Instruction asking to be admitted to the community as a "Postulant." The merits and credentials of the candidate are studied and a decision is reached. If the decision is a "yes" he would be admitted, usually in a public ceremony, to the Postulancy Phase of his training. For young men at the Brothers' prep school in Alfred, this "Postulancy Phase" of training began on February 22nd of their senior year. All of the final paper work needed for official entrance into the community would be completed before that date.

As I completed my second year at the juniorate in 1962, I really wondered about the possibility of my being accepted to enter the Postulancy the following February with the rest of my class. A full medical report of my visual condition was asked for and so an appointment was made with the specialist during the month of August when I would be at home. He gave me a thorough examination and wrote abundant notes during it. He even prepared charts for the Brothers illustrating, as well as possible, the nature and limits of my peripheral or field vision. The reports were sent in and the long wait began. I was almost sure that I would soon receive a letter advising me not to return to the juniorate that fall. I waited but no such letter, or any letter arrived for weeks! Finally, in late August a letter did indeed arrive, or rather an envelope arrived. I was disappointed as I opened it and found no letter inside. It was only a copy of the Brothers' latest newsletter issue. No letter. Was I to come back or what? I looked at the newsletter and there saw my "welcome back"! There on its front page was a picture of this year's seniors who had just received the habit as "novice brothers" and written in the margin was the note: *next year's your turn, Pawtrick!* FANTASTIC! I needed no other letter. I was thrilled!

I returned to the juniorate Labor Day weekend of 1962 and went home for my last vacation for three years at Christmas of that year. On February 22, 1963, with eight or nine others, I was received as a Postulant by the Brothers of Christian Instruction. A ceremony in the Brothers' chapel marked the occasion. Each of the candidates wore black suits, white shirts and black ties for the ceremony and that became our official attire as postulants in the community. During the ceremony each of us was given a lapel pin with the insignia of the Brothers on it. That was to be worn for the duration of our postulancy period.

Basically, our lives as students changed very little because of the postulancy phase of our training. We remained at the prep school for the completion of our senior year of high school. We did, however, begin to associate with the novice brothers at certain, specified times of the day. A special class for studying the office Rule of Life of the Brothers of Christian Instruction was begun for us and continued each afternoon during the postulancy.

Mom and Daddy drove all the way down from Limestone to be with me on Graduation Day from LaMennais Preparatory School, a day we had all wondered about for a long, long time. I graduated second in the class and so had to give one of the graduation addresses. Daddy wasn't a man of a lot of verbal praise but he did have one neat little way of letting us know he was proud of us as kids; he'd stroke us on the head with his great big carpenter's hand. On Graduation Day I was almost a foot taller than Daddy physically but that didn't stop him. I don't remember if I stooped down or he stretched up but I do remember standing outside the gymnasium as my brother took our picture together and I got a hug from Mom and that much-coveted stroke on the head from Daddy!

After graduation exercises instead of heading for Camp Boyland with the rest of the prep-school guys, the postulants made their official break with the prep school and moved across the street, bag and baggage, to the Novitiate building. From then until August 22 when we would officially become the class of "novice brothers" we lived with this year's novices, learning all the ropes, the traditions, etc. of the novitiate year so that we might uphold them during our year and pass them on well to the next group. One of the hardest things to get used to those weeks before August was simply calling each other "Brother." "Hey, Dick!" or "Bob!" slipped out so much easier than "Hey, Brother Richard!" or "Brother Robert!" But it did sound neat when we heard it addressed to us, "Brother Patrick!" Wow! I could hardly believe it. I thought often those days to three years earlier and all the anxiety over Brother Cyprian's visit and whether or not I would even be accepted for the juniorate. And now, the novitiate was all but here!

"Take as much time as you need..."

All major steps in formation with the Brothers were immediately preceded by "retreat days", days of silence and prayer aimed at helping the candidate for the step to prepare himself before God for the action he was about to take in his life. Before the Day of Postulancy we had made a three-day retreat. Now, as the day for our becoming novice brothers drew near we prepared for eight days of silence and prayer in retreat. A retreat master was brought in to give several talks each day during the retreat, to celebrate the Mass and devotions each day, and to be available for those wishing counseling, direction, and/or confessions. My first eight-day retreat was a *long* one! But it did finally end and on August 22, 1963, at St. Joseph's Church in Biddeford, Maine, I officially became "Brother Patrick Arthur Martin." We had each been measured for our black robes, "cassocks", and during the ceremony that August morning we were clothed in them for the first time. Mom and Daddy couldn't make it down for the day's celebrations because of Daddy's work but my sister, Lorraine, and, of course, my brother, Gerry, who now worked in Alfred with the Brothers, were both there with me. The August ceremonies took place at the Brothers' parish church in Biddeford, instead of at the chapel in Alfred, because of the crowds of family and well-wishers who usually liked to attend the ceremonies.

The "Novitiate" phase of formation for the Brothers of Christian Instruction consisted of a solid year of seclusion, prayer, study, and community living as the final preparation for the candidate's pronouncing vows for the first time as a member of the community. The year is intended to introduce the candidate to the living of the vowed life, a life of surrender to God and service to His people. During this intense year of seclusion from the world, its ideals, values, maxims, etc. it is hoped that the novice brother will pick up the new values, habits, maxims, ways of life that will enable him to live happily his vowed life of surrender to God and service to His people.

A year of seclusion it certainly was. There were no newspapers received at the novitiate and no radio or television programs were heard or seen. At least, that was the intended ideal. During our novitiate year, August 22, 1963, through August 22, 1964, a few earth-shattering events occurred that found their way even into the "inner sanctum" of our house. Pope John XXIII died and Pope Paul

VI was elected. The Second Vatican Council opened in Rome. And, on November 22, just three months after our Novitiate year began, President John Fitzgerald Kennedy was assassinated in Dallas, Texas. When that happened we joined the rest of the world in shock and silent vigil before the pageant on our borrowed television screen. Other than these world-changing events, however, the news black-out was held quite sacred. Except for day trips to the doctors, etc., the novice brothers never left the Novitiate grounds during their year of preparation for vowed life. If a novice remained outside the confines of the novitiate more than a day then he would be compelled to begin his novitiate year all over again if he still wished to follow his aspirations for the religious life.

The prayer life of the novitiate was, understandably, much more intense than that of the juniorate. Community prayer was supplemented by a much-encouraged program of private, personal and devotional prayer. Community religious studies and reading was also expected to be well supplemented by a great amount of private reading and reflection. Except on Sundays and major holidays all meals were eaten in silence. A simple sign system had been passed on over the years for the various dishes and foods at table. I had no problem learning the signs whatever but with the narrowness of my field of vision catching those signs from my hungry brothers was quite a problem at times. Happily they knew me and just as happily they were usually hungry enough to kick me under the table or jab me in the ribs to catch my attention! One of the funniest table instances happened about the third or fourth morning of our novitiate year. I had some sort of carmel jam in my plate when a hungry brother asked for toast. Since the toaster was right next to me I picked up two slices of bread and dropped them into the toaster, not realizing that as I moved my arm over my own plate I had dragged the low-hanging sleeve of my brand new cassock through that delicious carmel jam. Unknowingly I did it again when I went to retrieve the toast for the waiting, hungry brother. I hadn't seen the carmel dragging but the Brother across the table from me did see it and tried to point it out to me, maintaining all the while the silence that was the rule! Well, out of desperation, he finally kicked me under the table and then pointed to his own sleeve when I looked up at him. What followed brought us a "talking meal"! I raised my own arm to look at it, not knowing what was there, of course, I proceeded to drag the carmel stuff all across the front of my cassock, bringing laughter even from our Novice Master, Brother David Touchette, who up to that point had tried to overlook what was happening. We finished the meal with permission to talk and I had permission to leave and clean up!

A regular part of our novitiate life was our chores and work periods. Every morning after breakfast we usually reported to the kitchen to help in the preparation of the vegetables needed for that day. The kitchen staff prepared the meals for all the brothers on campus, the juniorate group, and the residential junior high school group of about a hundred students. That meant a great deal of potato peeling, carrot peeling and washing, peeling onions, you name it. I was assigned chores like the rest and proceeded to report for them. After a few scrapes and cuts with the potato peeler Brother David "warned me" strongly to be careful. Other less "dangerous" chores were chosen for me when they were available.

One of the jobs of the novice brothers on the Notre Dame Institute campus was "fire patrol." We were trained rigorously as the firemen for the property! The property had been carefully equipped with its own pumping station and reservoir and hydrants at strategic locations. We had our wagon with fire hoses and several drills during our postulancy summer taught each of us our assigned responsibilities in case of fire emergency. It was a gorgeous Friday morning in the spring of 1964, May 15, 9:15 a.m., when we heard the bell at the "Main House" start ringing. Almost immediately we also heard Brother Leo's voice scream over to us from the same place, "FIRE"! Within minutes our cassocks were thrown off and we were all at our stations. The fire pump was going, the hoses were connected and we had water shooting on the blazing main building on the Alfred campus. Grease from French fries or fish for that Friday noon meal had been boiling on the stove, had boiled over and flamed up and been pulled into the walls of the building by an exhaust fan. The wood frame building was no competition for the devouring flames. The rear wing of the building − housing the Provincial Administration Offices, Vocation Director's Office, many brothers' bedrooms, dining halls and huge bakery − went up first but could not be contained to that area of the building since the flames found "safe passage" to the front of the building between the slate roof and the 1930's style embossed-tin ceilings of the chapel which joined the rear and front wings of the huge building. By noon of that day fire companies from nine communities had answered the alarm for help! Miraculously, no one was injured in the catastrophe but the building was declared a total loss. Our novotiate year was certainly one event-filled year: it saw our Church's earthly leader die; our nation's leader was killed; and our Province's "mother house" burned.

The task of campus reorganization, clean-up, and reconstruction began immediately. The local Civil Defense Unit set up a portable kitchen and served meals for the entire campus that day.

Nasson College in nearby Springvale, Maine, invited the use of their cafeteria facilities for the emergency and hundreds of individuals and groups came to the stricken campus seeking to help in one way or another. The gymnasium on campus was taken over and set up as campus chapel while the recreation halls beneath it were quickly converted into the needed kitchen and dining hall facilities. We, the novices, quickly packed our gear and moved back across the street into the juniorate dormitory with the prep school students, thus making the novitiate building available for the brothers whose rooms had been destroyed by the blaze. Our daily routine as novice brothers was rather sharply modified those days of May and June, 1964. All night guard duty had to be set up to prevent the blaze from re-igniting. A storage room in the building had housed the paints and other such supplies needed all over the campus. We arose early those mornings and after Mass reported for work immediately – clean-up. The prisoners from the local county jail came in full force to help in the clean-up operation. And even through the tragedy some sense of humor was maintained. As I reported for work one morning not too long after the blaze Brother David said to me, "Whatever you do today, don't start running." We roared together as I realized, I had on a light blue shirt and dark blue pants; so did the prisoners!

The front section of the burned building was able to be restored for use in just one month! Working with local contractors we put a new roof on that part of the building and saved as much of the dining hall section of the center wing as we could with extensive renovations and reconstruction. All of the rooms were repaired, painted and refurnished so that they could be reoccupied by the Brothers one month from the date of the fire! In addition to learning many new values, new ways of thinking and praying, new attitudes, etc., we also learned many new skills during that year of novitiate. The emergency work schedule cramped our prayer life but somehow didn't take it away. We'd gather at 4:00 or 4:30 to pray morning, midday, midafternoon and evening prayer, to study the constitutions and rules of the Brothers, to complete our "spiritual reading" requirements for the day and then go to the chapel for the daily Rosary and visit to the Blessed Sacrament before the evening meal! In June the Brothers were able to move back into their quarters, we moved back across the street to ours, and life calmed down a bit for us to finish our novitiate year with some semblance of order! After all, it was already our turn to receive the Postulants and train them in the tasks and ways of life of "novice brother"!

At some point during the havoc of that spring each of us was asked to write an official letter requesting permission to make, for one year, the Vows of Poverty, Chastity, and Obedience according to the Constitutions and Rule of Life of the Brothers of Christian Instruction. I'm sure we wrote the letters to the Superior General or we could not have been accepted for vows but with all the commotion at that time I don't even remember writing! The vows pronounced by the Brothers are basically the same as those made by most "religious men and women" who belong to a "Religious Order" in the Church. Much simplified here, the vows – promises accepted by the Church but made to God – entail (1) the giving up of the ownership of goods of this world to be free to possess Christ Jesus only (Poverty), (2) the giving up of married life in order to be given totally to Christ and His people (Chastity), and (3) the total conformity of one's will to the will of God for him as expressed through the authorities in the community and the Church. The vows were studied, each in great detail during the novitiate year and then request was made by each of us to make and live the vows for one year.

Because of the May 15th fire the Alfred campus was now short of space for all of the Brothers who usually came for the summer retreat and ceremonies. It was therefore decided to hold the retreats and novitiate and vow ceremonies at the Brothers' residential high school, Mount Assumption, in Plattsburgh, New York. The eight-day retreat began for us on the evening of August 13th and ended on the morning of August 22nd. It was a beautiful but very lonely day for me, beautiful of course because that unbelieveable day had actually arrived: I was a Brother of Christian Instruction with vows! During the Vow ceremony each of us received, kissed, and began wearing for the first time the four-inch crucifix on our chest! We were now "Professed" – vowed – Religious in the Church! It was unbelieveable for me, but it was true, I had been accepted and I had made it this far! But that August Vow Day was a lonely day for me too. Because the retreats and ceremonies were in Plattsburgh, New York, it was too far for any of the family to be able to make it to celebrate the happy day with me and somehow a joy not able to be shared looses some of its flavor. I couldn't wait for the celebrations after the ceremonies to get over that day; it was a terribly long day but was finally ended mercifully with sleep. I hadn't been that homesick since I had entered the juniorate four years earlier!

A day or so after the ceremonies we all packed up and made the several-hour trip back to Alfred. There was somewhat of a grown-up feeling inside as we moved our gear out of the novitiate building, leaving it to the new class of "novice brothers" and taking our places with the "student brothers" or "scholastics", as they were called. The prep school students prepared and opened up Camp Boyland in Naples, Maine, each spring, and the student brothers closed up the camp each fall. So that's where we, the newest "scholastics", joined the rest of the student brothers as we moved out of the novitiate that last week of August, 1964. We would spend a couple of weeks at the camp, closing it up and securing it for the winter months, while resting and relaxing, too, before making the trip to the Brothers' college, Walsh College, in Canton, Ohio.

The "Scholasticate" phase of training for the Brothers of Christian Instruction was the final phase before the new brother was assigned to teach in one of the community's schools. The student brothers lived a community life, sharing prayer, meals, work and play, while completing their individual studies for bachelor's degrees in whatever areas of specialization each was majoring in. At the end of his first year of "scholasticate" the student brother renewed his vows for one more year; at the end of that year he pronounced the vows for a three-year period, and after that three-year period, or five years of vowed life, he was eligible to pronounce them for life.

The trip to Ohio in September, 1964, was the longest trip I had ever taken in my life and probably the most exciting too! I was absolutely spellbound as we hit the traffic around Boston and some of the sites along the way just totally fascinated this small-town boy from Maine! I remember writing home about the trip as soon as we got to Ohio.

The arrival at Walsh College, Canton, Ohio, was most welcome after the thirteen hours of driving there! I loved the accommodations of the student brothers' wing of the Brothers' residence. For the first time in my life *I had a room all by myself!!!!* The rooms were small, maybe six feet wide by ten feet deep from the corridor. Desk, dresser, sink and clothes closet were all built-in along one wall: the bed and chair were on the other. In addition to our bedrooms we had a common study hall, a dining hall and a recreation hall. We shared a common chapel with the faculty Brothers who had their own residence wing. The college, at this time in its history, consisted of this residence building and one other building known then as "College Hall." College Hall housed the Administration, the Library, classrooms, labs, cafeteria, book store, lounge, post office, and everything else that a college needed! The Brothers had moved the college from Alfred, Maine, to Canton, Ohio, in 1960, the year I had entered the juniorate. They had named the college, Walsh College, after the then Bishop of the Diocese of Youngstown who had invited them to come to his diocese. The campus consisted of about a hundred acres of treeless alfalfa land when it was bought and, except for the two buildings and few dozen planted trees, a paved parking lot and a few feet of sidewalk, it was still the same when we arrived in 1964. Today the small college boasts a campus center building, two 500-ft. dormitories, a science building, a gorgeous physical education center, cinder tracks and football and baseball fields, etc., in addition to *thousands* of trees that have been planted, watered and cared for by the hands of student brothers on campus! It was my work-period job for two years at college to cart around hundreds of feet of garden hose and keep all of the trees well watered each growing season!

Beginning college unburied an old, deep-rooted fear inside me: will the *blindness* get in my way? Will I be able to make it through college reading *letter by letter?* And, *if I do,* will I be able to teach with the *blindness?* I didn't know. I had no answers, as usual, to any of the questions and the fear that accompanied each question now came back at least as strong as it had ever been. The Provincial Superior of the Brothers in the U.S., himself brought up the final question as I prepared to register at college for my first semester. I had planned to major in mathematics because I figured that would entail the least amount of reading. I enjoyed math enough to be able to get through it, I was sure, and that's what counted at that point in the game! The Provincial Superior had other ideas, however, as he looked at my plans. "What if you *can't teach?*" he asked. What would I do with the math background? He suggested English literature as a major instead; that would be easier to fall back on for other than teaching work, he said. I couldn't believe it, but *English literature* with all its reading, became my college major! He did tell me to plan on taking as much time as I needed to get through college. There was no need, he insisted, for me to try to make it through at the regular student-brother pace of three years and summers, not with my letter-by-letter reading. Privately, *I saw red!* I wanted to teach. I wanted to be a *teaching* brother. And I wanted to be a *normal* teaching Brother! I had graduated from high school *second* of the class; I could make it through *here* just as well. I signed up for seven courses that fall semester and, quite frankly, surprised myself by making the Dean's List. Seven more courses the second semester put me well on my way! I was determined to make it through college at least as fast as any other student brother. Several courses during the summer session and seven more courses each semester of my second year at college really put me "near the end." It was excitingly close...and frightfully close too! Being near the end meant simply that I was nearing the final question: *Will I or will I not be able to teach a classroom-full of youngsters when I can't see one whole kid at a time?* That was the question I wondered seriously about and that was the question that ran through the mind of the Provincial Superior and all of the Brother Principals of the community's schools. *Is he going to be able to teach?* Each year as a class of student brothers prepared for graduation and assignment to one of the community's schools, we used to try and guess ahead of time which school each one was going to be assigned to. No one bothered to guess at my assignment; there was no clue available; the unknown factor was too great!

And so, with that "unknown factor" still looming in the now not too distant future, I began my third year at the college in the fall of 1966. I figured that with seven more courses each semester I'd be finished in the spring and the question would have to be faced by all. I guess I looked at the "question" in my life at that time in pretty much the same way I had come to regard all "big" moments of decision — like exams! I'd worry about them right up to the last minute; did I study enough? were my notes good enough? etc., but somehow as the deadline came upon me I'd calm down figuring, "well, I can't do anything else about it now, here goes!" It was always funny, because for me "relief" always came as I saw the exam paper on the desk in front of me rather than only when I had completed it. I guess that's somewhat how I began my third year at Walsh College in September, 1966. Registration day came and I received cards for my seven courses, picked up my books at the bookstore and quickly began to settle down for "another semester's work".

6

"Run, Brother, run!"

It was either the last week of September or the first week of October that year. The semester had just begun. We had had about a week of classes. We student brothers gathered for "night prayer" that night, completed the prayer and then filed out of the study hall where we had gathered for prayer in respectful silence. As I walked by our Director on my way to my room I heard him whisper as he tapped me on the shoulder: "Can I see you in my office right now?" I looked at him, surprised, and followed him down the corridor to his office, the last doorway on the left. "Come in," he said and motioned for me to close the door. I sat down not knowing whether to panic, rejoice, get defensive, "run with the ball" or what! It was highly unusual to be called in after night prayers. A very well respected tradition in all of the Brothers' communities was that of the "Grand Silence" which lasted from after night prayers until after prayer and meditation of the next morning.

"The Provincial called tonight," he began immediately. "the Brothers at Denis Hall need help: they're only eight Brothers and over a hundred boys..." He would have continued but I cut him off. "Tell him I'll come," I said, surprising both him and myself by my eagerness! "Wait," he said, "there's nothing definite yet. The Provincial just asked me to speak to you about it; no decision has been made yet. He's talking to the Brothers at Denis Hall tomorrow and will call me to find out your response and we'll go from there. But, he continued without giving me a chance to interject any questions or further comments, "aren't you supposed to finish up and graduate in May? This would delay you, you realize. You'd get your "student teaching" credits and possibly a "music appreciation course" while in Alfred but basically that would be it, so that would definitely postpone your graduating." "That's no problem at all," I said when he finally gave me a chance to speak. "right now I still don't know *what I'm graduating for*. If I get the chance to try my hand at teaching, a chance I wondered if I was going to get, then when I come back to finish up I'll know what I'm finishing up for!" "OK," he said, "then I'll talk to you tomorrow night when Brother Provincial calls back. If you do go it would most probably be *this weekend!* You'd probably be assigned to teach the sixth graders; they've only got twelve of them and Brother Provincial says there are no discipline problems among them this year, so it wouldn't be too bad for you."

"I'm all packed!" I said as I got up to leave.

"One thing, Pat," he said, "don't say anything to anyone about this until we know for sure tomorrow night. If it works out then we'll announce it." I can't tell you how excited I was that night as I went down the stairs to the corridor below and to my room. Did I sleep that night; I'm not sure, but that next day had to be the longest day in history. My classes didn't interest me; in my mind I was already going through the process of withdrawing from them all, packing up, *flying* to Maine, and I already saw myself in the classroom. It was the toughest assignment I ever got to maintain silence that day and say *nothing* to anybody about the "possibility" of my going out to teach! Putting my mind into my studies after classes that day was an outright impossibility. I deliberately avoided the Director's presence all that day; I didn't want him to see how preoccupied I was with the "dream." We gathered for night prayers and he came in to pray them as usual, as if nothing what-soever were in the air. I wondered if he were going to say something to the group during the prayer, before it, or after it. But he didn't. My heart was in my throat as I got up from my place and walked toward the door to head down to my room. Just outside the study hall door he was waiting for me. He touched me and motioned for me to follow. I repeated my steps of the night before and walked into his office, closed the door and took the chair in front of his desk. "Well?" I said before he had a chance to speak. "Did he call?" "Yes, he called and yes, you're going," the Director said quickly, knowing my anxiety. I would stay at least one semester at Denis Hall, he informed me, until the Provincial could arrange to get them other help at which time I would return to com-plete my studies. I would be flying up to Boston on Sunday and the Brothers from Denis Hall would drive to Boston to pick me up at the airport. He would make my plane reservations tomorrow, Saturday, and I should take care of seeing the Dean of Studies in the morning to withdraw from my classes. Did I have a suitcase or did I need anything, he wanted to know. No, I couldn't think of anything, but then again, I couldn't *think at all* at that moment. It had all come up so unexpectedly, so suddenly...Why, it was just last night, Thursday, that I had first learned of the "possibility" and I would be on the plane on Sunday! Wow! I was sure it was a dream. I would have been terribly disappointed but not at all surprised to have awakened at that moment and realized it was *only a dream*. But it *wasn't!* I kept telling myself over and over again that night as I went through the drawers and bookcase and dresser and closet in my room: *I'm going to teach!*

Grand Silence was a real penance the next morning as we

gathered in the study hall where we prayed morning prayer. I wanted so much to lean over and tell the Brother next to me *"I'm going to teach!"* Morning prayer was followed by our half-hour meditation time and that by Mass. Finally, we gathered in the dining hall for breakfast and after praying the blessing the Director announced my "good news" to the group! The surprise for them was as genuine and as great as it had been for me! We had a riot talking about how I had known since Thursday night but had had to keep silent about it until now! With packing, withdrawing from classes and saying "good byes" to the people I knew, that day passed rather quickly. A wrapped-up box of corn flakes, a "certificate of appreciation from "Corn E. Margarine" and a few hastily composed songs about what they called "my so-called jokes" added fun to the going-away party that underlined my last evening at Walsh College that year.

As I went to bed that night, my sleepless eyes agreed with my racing thoughts that it was a good time to think about all that was about to happen: my *first airplane ride, teaching, being part of a Brothers' community, seeing my folks!!!!* Yes, that's right! Mom and Dad now lived only six miles from the school where I would be teaching, but not only that, *Mom now worked in the school's cafeteria* and *Dad worked all over the campus for the brothers!* FANTASTIC!

In the spring of 1966 the Brothers in Alfred had completed construction of a chapel/cafeteria building to replace the facilities lost in the fire two years earlier. Mom and Daddy had talked about "moving down there" ever since our first trip to Alfred when we had stopped for Mass in the neighboring town. Daddy had worked two winter's for the Brothers to help pay my high school tuition and eventually my brother Gerard, had come to work in Alfred, too. Daddy had grown to really love the Brothers those two winters that he worked for them. He and I used to have all our meals together and I remember how he'd make me sing the hymns for him that he had just heard us sing in the chapel. He'd sit on the steps and listen to us pray and sing and when we were alone in the parlor for supper or lunch he'd talk about some prayer or reading or song he heard. I had never known my Daddy that closely; Mom and I could always talk about things like that but this was the first time I had come close to Daddy in this way. One day when they were still in northern Maine, Mom had said teasingly to Daddy, "What are you going to do when I die?" Daddy's answer caught her completely off guard. He hardly hesitated a moment before responding, "I'll move down and stay and work with the Brothers!" He loved them and many of them grew to love him.

As the new facility neared completion the Brothers decided to bring in a Brother from New Brunswick who had been trained as a chef. Was I ever surprised that spring when I got the news out in Ohio that Mom and Daddy had sold our house in Limestone – the house Daddy had built and they had lived in for some thirty years – and were moving to Sanford, Maine, that little neighboring town to Alfred where we had gone to Mass almost six years earlier! They had been asked by the Brothers to work with the chef in the new cafeteria, had jumped at the opportunity and decided to move! They had come down to Sanford, found and bought an old, two-family house (that Daddy could repair!) and they had moved in the spring of 1966. Quite discouraged by the condition of the house when they actually looked at it as "theirs", they would have moved back to Limestone immediately if they hadn't promised to work for the Brothers and if they hadn't already sold their house in Limestone! Daddy set to work immediately cleaning up, tearing down walls, ceilings, stairways, you name it, and putting up new ones. He and Mom worked tirelessly to convert the structure into "their home." My brother, Albert, now living with his family in South Dakota, came for a visit that spring and he and Daddy tackled some of the "two-man" jobs that had to be done. Gerard was there often, even bringing some of the Brothers and students from Denis Hall to help out if needed. And, thus, that spring it really did become "home" for the family. The new cafeteria in Alfred opened that spring and for a while both Mom and Daddy had worked in it with Brother Joe, the new chef. Daddy, feeling I'm sure like a fish out of water, eventually opted to get back to the repairs and remodeling jobs needed by the Brothers and the local parish in Sanford. Alfred, Maine, and the Brothers of Christian Instruction had really touched the whole family – through that one ad in a Sunday paper in 1960!

And so it was exciting for them in Sanford, too, when they got the news that weekend that I was on my way up to be on the Denis Hall staff! As I lay down that last night at Walsh I wondered what it would be like to be teaching so close to home. Since Christmas of 1962 I had been home only twice, once the previous summer for the wedding of my younger sister, Patricia, and this past summer I had seen the new home in Sanford for the first time. Now, I would be teaching "next door." That certainly did add to the excitement of the next day's trip!

In late forenoon the next day, the Director handed me an envelope with money for my ticket it it and then drove me to the Akron-Canton Airport for my first plane ride. I had never in my life been inside an airport terminal, let alone an airplane. When we arrived at the airport the noon-day traffic was horrendous. The

Director stopped the car, came around to my side and helped me get my suitcase, pointed to a door and told me I'd find the ticket counter just inside. He had to get right back, he explained, but he was sure I'd be ok. So we said good-bye and I was alone...in an airport terminal...for my first plane ride...Asking people directions as I went along, I did find the ticket counter and purchased my ticket. It was then that I discovered I would fly from here to Newark, New Jersey, on "United Airlines" and then change there to the "Eastern Shuttle" to Boston. Somehow I really did make it — all the way to Boston. It sure was some relief when I heard familiar voices behind me say "here you are! How did you get here?" They had been waiting for me at a different gate, but somehow we found each other! One of the Brothers grabbed my suitcase and we weaved our way through the airport crowd and finally found the car.

Now that the excitement of the first airplane ride was all over and we were only a couple hours drive from Alfred my mind became preoccupied with the next day's challenge: *teaching for the very first time!* The question was no different than it had been for years, just a little more forceful and heart-thumping now. *Will I be able to teach?* Visions of accidents occurring, kids hands raised all over the classroom, kids playing tricks on me,...suddenly, too, I found myself worrying about my preparation as a teacher...did I know "my stuff" well enough? Would they stump me and if they did what would I do? What would I be teaching? My major was English literature; you certainly couldn't teach that to sixth grade boys!

The principal of Denis Hall, Brother James Landry, and all the Brothers on the staff, and my own brother, Gerry, all made me feel really welcome. They made me feel like I was doing *them* a favor by coming; somehow I saw it quite the opposite at that time in my life! Monday morning was a scary ordeal for me, probably the most frightening day I have ever experienced in my life. The previous evening I had met with the Principal to find out my teaching and other duties at the boarding school. I was horrified and delighted at the same time: instead of the sixth grade angels I had been told about, I was assigned *40* eighth graders, some of whom were bigger than I was! Fear absolutely gripped me at the very thought of walking into that classroom but I was determined to hide it from both my students and my fellow Brothers. This was better than anything I had ever dreamed possible: if I could teach these kids, a class this size and not necessarily the "best kids" in the school, then I will have really achieved my dream: I will be a *normal teaching brother!* As for the subject matter, well, that sort of stunned me, too. My teaching day included American history, geography, general science, and French!

"Do you want me to tell the kids about your blindness when I introduce you to them?" the Principal asked me Monday morning. "No, please don't," I said, and to myself I added, "I want to be a *normal* teacher; I don't want their pity." The Brothers had prepared much of my beginning teaching for me and they were FANTASTIC in helping me to become *a teacher*. Tricks of the trade were shared willingly and without asking. They were all questions in the faculty room after each class that "I made it through" and with their help I learned teaching techniques that made it not only possible but enjoyable! I developed a few "compensation" techniques of my own that helped also. I never dared, for example, to stand in one place long enough for the kids to know where I was looking. I'd run or walk up and down the aisles as I taught, sliding between the desks and almost never calling on the student I happened to be looking at! I figured that if I could keep them guessing enough they wouldn't have a chance to get me guessing! I also learned to listen...paper rustling, and other movements and sounds took on a whole new importance.

Somehow I managed to settle down and become "a part of the school" that year. I really enjoyed the grown-up feeling it gave me to help out on school projects, weekend outings, etc. Because supervision wasn't exactly my gift, I took on the school's secretarial work in addition to my classes. Faculty outings and get-togethers were really enjoyable that year, too. The whole year went generally without incident. One of the Superiors in Alfred "observed" my classes for the college to aid me with critiques and helpful suggestions. We met one day for what I thought was our "beginning session" and during the course of our discussion the Brother said to me, "You don't mind, do you, when I walk into your classroom? Or, would you prefer that I observe from outside?"

"Oh no," I said, "walk right in any time. You can let me know when you're going to come in, or you don't have to, either way." He looked sort of puzzled by my response so I said, "Did I say something 'wrong'?"

You said, "going to," he said. "You mean you haven't seen me already in your classes???" He had apparently walked in and out several times that week, presuming I had seen him! "Well," I said, I guess you can say I was 'me' and didn't do anything special just because you were there!"

I hated to see that school year come to an end. I was scheduled to return to Walsh College in June for the summer-session courses. Having tasted the active work and fraternal fellowship of the Brothers' community at Denis Hall, returning to the student brothers' residence at the college was the *last* thing I wanted to do. I had loved the sharing of prayer and work, hard times and easy times, meals and recreation. I had really felt like a "Brother" there, and loved it. Somehow the student brothers' residence seemed to emphasize more the student status and much less the brother status. We were "brothers" to each other in the residence but our "still being in training" seemed to color our relationship with the "Brothers in the field." Going back to Walsh for me was like crawling back into the womb. The Director's "welcome" as I returned to Walsh confirmed my misgivings about returning. I was excited about my achievements of the year, achievements that a year ago, most had doubted were even possible; I was a hero in my eyes returning to the home front. My "swelled head" lasted all of about three minutes, however, as the Director reminded me that I had done "nothing extraordinary" and that I would be a "regular" student brother while there at Walsh for my last semester. The hero was shot down... Two courses during that summer session, seven during the fall semester and one additional course during that same fall semester at Kent State University Extension in Canton, enabled me to finish all of the requirements for my bachelor's degree by Christmastime, 1967. FANTASTIC! Another Brother who had been at the juniorate with me, and in the novitiate also, was still at Walsh that semester so the two of us often "comforted" each other. We both took the speech course at Kent State U. and that evening "out" helped move the semester along for the both of us. I think we shocked some of the Kent students with our speech topics. When "Brother Bob" delivered his "advertisement" speech on "Flush-a-by Diapers" the whole class roared! December finally rolled around, courses, papers, exams...were all over and the butterfly flew from the cocoon again! Back to Denis Hall.

Returning to Denis Hall I picked up most of the same courses I had taught the year before except ninth grade world history and geography was added. It was good to be back and now the fear of my first coming had subsided. When the students returned from their Christmas vacations and one of them came literally barreling down the dormitory steps and pounded on the faculty-room door and then asked excitedly if it was true that Brother Pat was back, I really felt good, and welcome!

Denis Hall had been founded by the Brothers of Christian Instruction in the 1950's as a residential school for boys. Just as a matter of course, many of the students for whom admission to the residential school was sought, came because of troubled family, social, or academic backgrounds. They needed the extra caring and supportive services that a small, residential school atmosphere could offer. Many of them needed simply a lot of that "big-

49

brotherly" love and confidence in themselves.

7

"Are you still there?"

The school year had begun after the Christmas holidays and I was back in the "grind" so to speak, again. One day after dismissal one of my students, waiting until we were alone, asked, "Brother Pat, do you have 'barrel' vision?" I hoped he hadn't seen the panic that ran through me as he asked his question. Had they discovered my "secret"? Had somebody told them? I quickly regained control of the situation. When you don't wish to answer a question, ask a question of your own! "Larry, what would make you ask a silly question like that?" I said. "Well," he went on hesitantly, "sometimes I have my hand up for a long time and you don't even seem to see it." "Well, Larry," I said trying to brush it off as "nothing," "If I called on every Tom, Dick and Larry that raised his hand, you guys would have me off the subject all the time and we'd never cover anything in the classroom!" "Yeah," he agreed, "we've tried it but you don't bite!" And he ran outside to recess, forgetting his question and not realizing it had never been answered. But I never forgot it. Larry made me really start thinking about what I was doing there at Denis Hall. How many kids out there needed the attention of being recognized when their hands were raised and had been neglected because I hadn't seen their raised hands? For every Larry who had the courage to come up and ask, how many others sat back and wondered if they weren't liked because they were never called on? Did I have any right to put my quest to be something I wasn't (normal!) in front of my students' needs? What was my *responsibility* to them for their education and upbringing in the boarding school as their teacher?

Larry's question and several other similar incidents kept me pondering that year but I didn't have too long to ponder before something more serious forced me to really look at what my dream really was. After reprimanding a student for rather abusive language one morning, I simply went on with the class. The bell rang ending the period and I proceeded to gather my materials from the teacher's desk. The student walked up, I didn't see his coming and I didn't see his fist until it planted the lens of my glasses in the flesh of my eye. Several times he hit and blood splattered. I left the classroom and walked out quickly to the principal's office. I was rushed to the eye specialist, the student was rushed out of the school for striking a teacher and drawing blood. As I lay in my darkened room hoping that more damage hadn't been done to my already rather poor vision, one question kept suggesting itself: *Would the student have struck his teacher if he had known his teacher was legally blind?* How many other kids might be affected by my trying to pretend I was someone that I wasn't: *normal!* What was *normal* anyway? Was it being a fully-sighted teacher? Then I wasn't *normal* and had no right to pretend I was. Was anyone *normal?* Was trying to be a *normal teacher* the only way that I could help these kids? What was I looking for in being a "Brother," to help others or to help me? Thanks to my very real "Brothers" on the staff that year and thanks especially to our principal, Brother James Landry, I was able to talk about a lot of these plaguing questions and even came to a very exciting and peaceful decision to leave teaching at the end of that school year.

The boarding school had no classified school library up to that point and it was much needed for service to the students. With my experience at the high school library for three years, I was excited about working to get "ours" set up. The Brothers prep high school had closed the previous year and the entire library collections and furniture was given to us for our new library. Daddy, who was still doing repairs and remodeling work for the Brothers now undertook the project of building me my first library, a gorgeous knotty-pine room, about 20 x 40 feet in size. I spent the summer of 1968, my first without studies, as school registrar in order to free the other Brothers on the staff for further education, and I spent much of the summer setting up the library, gathering all our own classroom collections and integrating them into the high school library collection that we had just received. By September the library's doors were open to the students and faculty and the work of classifying and processing all the materials we had went on. New materials came in, were ordered, and all had to be somehow tied into the one library collection also. I loved the work in the library; it brought back many "heavenly hours" spent in the library at the prep school not so many years earlier. It was sort of ironic that I now had the same library collection back!

Because of the special educational needs of many of the students at Denis Hall, we decided as a faculty to try and set up a specially equipped learning center next to the library for their needs. As "school secretary" the job fell to me to write to the various foundations and corporations to investigate the possibility of obtaining "grant money" for the project. A copy of "The Foundations Directory of the United States" was borrowed for the project and my work began. Letter after letter describing the proposed projects, its purposes and its vital need for our students was prepared and sent out. No grants were ever obtained for the project, but another, different grant did result directly from the project.

Going through the foundation directory one day in search of new places to request the needed funds, I came across the name and address of a rather well known "library foundation." "Wow," I thought, "I wonder if they could help me for funding for further studies in the library/learning center field? I decided to write. What did I have to lose? In my letter to the Chairman of the Board, I told briefly how I had "fallen into" the work because of my visual loss. I also mentioned that that same visual loss made it virtually impossible for me to enter into competitions for academic scholarships whose awards were based on time-testing scores. Was there any way, I asked him, that his foundation could help me in pursuing studies for master's degree work in the library/learning center field. Little did I realize that just a couple of weeks before that "Chairman of the Board" received my letter, he himself had undergone his own second cataract surgery, putting him in a rather sympathetic frame of mind to receive my request. He apologized that his foundation was unable to make grants to individuals but then went on to ask if he might be permitted to help me personally by writing to the Dean of the Library School at the Catholic University of America on my behalf. I figured I had nothing to lose with the Chairman of the Board writing for me, so I said in a letter to him that I would be most grateful for any help that he could give me. Not long afterward a letter came from Fr. James Kortendick, then Dean of the Library School at Catholic University. He told me of the letter he had just received and asked that I apply for admission to the library school at Catholic University of America. I should also complete the application for financial aid once admission into the university had been gained. If I made it that far, he said, he would see to it that I was given a fair chance to compete for available funds. The Provincial Superior gave me permission to apply for admission to the university, understanding of course, that I could go only if the funding somehow came through. All of the forms, fees, reports, papers and transcripts were finally gathered by early January, 1969, and the long wait began. A letter and card of acceptance into the Graduate School of Arts and Sciences was finally received and was followed by a similar letter admitting me into the Department of Library Science. No financial information was forthcoming for months and I simply admitted it had been a valiant attempt!

It was May 22, 1969, a Saturday afternoon. Several of us Brothers were in the Principal's office trying to talk a student into remaining at the school until the end of the year which was but three weeks away! The student had been in a fight with several other students who had verbally abused him and he had made up his mind he was going home. We were in that sort of an atmosphere when the telephone rang. Standing right next to it, I picked it up, "Denis Hall," I said, "may I help you?"

"Long distance calling for Brother Patrick Martin," the operator's voice responded. "This is Brother Patrick," I said, and waited for what I was sure was the parent on one of our students. As registrar at the school I was the one that many of the out-of-town families had met on visiting the school during the summer months. So, it wasn't unusual for a long distance call to come in for me. But *this* long distance call was unusual! "Brother Patrick", a deep, base voice began when the operator signaled, "this is Fr. Kortendick from the Library School at Catholic U. I'm calling to tell you that you are one of eight recipients of our Higher Education Act Fellowships this year! "The government grant," he went on, "will cover cost of tuition and fees, one round trip from Maine to Washington here, and will provide you with a monthly stipend for your room and board and books, etc..." I dropped the phone. "Are you still there?" I heard him say as I picked up the receiver again. "Yes," I said, "I'm just in shock!" "Go out and celebrate with your brothers," he said, "congratulations!"

I was like a mad man that afternoon. I ran all over the 300-acre campus. First to the Provincial's office where I found him in; he was as shocked as I was by the news. "Of course, you can accept it," he said "and yes, you have permission to go study for the year." Then I ran to every other building and told all the Brothers the fellowship had come through. I called Mom and Daddy. They were in heaven. I really think they were more excited about it than I was! I can still hear them asking me if I needed a typewriter or something else for the studies... They were so excited it made me more so! The grant didn't begin until the fall semester of 1969 but the Provincial suggested I go for the summer session at our own expense in order to get used to the university set-up and facilites. Georgetown University in Washington was sponsoring a workshop for Catholic schools public relations personnel. Since I was already heading to Washington and since my work at Denis Hall involved public relations, and finally, since it was expected that I would return to Denis Hall after my graduate studies in Washington, it was decided that I should attend the Georgetown University workshop as well. That didn't leave me much time to prepare. It was now already late May and the workshop began in early June. As I left Denis Hall in June of 1969, I looked back on almost three full very happy years there. I had graduated from Walsh College officially on May 18, 1968, and I had not dreamed then of ever going on for graduate studies, especially in librarianship. The

Provincial Superior had even suggested that I not bother with graduate studies if I was happy at Denis Hall since my being there in the summer would permit others to be free to go for studies needed in their fields. My plans were hopefully to complete the work for the Master of Science in Library Science Degree in one year and two summers. When Fr. Kortendick suggested that because of my vision I might wish to consider taking more time, I think I saw *red!* My area of specialization for studies at the university was to be the school library if at all possible. I hoped to write my master's research thesis on some aspect of school librarianship. Plans and dreams were flying high when I left for Washington that June.

Because of my summer studies I was forced to miss my youngest sister's wedding. Anita was marrying a guy from Sanford at the end of June and it would be impossible for me to get back for it. Her wedding "emptied" the house. There were fourteen of us living and the last one was now leaving. We were spread all over from Maine to Florida, from Washington, D.C., to California, and from South Dakota to Texas and Louisiana and Illinois! Just weeks before I received the good news of my grant and my year to come in Washington, one of my sisters and her family who had been stationed for four years in Labrador were transferred to Andrews Air Force Base in Washington, D.C. We were both really excited, then, when the news of my grant came through. I hadn't seen Germaine and her family in a good many years because we never made it home at the same time, and now we would be together in Washington for the year!

Summer activities in Washington, D.C., moved rather quickly that year. Almost before I knew it the Georgetown workshop was over and done with and I was on my way "across town" to Catholic University and my library science program. You can just imagine this small-town boy in Washington, D.C., all by himself! I loved it there! One of the Brothers that I knew was also studying at Catholic University so I made arrangements to meet and stay with him for the summer session. A community of priests, the Oblates of St. Joseph, had opened their Washington house of studies up to university students for very reasonable rates so Brother Guy Roddy and I stayed there. He had made all the connections ahead of time so that helped tremendously. Registration for courses took place mostly in the gymnasium; thank God Brother Guy was with me. That place looked like a zoo. The floor was like a maze; once you started down one track you hoped it was right because if you had to get out of line for any reason "your place" disappeared! But Brother Guy finally got me through it and that relieved me for the coming

55

semester registrations now that I knew "the ropes." Courses went well that summer and leisure time was spent touring the city which was really fascinating. I loved being able to find my own way around with the detailed street maps we bought. Before I knew it the six-week session was over and it was time to return to Alfred.

Dear Brother,

I have read several chapters of your manuscript, Patrick, and believe me you tell it well. I would have liked to have known you as a child...of course, at that time in my existance I would have had very little use for any human...and probably none at all for a blind little boy who couldn't walk a straight line. Ah, but we all change and grow, isn't that neat, Patrick?

All through the recovery stages from your meningitis and on into school and then into the brothers, you showed a remarkable tendency to stick to a course that would make you normal...no matter what. It seems to me that you must have been a little overbearing at times...trying so hard to be perfect. I am not sure that I would have felt drawn to you in those years, Patrick.

Of course, I would have liked to have been present to see you make a try at being an athlete...probably would have got a great laugh out of it. You see, I am thinking of how I was when you were at that stage of your life. Happily, I see things in a much different way now.

In my old existance, I would have found the trials and tribulations of the young novice rather amusing...now, I see them as they were to you, hard, bitter facts of life...stumbling blocks in your road to normalcy.

Personally, Patrick, I have never thought of you as normal...a little abnormal would be more like it. The way you rush around...the endeavors you get involved it...the way that people, handicapped and non-handicapped alike, are drawn to you...that isn't exactly normal for so-called normal people, is it?

I must read more, Patrick, I must find out when and why you began to change into the loving and caring Patrick that I know now. It must have all been there, hiding under the mask that you wore constantly... I must find out where and when the 'real Patrick' was born.

With the peace and love of the great I AM

The Spirit of the Handicapped

8

"Patrick, you have to call your Mother..."

The summer of 1969 was one event-filled time of my life believe me! In addition to the May 22nd excitement of winning the grant and then going to Georgetown University for the workshop and then to Catholic University of America to begin my master's degree studies, that was also the summer for my "Perpetual Profession" or "Final Vows" as a Brother of Christian Instruction. I had entered the Juniorate in September of 1960, had become a Postulant on February 22, 1963, a Novice on August 22, 1963, had made First Vows on August 22, 1964, and already it was time for Final Vows, August 22, 1969. Strangely, there was no more fear of being accepted or rejected at this point in my progress with the Brothers. I am sure that my "growing up" at Denis Hall with respect to my calling had much to do with the lessening of fear as also did my at-homeness with the Brothers and theirs with me after these nine years. The fact that I had now lived the vowed life for five years also made me at home in asking to renew those vows for life. The decision to make my Final Vows was not a difficult decision for me at that time in my life.

Mom and Daddy seemed quite excited over the coming ceremony. They had seen the baby of the family get married in June, and now the baby of their boys was preparing his Perpetual Profession as a teaching brother. My sister, Patricia, whose wedding in August of 1965 was the occasion of my first home visit as a Brother, was really excited about my Final Vows, too. She and her husband, Jerry Kozar, surprised us all by announcing that they were going to drive up for the occasion all the way from Amarillo, Texas! They had just adopted a baby boy in July and they would bring him along. Patricia and Jerry wrote ahead of time that summer and offered Mom and Daddy their first "Honeymoon" after forty-seven years of marriage! They asked Mom and Daddy to go back to Texas with them after my vow ceremonies. None of us believed Daddy would go; we knew Mom would if he would so we started praying. The vacation would be great, FANTASTIC, for them. They deserved it. We thought of every possible persuasive argument in the book — but didn't really have to use any of them! Daddy said he'd go! We couldn't believe it. He worked hard all summer finishing up all of his repairs for the parish and for the Brothers. He had the house all done over with aluminum siding and brand new aluminum frame storm windows and screens. He had all the little repairs around the house in order. That summer he decided not to renew the registration on the station wagon. "I'm not going to drive this anymore," he had said and we had simply accepted it because Dad had had glaucoma for many years. We knew this bothered him more than he let us know. Daddy never complained about pain. In Sanford they were walking distance from town and right across the street from the Church, so they really didn't need the car that much. In short, we didn't think too much about it when he decided not to renew the registration.

Final Vow Day was preceded, like all of the other steps that had led up to it, by an eight-day retreat, a time for prayer, reflection and openness to God in preparation for the gift of one's life under vows in response to His love. The family had never been able to make most of my "ceremonial steps" into the Brotherhood because of distance or work. But when Perpetual Profession Day arrived, sunny and warm, they were there! Mom and Daddy, Gerard, Lorraine, Anita and her husband, Al, who had just been married two months earlier and Patricia and Jerry had come from Texas with their newly adopted little Andrew David Kozar! Another Brother, and another Martin, made Final Vows with me that day too. Brother Joseph Martin, from the Detroit, Michigan area, and I had gone through the Novitiate and Scholasticate together. And so now, we made our preparation retreat and planned our vow ceremony together. Brother Joe's family came from Michigan for the celebrations. It was a happy day for both families.

Patricia and Jerry and Mom and Daddy decided they'd leave Maine early on August 23rd, the day after Final Vows. The night before that Brother James, Principal at Denis Hall, brought Gerard and I down to say our good-byes. It was a quiet evening after an exciting day but we were especially excited for Mom and Daddy. They were planning to take about two weeks to get to Texas. They wouldn't rush it. Mom and Daddy knew Jerry's folks in Pennsylvania quite well and so they were going to spend some time visiting them. That would break up the trip and hopefully not make it too tiring for them. They left on schedule the next morning and postcards from along the way came to tell us how they were enjoying the trip. They were seeing things Mom and Daddy had read to us about a good many years ago up in Limestone! They arrived in Texas to find my brother Philip from Illinois there waiting for them as a surprise! A letter came telling how much they were enjoying... It was Sunday morning about 8:00 a.m. Brother James had come over to the faculty residence where I was staying to get me. It was September 7th. "Patrick, you have to call your mother. Your Dad is pretty sick," he said very soberly. A call to Mom told me the story of how they had gone to bed early the night before, how Daddy had insisted on talking seriously for a long time about where all the legal papers and deeds and policies, etc. were, how Mom should take care of herself and watch out for her money, etc., etc. "Oh Dad, let's go to sleep," Mom answered several times but he'd go right on talking. Finally, they had gone to sleep and he had suffered a massive cerebral hemorrhage at 6:00 in the morning as they were getting up! Police and ambulance were there in minutes and he had been rushed to a large Catholic hospital in Amarillo. She didn't have any other news, except that it didn't look good. Several calls that day and the next morning revealed less than a ten percent chance of survival. He had never regained consciousness from the moment of the hemorrhage. By Monday night I had notified all of the brothers and sisters on the east coast while Philip took care of the west. We kept in close touch to make sure everyone had been reached. On Tuesday Gerard and I flew down to be with them. Albert flew in from South Dakota; Martha and her husband, Andy, flew in from California; Theresa and her husband George and their kids drove up from near Dallas, Texas; on Friday, September 12th, my brother Paul flew in from Columbus, Ohio, and five minutes after he arrived at the hospital Daddy died, at 3:00 on his own "Good Friday" afternoon!

We went through the motions of things, holding up marvelously well, all of us, under the circumstances. The Chaplain of the hospital was FANTASTIC in helping us to make all the necessary decisions and arrangements for a funeral Mass there in Amarillo the next morning, so that all those who had traveled so far wouldn't have to travel way out east now. Flight arrangements were made for some of us to fly back with Mom and Daddy's coffin for funeral services and burial in Sanford, Maine. Everything moved smoothly those few days. For everyone it had all just happened *too fast.* We really weren't entirely conscious of what was going on. The brothers and sisters who hadn't made it out west began to arrive in Sanford. Annette, the first child in the family, came down with Fern, her husband, and they brought Isabelle, their daughter and Mom and Daddy's Godchild; they came down from Presque Isle, Maine, which is about a half hour from the old home town, Limestone. Germaine and Ted drove up from Washington and Willis, my oldest brother, and his wife Mary, drove all the way up from Florida. Anita and Al had been there to meet us all at the airport when we flew in. Lorraine, my sister from Portland, Maine, came in as we arrived also. Mom's sisters and their husbands came down from Limestone and other relatives began to arrive also. I hadn't seen Willis, my oldest brother almost since I was sick in the hospital or shortly afterwards. We just never made it home together, until Daddy's death. Willis had never been to the new "home" in Sanford so he called when he arrived in town, told us where he was and a couple of us went out to meet them. I shook his hand and he said, "Wait, you're going to have to tell me which one of my brothers you are!" We hugged as I told him I was Patrick, and he couldn't believe it! He had gotten emergency leave from Korea to come home when I was in the hospital and it didn't look too good for me then. He looked at me now and shook his head. Brothers, we hardly knew each other! The age difference separated us but also the fact that Willis' health was not good and traveling was rather difficult for him made the gaps between visits even greater.

Daddy's funeral Mass was celebrated by one of Mom's cousins, Fr. Clement Thibodeau, who was chaplain for the Brothers in Alfred at the time. The services were held in Holy Family Church, the same church in Sanford where nine years earlier we had stopped for Mass on our way to the Brothers! After the burial services on Monday, September 15, 1969, Mom decided that she'd go back to Texas to be with Pat & Jerry for a while rather than to stay at home alone. But, no matter where each of us went or with whom, it was like we were now alone, Daddy was dead. All of the aunts and uncles and cousins, and all the brothers and sisters went back "home" again...to be alone and realize the hurt unconsolably inside over what had just happened. Our Daddy had died. Mom went back to stay with Patricia and Jerry for a while in Texas; from there she went back home to Sanford and from there traveled each year to visit this one or that one...but no matter where she went we all came to realize that we could never replace for her the dear one she had lost, her spouse.

On Wednesday, September 17th, I flew from Portland Airport to Washington, D.C., to continue the studies I had begun at Catholic University that summer session that now seemed so long ago! I had made arrangements to live with the Christian Brothers at their residence at De Lasalle College right near Catholic University. I didn't know any of the Brothers so I simply went to work unpacking my things and settling my room for the year. And for the first time in an awful long time I was physically *alone* and all that had just happened came rushing at me. For the first time since Daddy had gotten sick, I sat down and cried.

9

You've got nothing to lose..."

Most of the courses in the Library Science Department at Catholic U. were two-credit courses instead of the regular three-credit ones. That meant that to get the same number of total credits for the degree you had to take more courses. I ended up with *seven* graduate-level courses my first semester and my second semester at the university. Somehow, even with the letter-by-letter reading I managed to make it through, with good grades besides! I was all enthused with the program and was even eager to begin the research on the school library project for the degree thesis. There were about eighty or so full-time students in the department, not to mention the much greater number of part-time students. We became a very close "family-like" group that year, sharing many of the same courses together, preparing reports and exams together, sharing lunch together, shopping, going to a movie... I loved the specialization of the degree; I mean, I was "surprised – pleasantly – not to see "core requirements" like sciences, history...the liberal arts undergraduate program. The maturity of the students and of the approach to the program work and goals was excitingly refreshing. I loved my year at the university!

One of the elective courses I decided to take my first semester at Catholic U. was entitled "Principles of Adult Book Selection." The Professor was a Benedictine priest whom veterans in the department advised me I would thoroughly enjoy. It was an evening course also, which meant I would get to meet many of the part-time students who came only in the evenings. The course did indeed prove to be rather interesting and enjoyable. Fr. Theall, the professor, asked in class one night, "What do you people think about being 'read at'?" He then proceeded after a few comments to tell us why he absolutely detested someone reading aloud to him. At one point he brought up examples of mispronounced words that can make the listener lose the entire flavor of the reading. A student in the class commented that he worked at the Library of Congress and that in the Library's Division for the Blind and Physically Handicapped they had hundreds of thousands of "recorded books" that were FANTASTIC to listen to. He told briefly how he had had the opportunity to listen to a few selections and how sophisticated the equipment was and how professional the reading voices were. His comments certainly didn't seem to convince Fr. Theall of anything but they ran me over like they were a two-ton truck of bricks! I had never heard of these "talking books," as he called them! Why, they could solve an awful lot of my reading needs if the titles I needed were available! I cornered the student on the stairway of the library as we left class that evening. He really didn't know too much more than he had shared in class, but he did tell me who to call to get all the information I wanted, and I called her the very next morning and visited her at the Division for the Blind and Physically Handicapped of the Library of Congress that very afternoon! It was like walking into a make-believe, a fairy-tale land for me. Why, they had thousands of book titles on hand for free borrowing, the record players for listening to the books were available on free loan, dozens of magazine titles were also available, and texts *needed by students or professionals would be done for them at no charge!!!* The service was available under Public Law for disabled Americans who could not read *normally* because of their visual or physical disability. Millions were estimated to be eligible to use the program; thousands were actually using it; millions did not know — like myself — that it even existed! It was FANTASTIC. By Friday of that very week I had my application for talking books completed, signed by Fr. Kortendick, and delivered to the Division for the Blind and Physically Handicapped, and I walked out that afternoon with my own talking book record player and two shopping bags of talking books! I was in heaven. Some of the required reading for my Adult Book Selection, Young Adult Book Selection, and Children's Literature courses were available already in the recorded format. With the talking books I could "read" eight to ten times as fast as my letter-by-letter approach. And no one, not one of the many specialists, none of the State personnel who had kept in touch with us those early years after the illness, no one had ever told us about all this! It was literally digging up a buried treasure *completely by accident!*

I remember well the first talking book I read that year, Kamala Markandaya's "Nectar in a Sieve." The records were playing and I was doing manual chores about my room. All of a sudden I realized I was standing perfectly still in the center of the room totally entranced by the story. I know not how long I had been standing there but I had very evidently been pulled right into the book from the real world where I had been doing little chores.

As I look back at it now, that "accidental" discovery of talking books was perhaps one of the most momentous happenings in my life since my illness itself. That discovery changed and affected my life right down to this day. One day while I was enjoying a talking book in my room I began to wonder if perhaps there might not be other "treasures" out there that I could be taking advantage of but knew nothing about. An idea was born, a thesis topic was approved in Maine, and the Director of my thesis project accepted the outline for it, though he thought it a bit big for a master's degree undertaking. The idea was to research *everything* that Maine, my home state, had available for visually and physically handicapped readers! The project was excitedly received by authorities at the Division of Eye Care and Special Services in Augusta, Maine. The project, when published, would be an invaluable tool for acquainting people with available resources and also for pointing up needs for additional resources. The project had never been undertaken before so that made it especially suitable as a degree-thesis project. And, finally, the project would tell *me* what else might be available for use.

The "school library thesis project" that I had originally intended to research wasn't even given the courtesy of a "decent burial;" it was simply *forgotten!* The thesis project, picked up very early in the year, was excellent in that it tied the whole year together meaningfully for me. Smaller projects for individual courses were somehow tied in with this larger one. When a "Bibliography" course assigned each student to compile a bibliography (ordered list of titles) on a particular subject, I simply chose to prepare mine on "Services for the Handicapped in Maine". That list put me in touch with most of the existing literature – very little at the time – that might be helpful in preparing my own work.

In December, 1969, while on semester break from the university, I traveled to the State Capitol in Augusta, Maine, and met with the authorities who had approved the project, discussed its scope, direction and publication. Shopping bags of materials, brochures, survey forms, etc. were picked up while on the trip. At the same time visits and interviews were arranged at "service centers" for the handicapped readers in Maine. Service providers were interviewed for inclusion in the completed work. Statistics, geographical data, survey information, all had to be gathered. The project got more exciting with each new phase that suggested itself.

Some results of the research seemed apparent and appalling long before the final report was prepared – the great disparity between the number of potential users of every given service and the number of actual users of the service! It hurt! I was far from the "only one" who had gone without merely because I did not know! A haunting question followed and would have to be given consideration in the "Recommendations" section of the final thesis report: *What do we do about it? How do we wipe out the ignorance that keeps most from the services that could enable them to live more fruitful, enjoyable, giving lives in their world?*

I don't recall the exact sequence of events but somehow at the same time as all the thesis research was going on, I found myself more and more involved in the quest to "wipe out the ignorance." The idea, dream, of helping to wipe out that ignorance personally begins to form. Leaders in the field that I interviewed suggested the need for someone fulltime "on the road," others suggested more specifically, "someone who would be free to go and find them whenever and wherever they are to be found," and the then "Chief" of the Library of Congress's Division for the Blind and Physically Handicapped asks "why don't *you* go out and do it?" It was an intriguing, enticing, but totally unrealistic suggestion at first. As I look back on that year I find it absolutely incredible what was accomplished in the one year. While carrying the seven courses each semester and continuing to do most of the reading letter-by-letter because it was too late that year to get many of the specific texts recorded, I also managed to complete all of the research, travels, interviews, surveys, etc. for the thesis. I organized all of the materials and got the first draft of the 125-page report typed – all by the beginning of the 1970 summer session! I guess I was too closely involved in it at the time to see the outright "miracle of God" that it really was!

As the thesis research neared completion the idea of my possibly dedicating my life in service to handicapped persons began to seem more and more "real." I talked more seriously now with professionals in service to the handicapped and they couldn't encourage me enough. Several of them advanced two specific reasons for their "backing" of the idea: first, I myself was handicapped, a fact that could be a tremendous gift in such work; and secondly, I was a religious, I had no family and I didn't work a "40-hour week" but supposedly had dedicated my life to service; many of the handicapped would be able to be reached only in the evenings, on weekends, etc., when it would be rather difficult for a family man or woman to be "free" to be there for them. I also began talking with several brothers in the community. What did they think about a Brother doing specialized ministry like this? Should I consider requesting permission of superiors to try the work? The encouragement received from my Brothers in the community was at least as strong as that which I had received from the professionals in the field. Several of them even went so far as to point out that, in their view, the ministry with the handicapped seemed to be the natural "next piece" in a whole chain of events that had brought me to this moment. I had survived the meningitis, my central vision had returned, the success in school with letter-by-letter reading, getting into the Brothers, the growth through teaching, getting into library work, writing just *one* letter and coming up with the grant that had brought me to Washington in the first place, discovering the talking books by "accident"... Were there really any "accidents" or was this not perhaps the natural calling of my life? I had come to Washington to prepare to be Denis Hall's first full-time professional librarian. The Georgetown University workshop and all of my studies at Catholic University were intended to prepare me for my return to Alfred, Maine. Now I began to wonder just what I was indeed being prepared for.

After much hesitation and prayer I finally decided to ask permission to try the work for one year. Too many things pointed towards it; I had to try it. Upon receiving my request in early 1970, the Provincial Superior wrote and explained that a new superior would be taking over with the "General Chapter" of the Brothers in March. He said that he'd rather not make this decision, so I should continue to pray about it and he would discuss with the newly appointed superior my request. The "General Chapter" was like the "top governing body" of the world-wide congregation of the Brothers of Christian Instruction. Superiors from all over the world plus elected delegates convened every six years to renew the congregation in the spirit of its founder, Father De La Mennais, the spirit of the Gospel of Jesus Christ, and the needs of the Church at the present time. The "Superior General," and his council were elected by this "General Chapter," to serve and guide and administer the world-wide community of the Brothers of Christian Instruction. The new "General Council" would then appoint or reappoint the major superiors for the Brothers' communities in the various "provinces" of the world-wide congregation of teaching brothers. And so it was that with the General Chapter of 1970, a new Provincial Superior for the United States province of our Brothers was expected.

The new Provincial Superior wrote to me from Europe where the General Chapter had been convened. He pointed out that many of our own schools needed librarians and, therefore, he could not see releasing me from our school system to work in something completely different. I was very disappointed in his response; I was very torn as I read his letter. I had made Final Vows just the previous summer as a Brother of Christian Instruction and yet, the more I and many others looked at the whole prospect of my working in services with handicapped persons, the more clearly it seemed to be my calling. Were the "needs of the schools" the only consideration to be taken into account, I complained to myself as I read and reread the letter. They hadn't been that "eager" for me when the prospect of my teaching had been the consideration, I continued my meditative complaints. When I insisted, it was finally agreed that I should try the work for *one year* and then return to our communities.

Dozens of resumes were sent out and numerous trips were taken that spring in search of a job in services with the handicapped. I now had the permission to accept the job; I had to get the job to accept! One by one the responses to my inquiries for the job came in. Every area where we had schools was checked out first since the Provincial had insisted that if at all possible I live with our own Brothers while carrying on the work with the handicapped. One by one, every area where we had a school responded negatively to my inquiry for work. The work would have to pay for my needs and my support for the community so I had to find a paying job somewhere.

My job file was very carefully kept that spring. I kept a carbon copy of each resume I sent out and as the responses came in they were neatly filed with their requesting letter. If a response held some hope, I pulled its carbon request letter and the request and response went in a "maybe file." As long as I had correspondence in that "maybe file" my hopes stayed high. Eventually I even had to start a "yes file" and then life got exciting. In the end the tough decision had to be made: which "yes" do I say *"yes"* to?

The New York Public Library had sent its Personnel Recruiter to the university's library school early that year. He had spoken to us about the various types of services offered by the library system and had caught my interest when he mentioned in passing that the system did operate a "Library for the Blind and Physically Handicapped" as part of the nationwide service to handicapped readers. I had an interview with him along with many other job-seeking students of the library school. My thesis director, Dr. Elizabeth Stone who later succeeded Fr. Kortendick as head of the library school, really encouraged me to go in and see the recruiter. "You've got nothing to lose," she had said. *I gained a job!* I told the recruiter of my wish to find the handicapped and wipe out the ignorance that keeps so many of them from the services they could be enjoying and using. I told him "my own story" and he took copious notes during the interview. I filled out an application for work at his insistence, gave him a copy of my typed resume, thanked him for his time, went home and wondered, what file will this one end up in, "no thanks," "maybe," or "yes?" It made it all the way to the *"yes"* file by mid-April, 1970, and I had promised him a response within a month of the offer! On May 15th, 1970, I looked at my "yes" file and decided to place my *yes* with the New York Public Library's offer. They were the closest to any of our Brothers' communities; I knew

66

from talking with the recruiter that there was plenty of public transportation in the city: a car wasn't desirable! My "yes" was greeted warmly by return mail and I was advised to report for work on Tuesday after Labor Day that September! I was hired! FANTASTIC! New York City here I come!

With a job in hand, I buckled down to the work of completing the thesis research and the other degree requirements. Second semester finished in early June and I packed up all of my notes, articles, survey forms and other needed supplies and headed for Denis Hall in Alfred. The Brothers there had graciously offered me a room, a typewriter, plenty of privacy and warm encouragement for putting together the final copy of the thesis. In a little less than three weeks the data was all organized and the first draft of the research project was typed! Since I was in Maine, I took the package of 125 typewritten pages to Augusta for the approval of the Division of Eye Care and Special Services. They quickly gave their approval and I left for Washington to obtain university approval before typing the final draft of the thesis. It's amazing what goes through your mind at moments like this. I personally carried the finished copy with me at all times for about a week and a half until a Xerox copy could be made. I had visions of losing the thesis and having to begin it all over again. I wouldn't even leave it in my room for fear it might be stolen! With final university approval the thesis was sent to the Division of Eye Care and Special Services in Augusta, Maine, where it was published for State use under the title: "Library Services for the Blind and Physically Handicapped in Maine: A State-of-the-Art Report, August, 1970.

The summer session, 1970, was spent preparing for the Master's Degree "Comprehensive Examinations," eight hours of testing given in two 4-hour sessions on the entire field of librarianship, Since the grant covered tuition for all courses, I took one more course that summer session and spent as much time as possible working as a volunteer at the Library of Congress, Division for the Blind and Physically Handicapped. That volunteer work was the most practical introduction to my upcoming work in New York City that I could have asked for. Much of the practical, how-to-do-it knowledge for working with the talking books, equipment and nationwide program came from those few weeks of volunteer work.

Comprehensive exams finally came, were taken...and passed...in late July, 1970, and my studies were over, the degree was awarded in August and immediate preparations were begun for my work in New York City.

10

"You know what you were hired for..."

When I look back at the year 1970 in my life I sometimes wonder how I made it through! In addition to the seven courses of study that spring semester, the thesis research, writing, and publishing, the comprehensive examinations and other details for completing the master's degree program, that year also brought the somewhat agonizing decision to begin work with the handicapped. Then the decision as to where that work would be done, and finally, the decision concerning living accommodations. This was really a "growing-up" time of my life. I had never made so many important decisions of my own before. Was this *really* the life-work I was being "called" to? Five or six job offers eventually came through. Which *one* should I take? And once New York City had been selected as the "scene" of my new life-work, where did I begin to find a place to live?

As a Brother of Christian Instruction all such decisions would have been spared me normally. The needs of the community's various schools determined where I would be assigned and what I would do there. By my vow of obedience I had promised to comply with all such assignments. The Brothers working at a particular school or institution lived in a "community residence" so if a brother was assigned to that school he "moved into" the community residence. In 1970, however, with the permission to try the new work being granted and the job site finally selected, I now found myself looking for a place to live. Since the Brothers of Christian Instruction had no community houses in the New York City area, I decided to seek housing with another community of teaching brothers in the city. It was sort of ironic that I had made Final Vows with the Brothers of Christian Instruction in the summer of 1969, just before leaving for Washington for graduate studies, and I would probably never live with one of the brothers' communities again! In Washington I resided with the Brothers of Christian Schools (Christian Brothers) for the first semester of my studies at the university and then with the Oblates of St. Joseph, another men's religious community, closer to the university campus, for the second semester and summer session. In New York City it was the Irish Christian Brothers teaching at Sacred Heart Grammar School in mid-Manhattan who opened the doors of their residence to me.

Until August, 1970, there were just too many things happening and decisions to be made to allow me any leisure time for wondering about or *fearing* what was coming next! It was like all the pieces of a puzzle fitting together *fast!* I hardly had time to contemplate one piece in place before several others had already fitted themselves around it!

On the Saturday of Labor Day weekend, 1970, my brother, Philip, drove me from Maine to New York in his red Mustang. That trip was a "new beginning" for the both of us. Phil had been an older teenager already when I was sick in 1953. I remember it was he and Dad who had picked me up at the hospital that FANTASTIC, snowy December 22nd morning when I had finally returned home! How many times that next year it was he who brought me to the doctor's office for those horrible penicillin shots or examinations! Or it was he who would drive Mom and me to the train station for yet another trip to an eye specialist or clinic when Daddy couldn't get off work. When I was a freshman in high school Phil had entered the Air Force. I remember well when he stopped in to visit me at the Brothers' prep school several years later on his way to Turkey. Since the prep school was so far from home, visits from the family had been few and therefore, always welcomed and well remembered! Now, the same year that my own life was taking a somewhat new direction Phil's life also was being redirected. He had decided to leave all and to enter the seminary to prepare for ordination to the priesthood. No one knew then all the circumstances that would lead him ultimately to the Archdiocese of Santa Fe, New Mexico, where he was ordained a priest in October, 1979!

Phil beautifully scheduled his drive to the seminary in Lexington, Kentucky, to give me a ride as far as New York, my new "home." The trip down from Maine was both too long and far too short! As the miles sped by I couldn't wait to get there to begin this FANTASTIC new adventure in my life, but I also wished the trip wouldn't end because I knew that when it did Phil would continue on his journey alone and I would be left *alone* in New York City. Now I *did* look ahead and secretly I was *scared stiff!* We did eventually arrive in New York, found the Irish Christian Brothers' residence at 416 West 51st Street, and unpacked my suitcases and boxes. Phil was FANTASTIC. He brought me to a subway station — my first time — showed me how to purchase the "tokens", deposit them in the turnstiles, board the *right* trains, read the subway maps, etc. We even found the Library for the Blind and Physically Handicapped together. I sure hated to see him leave the next morning. I dreaded that moment when I'd be left alone in the city. I even asked myself how I had ever gotten myself into "this mess"...

Somehow, Phil's departure brought me back vividly to exactly ten years previous when Mom and Dad and Gerry had left after bringing me for the first time to the Brothers' prep school. It was like starting all over again.

The bout of loneliness and homesickness lasted but a few hours, however, this time. Unpacking and setting up my room on the fourth floor of the brothers' five-story brownstone "walk-up" killed a few hours of that Sunday. Meeting and getting acquainted with the Brothers themselves pretty much occupied the remainder of that first day in the big city.

Monday was Labor Day and I wasn't scheduled to begin work until Tuesday morning so I decided to do some "exploring." As I left the Brothers' house that morning a real thrill of excitement ran through my whole being. Suddenly it hit me that my new life was beginning...it wasn't a dream...it wasn't someone else's...it was mine...I was in New York City – *alone* – and now "alone" was a FANTASTIC gift! My mind quickly raced along the footsteps of my life since the meningitis in 1953...the blindness..the can't-do's...the fear of not being able to do *anything* with my life...the questions about what I wanted to do after high school...the brothers...teaching...the boarding school library...Catholic University...talking books...a thesis...a lifework...here and now! But the excitement was even deeper. Suddenly I discovered *I was on my own.* I came and went from the Brothers' house as I chose...I didn't even have to ask someone to drive me...the Brothers had no car. "We" all used the subways and buses.

Very carefully I tried to retrace the steps Phil and I had taken the morning before and what a wild, thrilling moment it was when I came up the subway steps and found myself in front of the Library for the Blind and Physically Handicapped! It was truly FANTASTIC! I had done it alone! I even found my way back "home" again! This was really great! I kissed the sidewalks of that city that Labor Day as I realized I *could indeed* get wherever I had to go *by myself!* I had been hired by the Library to travel and find the handicapped throughout the city and all over Long Island. Maps of the city and Long Island had been sent to me and had given me many a second thought – and nightmare – about my new lifework! But now, after a day of exploring I kissed those concrete sidewalks with *relief.* I could do it and I could do it *alone! I needed no one* and that was somehow quite thrilling for me! For a while I was like a kid with a new toy. I'd find myself on the street map, transpose it to the subway map with all its green and blue and red lines and black dots...then I'd pick a place I wanted to find, locate the proper subways and transfers I had to take and off I'd go to see "if it really worked." And it was like magic; it really *did* work. Coming up from underground I'd "miraculously" find myself exactly where I had *hoped* to end up. FANTASTIC!

One of the things I liked best about the subways was that they made every stop whether people got on/off or not. That meant I could find the stop I wanted on the subway map, count the number of stops from where I was now, and that made it easier to get off at the right stop; I didn't have to worry about trying to read the station stops as the train zoomed in and out. My first day on the job taught me just how valuable this *gift* was!

I reported for work that Tuesday morning at the Library's central offices, to my surprise with dozens of other new employees of the library systems. I felt like a new little monkey in the zoo that everybody and his uncle wanted to see. After hours of filling out medical, personnel, financial, and governmental forms and more hours of interviews with various supervisory personnel I was finally put in a New York City taxicab and sent off to the Library for the Blind and Physically Handicapped at 166 Avenue of the Americas, in lower Manhattan.

One of the New York Public Library's eighty branches, the Library for the Blind and Physically Handicapped was responsible for providing Braille and talking-book services for visually and physically handicapped readers throughout the five boroughs of the City and all over Long Island as well. It was primarily a mail-order service with readers telephoning or mailing in their request from catalogs and librarians and clerical staff responding to these requests. Thousands of volumes were sent out via "free mail" each week.

"You know what you were hired for," the Branch Librarian told me after formal introductions were over and we were seated at her desk. "The library is presently serving about six thousand five hundred readers. It's your job to get out there (she pointed to the door) and find the thousands we aren't serving and acquaint them with our services. The sooner you get out — the more you stay out there — the better you will be doing your work!" Wow, what a job description! I was excited as I heard her speak. I found it hard to believe she was talking to me! Her talk removed all vestiges of fear concerning my new life-work that still remained! As I left the library for "home" that evening I was walking on air. It really seemed like everything I had hoped it would be.

As I prepared to leave the library at 5:00 p.m. no thought of the New York City "rush hour" crowd occured to me. Brought up in Maine's small towns, no idea of the immensity of those crowds was possible! I carefully re-examined my subway map, counted six stops of the "Eighth-Avenue local" which would take me closest to the Brothers' residence, said my "good-byes" and walked out the front door of the library, turned left on the sidewalk and started down the subway stairs. I could not believe the crowd on that subway platform! I am sure that there were more people on that concrete siding that night – and every working night – than there were in my entire home town in northern Maine! I wormed my way down the crowded stairway and up the platform to about the middle of the station. Trying not to appear too conspicuous, I surveyed the ocean of people all around me and the similar one on the other side of the station. It was simply incomprehensible! And to think that this was but one out of hundreds of such platforms equally as crowded at this exact moment all over the city. It was mind boggling!

As I stood there I suddenly felt a rush of cool air across my face and then heard the thunderous approach of the train. It was frighteningly loud! It stopped. The doors opened. And what happened next I'm still not sure but all of a sudden I heard the doors close again, but they were behind me! I hadn't taken a single step but somehow had been *carried* onto the train. "Panic" would be a mild description of my state at that moment. I hadn't even had time to focus and *try to read* the train identification. Was I on the *right train?* Did other trains besides the one I had wanted stop at this particular station? Would this one make all the same stops the map said it should? Was the map valid for "rush-hour" trains? Before I knew it we had stopped at another station; I couldn't believe they could crowd more people onto that train but they did and at least as many as had gotten on at our station stop! I counted the stops and held my breath as I fought my way off the train at the sixth stop. Trying to get off the train with hundreds trying to get on through the same doorway was all but impossible. Somehow, I made it. Finding my way about ground I looked for the nearest street sign – another blessing of New York, every street corner has them! Whatever fears of "big city living" I might have still had up to that moment were instantly *wiped away* as I read the "Eighth Avenue" and "West 50th Street "signs! I was as good as home! I knew my way from there; I had made it "home" in the rush hour! FANTASTIC!

Five Irish Christian Brothers lived in the community on West 51st Street where I took up residence that fall. They were FANTASTIC in helping me to get to know the city and its "ways." I quickly learned that the "big city" was like a conglomeration of "small towns." The Brothers all taught at the Catholic grammar school "around the corner" on 52nd Street. The parish church was at the end of the block, a hospital was just across the street from the residence. One apartment building on the block had as many families living in it as we had had in our town in Maine. The parish covered only a few blocks. I was amazed to find so many churches so close together. The conveniences of the city were fascinating. The corner grocery store, shoe repair, dry cleaner, hardware store, you name it, they were all there at your fingertips! You didn't have to "send something away" to a service center; the service center was right there in the city. It was neat recognizing addresses I had heard so often on TV and radio. Impressed with all of these "conveniences at your fingertips", I decided to make use of one of them my second Saturday in the big city. I had a tape recorder needing repair so I looked up the nearest service center in the Manhattan Yellow Pages – 1184 Madison Avenue. By now I saw myself as somewhat of an "old hand" at getting around the city. I remembered that Madison Avenue was "a few" blocks "that way" so I figured I'd walk to Madison Avenue and then follow it until I came to 1184. I loved the convenience of it all! Well, the walk from Tenth Avenue to Madison Avenue took long enough; I found a building number and saw that I had to walk "uptown" to reach 1184. Religiously I watched for building numbers as I began my hike up Madison Avenue. Block after block, ever so slowly those numbers climbed toward 1184. When I finally reached it I had walked from 51st Street to 96th Street! It was both a thrill and a relief to find the name of the store to coincide with what the Yellow Pages had said it should be! I left the recorder there for repairs and began my long hike home. Remembering that on my crosstown walk to Madison Avenue I had crossed Fifth Avenue, I decided to go back on 96th Street and find Fifth Avenue for my downtown walk to 51st Street. I had only walked one block, however, when my limited vision was literally stunned by the scene in front of me: *green* grass, trees, leaves... I seriously wondered if I had walked out of the city! It was only that evening when I plotted my day's journey on my street map that I discovered that my day's find was called *Central Park!* The Brothers at the residence had many a chuckle over my "finds" those first few months of my stay in the big city.

I spent my first few weeks at the library learning the various routines of the library's procedures and services. In addition to finding my way around the library, my days were spent talking with readers on the telephone or in person if they dropped in, filling their requests for more reading materials, familiarizing myself with available reading materials and procedures for getting them to the readers, handling the books themselves and preparing them for mailing or returning them to the shelves when the mail trucks brought them in. One specific "in house" assignment was to get to know the talking-books equipment well enough to advise users with problems over the telephone! It was some challenge to explain to a totally blind reader how to change the needle on his record player! The patience of the readers with their new "technician" was phenomenal! Each time a new reader received a machine he had to be helped over the phone to unpack, set up, and operate the record player or cassette player. It was always deeply gratifying to hear the new reader's excitement of having succeeded in setting up and now hearing for the very first time a real "talking book!" After a few such weeks at the Library for the Blind and Physically Handicapped learning the ropes, I knew it was time to "get out" and do what I was hired to do – to find those who knew nothing about the library's services. Other than a speech course while in college and three years of teaching I really had no experience whatever in public speaking. I had never done this type of work before and I had no predecessor at the library who had done it so I had no shoes to step into. How would I get appointments to speak? What would I speak about if I did get an appointment and how would I answer all the questions? I procrastinated for a few days, weeks... I spent time preparing a slide tape presentation of the library's programs and services. I studied all the available equipment and services and their use. And finally, one day I sat at my desk in the back corner of the office at the library and dialed four numbers on the telephone, four agencies serving the handicapped...and I ended up with four appointments to "come out and speak about the program!" I thought the worse was over I had crossed the threshold. While preparing the first talk an idea came to mind, I would simply tell my own story, but in the third person. I would tell the story of "a little boy" who had had meningitis, etc. right up to the point of that little boy discovering "talking books" while in graduate school at the Catholic University of America in Washington, D.C. Then I would reveal myself as that "little boy" and go on to tell my audience what talking books now meant to my life. I would end the talk with a demonstration of the talking book record player, cassette tape player, talking books, magazines, catalogs, workings of the program, eligibility requirements, etc. I had given a similar "third person speech" while in speech course in college, telling why I had become a brother, and it had gone over quite well. It was worth a try in this situation. It worked, far better than I had dared anticipate. Each of my first four talks brought invitations to speak to other groups and the long road to today opened up before me. Rarely after that did I have a chance to sit at my desk and make telephone requests to "come out and speak." Most of the requests came to the library. A calendar soon began to fill with daytime, luncheon and evening programs. I loved the work immensely! I was at home in it.

In November, 1970, as my speaking work and other work with the Library for the Blind and Physically Handicapped was just beginning to "take off", the head librarian at the branch announced her retirement. It was she who had welcomed me my first day on the job and had told me warmly, "You know why you were hired...get out and do it!" I had hardly gotten to know her these short few months but I did know her enough to know that I would truly miss her when she did retire.

I had been working for the New York Public Library for about a year when in August, 1971, I received a telephone call one morning from one of the personnel supervisors in the system. She informed me that a reporter and photographer from the New York Daily News would be down later that day to interview me. They had decided to "do my story" in the paper. I said "no thanks" and hung up the phone. In less than a minute it had rung again. It was the same supervisor. "You came here to spread services for the handicapped," she said promptly, "and your story in the paper will do just that! I'm sending that reporter down." I had never been interviewed before. Just about the time I began to wonder when the interview was going to begin I realized it was over! I was scared as I watched them leave the library. What were they going to say? How was the article going to be worded? Would they let me see it before "going to press?" What would the family, the Brothers say about it? The article came out, "Brother Martin's Mission To Spread the Recorded Word." I hurried to the newsstand early on the day it was supposed to come out. I bought a copy of the Daily News, walked away and found the article. I read it, letter by letter standing there on the street corner. A deep sign of relief told whoever happened to be watching that I liked what I read; my purchase of a hundred copies told the newsstand vendor that I loved it! I sent copies out to everyone in the family, the Brothers, and I gave copies to anyone and everyone who wanted, or would take one! And then the responses began to come in. A hundred and sixty-five traceable responses came from the single article! People wrote and called asking for information about the talking books they had read about in the paper. Organizations called and wrote asking for speakers and programs about the talking books. One lady called and asked me to send her a copy of "The Godfather" which had been mentioned in the article. When I suggested that perhaps it was not the type of book she thought it was, she responded sweetly, "Oh, Brother Martin, I'm sure if you enjoyed it I will too." I sent her the book. The article also brought a number of requests for visits to families of handicapped individuals. The responses certainly verified the supervisor's words, "your story in the paper will do just that!" More and more that summer and fall I came to see that my story was perhaps the most powerful tool I had for spreading the services to those in need. Each time I told it or it appeared in a paper more requests came to do it again.

11

"Couldn't you do both?"

In "official circles" at the New York Public Library I was addressed as "Mr. Martin" when I first arrived on the scene in 1970. That had been their choice and I hadn't really objected to the use of the title "Mr.". The Daily News interview, however, a year after my arrival in the city brought out the fact that I was a "Brother" a member of a Catholic religious community of men. Because of that "revelation" a new type of request began to come in to the library. Individuals and families just needing someone to talk to began calling. Religious organizations asked that I come and speak. Some homebound handicapped even asked if I could come and "celebrate the Mass" for them. I would explain that I was a "Brother" and not a "Priest", that the two were different like a doctor and a lawyer, that a Brother did apostolic work like teaching, hospital work, or work like I was doing, whereas a priest was ordained for sacramental, worship ministry – serving the people of God through the various sacraments, preaching, teaching and counseling. They would listen and then add, "couldn't you do both?" I'd laugh gently and say no. As a Brother I could not become a Priest. The Brothers were founded strictly for teaching and related work and part of the Constitutions of the Brothers of Christian Instruction specified that the Brothers should not go on for ordination.

At first when the discussion of priesthood/brotherhood would come up it was just that, a discussion that made an interesting evening but not much more. The priesthood wasn't much more than a topic of idle conversation for me at that time because religion itself had become little more than just that in my life! It was a strange time in my life, to say the very least! I was a Brother in name but certainly not in living style! I rarely met with the Brothers those years, rarely visited our own communities or took any interest in things of the Brothers. "My" life and "my" work had pretty much become "my all!"

If I'm truly honest, I'd have to say that even God was shoved to the back seat – or out altogether – those years. I had prayed to Him in times of trouble in my life. He was the one I had turned to when everything I had tried failed and I had no other recourse. When the Brothers had discovered my blindness, then I'd slip into the chapel and sob my "Why don't You cure my eyes so they'll accept me?" But each hurdle I made, I found myself needing Him less and less, turning to Him in real prayer less and less frequently.

Prayer gradually became little more than "words I said" or "times spent in the chapel." When I arrived in New York City and found the thrill of *independence* from family, friends, Brothers, I also seemed to have found *independence* from God as well. Those were the days when I'd go into the Church with the other Brothers, make the Sign of the Cross and then wake up from my daydreams at the end of Mass and wonder with embarrassment whether I had taken part at all with the rest. Did I stand up and kneel down at all? Did I go to Communion? Or did I just sit there, lost in my plans and daydreams of the day ahead? I honestly couldn't tell you. Even my vowed religious life had come to mean very little at this time. Obedience? I did *my* thing: it was *my* work; I carefully protected myself those days from the advice and counsel of family and Brothers. Obedience? Poverty? My salary with the city was nine or ten thousand dollars. I had a bank account, paid my room and board, took care of *all* my incidental needs, travels, etc., and, *if anything was left over,* I sent a check to the Brothers. Poverty? Chastity? Well, I wasn't married. Chastity? Community prayers with the Brothers I lived with were few and usually hurried; on holidays they were to be said privately which meant I didn't say them at all.

Yes, it's little wonder that the issue of brotherhood/priesthood was little more than a topic of discussion for me at that time in my life. The real, amazing wonder is that it seems to be precisely through the call to the priesthood that I was "bull-dozed" out of my total laxness in religion!

After the Daily News story I began receiving more and more invitations to speak and do programs for Church-related groups and societies and organizations. More and more I began to see the FANTASTIC beauty of "that world" that seemed so foreign to me. More and more I found myself wanting to become part of them. How many times, after speaking for an organization affiliated with the Catholic Church and serving the handicapped, I would leave an application to join its staff! I didn't recognize the real hunger inside me at that time. I really thought that what I wanted was to leave the city's employment and work for the Church. That was it, I thought.

Meanwhile thoughts and urgings toward serving the handicapped as a priest keep coming up. In November, 1971, Brother Hervey Brooks who had been a powerful inspiration in my life with the Brothers from my first year at the prep school, announced his decision to leave the Brothers to be ordained a priest. I attended his ordination and first Mass as a Priest and that seemed to give new life and substance to the call I seemed to be hearing from the handicapped back in New York. As I found myself in the homes of the handicapped persons in the city I began to see more and more how I could serve them more fully as a Priest. Their religious, spiritual needs seemed to take on a greater importance and the neat thing was that I was sure I could do both things — serve them as I was now, and as a priest at the same time! One fact, however, cast quite a negative light on the whole possibility of the calling to the priesthood. I was a brother, a Brother of Christian Instruction with Final Vows. The Constitution of the Brothers specifically stated that the Brothers would not be ordained priests. And that seemed to take care of that! Except that the idea wouldn't "go away." Situations, needs, circumstances kept bringing it up.

Finally, in March of 1972, after a whole series of these "calling events" I decided to go to Maine for a private "retreat" at the rectory of a priest friend, Fr. Roger Bolduc. I knew that Fr. Roger knew me quite well and I hoped that somehow he'd be able to help. His first parish as a priest had been my family's parish in Limestone, Maine. His first wedding as a priest was my sister, Martha's wedding in July, 1962. He and I had spent six weeks together in Washington, D.C., in the summer of 1970, my last summer session at Catholic University. He had been attending a religious workshop there and so we had managed to share quite a bit of time together that summer. He had often since invited me to come up and spend time with him at his new assignment in Old Orchard Beach at St. Margaret's Parish. So, now, I decided to do just that. Fr. Roger was delighted at the idea when I called so off I went in late March.

Old Orchard Beach, a FANTASTIC summer resort, is deserted in late March! I had the beach all to myself. While Father Roger carried out his normal priestly and parish duties I spent time wandering up and down the miles of deserted ocean beaches. At first my intent was to "can" the idea of the priesthood once and for all. I had done pretty well at canning it, I thought, until one evening when the two of us sat talking for a long time and the "call" came stronger than ever before. I broke down and shared the whole story with Father Roger. What did he think? Was I stupid...running...or was the call perhaps for real? It had persisted for an awful long time and somehow I wanted it settled, I told him. Little did I know then, thank God, how many more long years it would persist before it would finally be settled! Father Roger was beautiful. "Patrick," he said, "I'd love to say *come and join me as a priest!* but I cannot; that wouldn't be fair to you. All I can say is that I will be here and will be willing to help you in any way possible as you seek the discernment and help you need in this whole area." He offered to take me to meet and talk with the "vocation director" for the Diocese of Portland so that I might discuss with him the possibility of a vocation as a "priest for the handicapped." We prayed together that night and the next day I decided to take him up on his offer to visit the diocese's vocation director. It was an exciting visit. I simply described to him the idea that kept calling me, the idea of a priest ordained to bring the Church to those who could not come to it. The more we talked, the more excited he got. "I'm supposed to play 'devil's advocate'," he said at one point, "and I'm more excited about the whole idea than you are!" That afternoon while Father Roger and I were at lunch he spoke with the bishops of the diocese about my calling and brought back the message that they would be happy to receive my application to enter the diocese with that calling in mind if I decided to follow it through! I couldn't believe it! I had come, I thought, to can the idea and now I was leaving with an invitation to follow it! FANTASTIC!

After a brief visit with Mom at home in Sanford, Maine, I flew to Canton, Ohio, where the Brothers were gathered at Walsh College for our Easter Retreat. That Holy Thursday night was one long night! Should I, or shouldn't I? I kept asking myself. Finally I decided to talk to Brother Francis Blouin, the Provincial Superior, about my wish to leave the Brothers in order to pursue the calling to serve the handicapped as a priest. Once the decision was made, I think I got some sleep that night. But, Good Friday morning, 1972, I will never, never, never forget. Brother Francis and I walked back and forth on the sidewalk outside College Hall for several hours. I shared with him the whole idea, how it kept coming up, the FANTASTIC beauty of the calling, if it were possible, the reaction at the vocation director's office in Maine. No, he told me categorically, he could not back my move to become a priest, because I had recently taken final vows. He did not see how God could be asking me to move away from them so rapidly. He was sure it was only because I was a very emotional person and prone to act fast or compulsively. He asked me to wait a month before even considering the idea again. A lot of heat but little light was generated in our discussion on the sidewalk that Good Friday morning. His final request, that I wait a month before taking any action...well, I agreed to it, but very reluctantly. I had so much wanted him to be as excited about it as I had been, his reaction had really discouraged me. Good Friday afternoon just dragged on and on like it would never end.

That evening the retreat director, Father Ralph Ragowski, a Dominican priest from South America, announced that he would be available if any of the Brothers wanted to see him about anything. I decided to go in and lay out everything before him. He was a total stranger, I reasoned, he could be objective in his counsel. After I had shared "the whole story" with him, Father Ralph said, "Pat, can we pray?" "Sure," I said placing my hands in his that were reaching out to me. We, or maybe "he" (I really don't remember) prayed for some time and then he looked at me with a strange but beautiful look of peace. "I've got two things to say," he said after a brief pause. "First, you're going to be a priest for the handicapped! No, I don't know where, when, or how, but don't worry, it will come." He paused and then continued, "Secondly, you've got to learn to share your prayer with others. I'm going to give you the address of the Fordham Charismatic Prayer Community in New York. Look them up when you get back. They can be a great support to you in your calling." He took out a small, pamphlet-like directory, copied an address and handed the slip of paper to me. We shook hands. I thanked him warmly and left, walking, somewhat, on air. I couldn't believe his "prophecy" — "First, you're going to be a priest for the handicapped..." He had said the words so distinctly and so deliberately. I repeated his words over and over again with utter disbelief. He had said them...with authority! I was baffled and excited at the same time.

Back in New Ycrk I gave Brother Francis his requested one month, and even added ten days to it! Finally, on Ascension Thursday, 40 days after Easter, I sat down and wrote him a long, typewritten letter begging his brotherly support in this calling and informing him that I had indeed decided to apply for admission as a candidate for Holy Orders in the Diocese of Portland. On the same day I completed and sent in the application form with all other necessary documentation accompanying it. Both envelopes in the mail, I now could do nothing but wait. How often during those weeks of waiting I would recall with excitement that prophecy of Father Ralph Ragowski. I had never bothered to look up the Fordham Prayer Community, his second request. In fact, on leaving his office that Good Friday night, I had nonchalantly thrown the address in the washroom wastepaper basket. After some three weeks the wait ended abruptly, I wished afterwards that it hadn't ended at all, for with the end of the long wait came also the apparent end of hope! Two letters arrived the same day — mysteriously — one from the diocese and one from Brother Francis. I read Brother Francis's letter first. It was brief and very much to the point stating simply that he could not in any way give the "brotherly support" I had asked for in my letter, because he still was certain I was making a mistake. In fact, he went on, he had not recommended that I be accepted by the Diocese of Portland for two main reasons. First, he truly believed that the decision to move from the brotherhood to the priesthood was too rapidly a change of life's orientation. Secondly, he reasoned that because of its extensive size, Maine should be the last state to select if I did move to ordination. Its size would only complicate my transportation problems.

He had not, nor would he veto their accepting me, but the vocation director had said that I would not be accepted without his recommendation. He continued, that in all honesty, he could not recommend me. The diocesan letter added nothing new to the day's bad news, it merely confirmed that I had read the first letter correctly.

I became an embittered man, a hate-filled man, that night. Angrily, I ran up and down every block between 34th Street and 57th Street and between Eighth Avenue and the Hudson River. I was angry and I nursed the anger well as I ran frantically up and down each block. I must have been some sight to see. I told myself that my life had been played with like a pawn on a chess board, that a major decision had been decided for me and I hadn't even known that the meeting to discuss it was taking place. He had no right, no right, I repeated to play with my life or anybody's life that way. I filled my pocket with the needed coins and stopped at a pay phone to call and tell him off! I wanted to tell him to "process me out of the order" immediately; I wanted to have no part whatever with a community that treated its members that way! I was mad and rehearsed my words as I dialed and waited for it to ring and then waited for the ring to be answered...but it never was. Why? How come? What was the Provincial House number? Somebody was *always* there to answer in case of emergency. But no matter how many times I dialed *nobody ever picked up that phone!* It was as if 400 miles away in Maine they knew I was calling at that precise moment and decided not to answer! That only enraged me more. I tried for days to reach Brother Francis by phone, but always no answer. I tried writing. I'd begin a letter when I got home from work, continue it in the morning before leaving for work but by the time I'd get home from work to continue it again I had lost my train of thought and so I'd have to rip the pages out of the typewriter and start all over again. I had so much that I had to tell him. He just had to be "told off" before he ruined some other brother's life as he had now ruined mine! Several days — weeks? — of this trying to make contact with him elapsed with no success. It was almost the end of May when I received a call at the library one morning. The mother of a handicapped child was calling at the recommendation of a woman who worked at the Xavier Society for the Blind in New York. The worker had told this woman that "if anyone could help her daughter this 'Brother' who worked at the Library for the Blind and Physically Handicapped could!" Yes, I told the woman, I'd be happy to come and visit the family, in fact, I'd come that weekend, the Sunday before Memorial Day. I didn't know what I could do for the child; I was flattered by the recommendation by Patty Mount at the Xavier Society but I'd like to visit and observe the child before saying or doing anything. I was asked to come and spend the afternoon with the family and then have Sunday dinner with them. That sounded great so I said I'd be there. The visit was FANTASTIC: I fell in love with the whole family and still treasure their friendship to this day. Watching and talking with ten-year-old Justine, who had almost no useable sight and only one functioning hand, a number of "dreams" suggested themselves in the course of that afternoon — like learning to touch-type with only the one hand and no sight; like learning to operate reel-to-reel and cassette tape recorders so she could "listen" to her textbooks which were obtainable in talking-book format, etc. The family was excited and so was I as we planned the calendar for typing lessons that I would come and give Justine as a volunteer one evening each week. It was Wednesday morning after Memorial Day before I got around to calling the Xavier Society for the Blind to thank Patty Mount for her recommendation. She listened as I described my afternoon with the Hopper family. When I had finished she commented briefly and excitedly and then said simply, "Brother Pat, I'm going to a 'prayer meeting' tonight. Would you like to come with me?"

"No thanks," I said without hesitating a moment. "Patty, with my volunteer work on top of my regular work I'm on the road 80 or 90 hours some weeks. I'm sure my calendar's booked for tonight already."

"Would you check?" she persisted. I checked and found the page of my calendar wide open. Without telling her that, I said simply, "Where are you going, Patty?"

"Fordham," she said nonchalantly. "The Fordham Prayer Community meets every Wednesday night. Can you come?" Was it mere coincidence or was there some message here for me — the same prayer group that Father Ralph Ragowski, that Dominican priest from South America preaching a retreat for our Brothers in Canton, Ohio, six weeks or so earlier, had recommended to me... And my calendar was wide open. I had thrown away the address; it had come back to me. What was this all about? "Yeah, I guess I'll go," I said not very enthusiastically and wondering as I said it just what I was getting myself into!

I was still trying to reach Brother Francis those days, still unsuccessful, and still determined to process out of the Order as soon as possible. What was I doing going to a prayer meeting now?

Well, it was too late to back out now. I was sure Patty would read through whatever excuse I came up with for cancelling so I decided to go and brave the prayer meeting. I went, looking as unclerical as I could, wearing plaid trousers and a striped shirt or some other unruly combination. I didn't ask too many questions when I met Patty at the train station. She didn't say too much, if anything at all, about the upcoming experience.

We arrived. All I really remember about the night is that there were literally hundreds of people there for the prayer meeting and that in itself baffled me. From my point of life where prayer was something I did "because I was a brother and it was expected of me", I simply couldn't comprehend these hundreds of "fanatics???" who came every week for an *extra* night of prayer... It just didn't make sense. It was like being in another world. The whole group, perhaps two or three hundred stong, sat in a circle and simply prayed and sang together, shared scripture passages and personal experiences for a couple of hours. The Mass which climaxed the whole prayer meeting was simply one of the most awesome events of my life up to that point. Far from daydreaming or sleeping through it, I even found my eyes embarrassingly wet at times! I simply did not know what to make of the whole affair. The people seemed most sincere and rather sane when you talked with them but they strangely talked *excitedly* about the Lord and religion. That was just a totally different ball game for me and I simply didn't know how to handle it. I stood around waiting, hoping that Patty wouldn't take too long with all those hugs and goodbyes which flooded the place as people began to head for the real world again. All of a sudden I watched a lady turn around and head right for me. I knew she was coming to me but I didn't know what to do, where to go, how to escape! She spoke quickly and introduced herself as Marie Meagher and invited me to come to the "Core Meeting" on Sunday night! "Lady," I said, "this is my first prayer meeting; I don't know if I'm ever coming to another one of these, let alone your 'Core Meeting'! "Besides," I went on before she had a chance to interrupt, "I don't even know what a 'Core Meeting' is!"

"That's strange," she said when I finally gave her a chance to talk. "I don't even know why I asked you! The Core Meeting is simply a group of 'veterans' who have been with the prayer group for a year or so,who dedicate one extra night a week to prayer, asking God's guidance and blessings on this Wednesday night prayer meeting. We never ask strangers to it, so I don't really know what made me ask you, but I did, so please, feel free to come!" "*Another extra* night of *prayer?*" I wondered as she was taken away by someone with a question for her. These people were just *too much*.

One extra night of prayer a week *might* be conceivable, but now, another one on top of that??? Patty finally did get through all the hugs and goodbyes and we headed for the subway and home. I didn't talk too much, if my memory serves me correctly, on the way home but my mind certainly wasn't unoccupied that night. I kept trying to understand what I had experienced that night. It was without doubt the deepest, simplest, and most beautiful community-prayer experience I had ever had in my life! I had to keep telling myself that it had really happened. The timeliness of the experience bothered me terribly. Was it mere coincidence that it had happened then when I was in the middle of one battle royale in my life and faith and commitment to religious life? Or was it *arranged* that way? But by whom? Patty knew nothing of what was going on in my life, and I knew nobody else at the prayer meeting. By God? But did He do things like that? Did He really get involved in our day-to-day life? And if so, *why?* What was He trying to do with/for/to *me?* The questions were too many; the answers, too few. The following Wednesday night's space on my calendar remained unasked-for all that week. I almost prayed that it would stay that way. It's like I wanted to go back to Fordham just one more time to see if that make-believe world was really still there. Would it be the same? Had they, perhaps, staged a show for me? No, I was as taken by the second night at Fordham as I had been the first. And on the third Wednesday evening I found myself headed for the subway after work and Fordham University's prayer meeting once again! There was something fresh, spontaneous, genuine, simple, sincere..whatever it was, I found myself wanting more of it!

After three prayer meetings in a row I still found myself fascinated by the whole experience and really wanted more of it. What's more, it had already 'done something' to me; I had stopped trying to reach Brother Francis! I had not yet reached him since receiving his letter several weeks earlier and now I simply stopped trying to reach him. The Sunday after my third Wednesday at Fordham I found myself free and so I decided to go back to the University that night and find out what that "Core Meeting" was. I walked into a small room filled with about two dozen people, some of them somewhat familiar faces after my three weeks at the prayer meeting. It was very simply just another prayer meeting but its intent was clearly to pray for the guidance of the Lord on the larger Wednesday night prayer group. As we began to pray, eyes and hands somehow focused on the Lord, I recognized the voice of the priest who had celebrated the Mass each Wednesday at the end of the prayer meeting. He was now speaking to us as a group. "My brothers and sisters," he said, "let's pray tonight for someone in the group who's carrying a very heavy burden. I don't know who it is," he went on, "but I've felt a very heavy burden on the prayer group for the past three weeks. I don't know what it is but let's ask Christ, Who said 'Come to Me all you who are burdened and I will give you rest,' to come and take that burden whatever it is." We all assented silently and began to pray spontaneously and sincerely for whoever it was that was suffering so. I watched rather curiously as I saw a lady do something that seemed rather silly – she took her Bible, opened it without turning to anything specific, but just began to read wherever the book opened, "If one branch suffers the whole tree suffers..." I didn't listen to any more. The burden talked-about suddenly came clear, *me*, my quest for the priesthood for the handicapped, my anger, hatred and bitterness towards Brother Francis, and my determination to leave the brothers because of it all. Without taking time to rationalize, I simply blurted out, "You want your burden? I think I've got it!" And I told my story briefly. I ended the account, however, in a way I would have never dreamed ten minutes before! I didn't ask that group to pray that the Bishop would decide to override Brother Francis' veto. I didn't ask them to pray that Brother Francis would change his mind and decide to grant me the brotherly support I had sought. No, I simply asked them with a flood of unexpected tears to pray that my own heart would be melted and that one day I would be able to love the man I now hated so desperately, that I would one day be able to hug in love the man I now hated enough to attack physically had the Lord not kept some 400 miles between us! The beautiful priest who had spoken at the beginning of the prayer meeting now rose to his feet and addressed me directly and ever so gently, "Brother Pat," he began, "in all my years of priesthood I have never heard a more beautiful confession! Can I give you absolution in community as you have confessed in community?" My tears were warm and flowed freely now as I said, "Please," and those words of absolution were the most beautiful words I had ever heard. Hundreds of times I had heard them before in my life as a Catholic but somehow now they seemed so much richer and gentler and so much more real for me. That Sunday night had to be the most beautiful night of my life.

I don't remember the rest of the prayer meeting; I don't recall at all the subway ride home or even going home at all that night. Nothing else seemed important after that moment of absolution. It's like I was truly set free, free from what I wasn't really sure and it really didn't matter at that point! I was free. Now I simply, deliberately decided not to try any more to contact Brother Francis but instead to leave everything just as it was and let the Lord handle it. Over that summer I can say honestly and gratefully that the bitterness and hatred in my heart for the man who had stopped me cold in my tracks earlier that year truly did begin to melt and disappear. A gentle peace began to steal over me. I wondered what lay in store for me. What should I do? or, should I do anything at all? I decided simply to go on working and just wait and see what would happen. I did my best now to keep my Wednesday night calendar space open and found myself looking forward to those weekly returns to the Fordham Charismatic Prayer Community. I who had found it strange that people would actually give up an extra night a week for prayer, now found myself each Sunday night also at the prayer group's core meeting! I wasn't totally sold on all the goings-on of the prayer meetings or all the hugs and kisses on arrivals and/or departures...but something – someone? – there kept drawing me back and making me hunger for more. I even found myself getting uncomfortable somewhat about the routineness of my prayer life with the brothers where I lived; I seemed to thirst for more prayer-meeting-like gatherings.

In August of that year, 1972, when the roaches that were so common in the buildings of the area finally made it to the fourth floor of the house – where I lived – I decided to let them have my room! I picked up a copy of the newspaper, opened to the classified section, laboriously went through the "Apartments for Rent" section letter-by-letter and found one that looked just right! I called the given telephone number only to find out it was an agency. They said they had many apartments for rent, why didn't I come out and let them show me some. They were sure they had the one I was looking for! They did! A two-family home in East Elmhurst, Queens Borough, with the owner, a widow, living in the upstairs apartment and the downstairs, street-level apartment available for rent!

On August 15th I signed the lease for one year to begin on September 1st! The house was "walkable" to the subway station and right on the bus route which was convenient for inclement weather! Many of the people who attended the prayer meetings at Fordham regularly, also lived in the area; in fact, the lady who had invited me to the core meeting my first night at Fordham lived but a few blocks away with her family. The setting was just FANTASTIC! and everybody wanted to help furnish the place. I had nothing to furnish a bedroom of my own, let alone a five-room apartment! But, in two weeks it was furnished. The Hopper family in lower Manhattan found me a FANTASTIC "deal" on sixty five yards of wall-to-wall carpteting – $75.00 for the whole thing providing I'd install it myself! So, I did! Chairs, table, bed, dressers, dishes, linens, living room furnishings, you name it, it all came in from and through members of the prayer group and other friends like the Hoppers!

I moved into the apartment on Labor Day weekend just two years after I had first come to New York! We planned a Friday night prayer meeting in the apartment's large living room for people of the Fordham Prayer group who lived in the area and any of the neighborhood people who wanted to come. The first prayer meeting was scheduled for Friday night, September 15th. That happened to be the religious feast of Our Lady of Sorrows so the prayer group that developed became known as Our Lady of Sorrows Prayer Group. I ran around frantically after work that Friday preparing for the first prayer meeting at the house. I was excited but the nitty-gritties pushed the excitement into the background. We needed chairs, song books, coffee cups, coffee, tea, milk, sugar, and what else? Oh,...it suddenly dawned on me, I had no coffee percolator to prepare the coffee for after the prayer meeting. It was too late to do anything about it; the people were already on their way. I was dumbfounded, totally speechless when two ladies walked in that night carrying a "gift for the house," – a 36-cup coffee percolator!

The week after our first prayer meeting at the apartment I received a letter in the mail...from Brother Francis! He'd like to come and visit me the following Wednesday, his letter informed me. If he didn't hear from me to the contrary, he'd plan on arriving at about 5:00 p.m. that Wednesday evening. We could have supper together, he went on to suggest, spend the night together and then he would have to leave the next morning for Canton, Ohio, where he was due to visit the brothers at the college. I read the note not knowing really whether to be excited or to panic! "Father Joe," I said to the leader of the Fordham Prayer Community that Sunday night at the core meeting, "I'm scared! I hated that man last summer enough to attack him physically! Sure, the hate and bitterness seem to have been melted over this summer, but the melting has never been put to the test! That test is coming this Wednesday! What do I do? How can I be sure the bitterness and hate won't flare up again? And, secondly, Father Joe," I went on, "what do I say to convince him that the handicapped need a priest?"

"Patrick," Father Joe began, "do you dare fast and pray?" Why not, I had tried just about everything else, hadn't I. "Fast and pray these next three days before he arrives," Father Joe went on, "to take control over your own body, emotions, and life so you can give that control to Jesus Christ. If Jesus Christ controls this meeting with your provincial superior, I guarantee you," he said emphatically, "that there will be *no bitteress or hate*. Secondly, "he kept on going without giving me a chance to butt it, "as far as what to say to your provincial superior, *shut up and say nothing!* Trust totally that if the Lord wants the priesthood issue brought up He'll bring it up! Let him!" That was asking an awful lot but I decided that I really had no other alternative. I fasted and prayed like I had never prayed before those next three days.

On Wednesday afternoon I had just arrived at the apartment, had my key in the front door of the house, and I heard a car pull up behind me. What timing, I thought to myself as I recognized the provincial's pale green car, I had come home from Manhattan, he had come all the way from Maine, and we had arrived at exactly the same moment. I heard *two* car doors close. I looked back again to see one of the older brothers walking up beside him. "Huh, he brought 'protection'," I snickered to myself as I opened the apartment door and then turned to welcome them. They had driven almost seven hours to get here so they suggested strongly that we walk to a restaurant somewhere rather than our riding. It was a warm September afternoon, the sun was still up and I knew a restaurant a few blocks away that was supposed to be "ok", so we brought in their suitcases and then left for dinner. Conversation was light and somewhat guarded on the way to the restaurant and during dinner. The fact that I still remember what I had for dinner that night – eight and a half years ago – tells you that not too much else of importance could have been going on! The "ham Hawaiian style" absorbed my interest and probably tasted extra-specially good because of the three days fasting that preceded that meal! We finished our dinners and started for the apartment only to discover a deluge outside the restaurant. It was raining hard like it had been raining all day – except that the sun had been out when we had walked in an hour or so earlier! The older brother promptly reminded us that he could not run but also that the two of us should not get soaked waiting for him. Run on up ahead, he told us, and he would follow shortly. Brother Francis suggested that he and I would indeed run on up ahead and that he would then come back with the car to pick up the older brother. That sounded good to all so the two of us began running side-by-side.

As soon as we were alone, he said to me, "Are you still interested in going on for the priesthood?" I couldn't believe it! "He" really *did bring it up!!!!* I was dumbfounded; all I could say was "It's still needed, Brother Francis." He went on to explain that after conversations with the Superior General of the community, in Rome, it seemed quite evident that a decision to allow the brothers to go on for ordination to the priesthood seemed very likely in 1976, when the worldwide community would next convene its General Chapter. The General Chapter of the order was reconvened every six years almost since the beginning of the order back in the early 1800's and it formed the top governing body of the worldwide religious community. It had the authority to change rules as basic to the community as whether or not the members of the community should be ordained to the priesthood. The order had been founded by a French priest strictly as teachers of the poor and up to this time all of its General Chapters had sought to preserve this original intent. Now, however, because of the shortage of priests in the church and the need for priestly services in the brothers' various residences and institutions it seemed quite likely that the next scheduled General Chapter would choose to depart from that tradition in order to better meet the needs of today. "Would you be willing," Brother Francis continued, "to begin your studies toward ordination now and complete them in 1976, remaining a brother all the while? You could get a master's degree in theology but with special guidance toward ordination preparedness. In 1976, if the General Chapter allows ordination for the brothers, you would be able and ready to be ordained *within* the community. If the chapter decides negatively toward the priesthood," he concluded, "then at that time I would personnally help you transfer to whatever diocese or other religious order you choose in order to be able to serve the handicapped as a priest." I couldn't believe what I was hearing! It was like having my cake and eating it too! I had to complete the program of studies anyway no matter where I would go and that program would be about 3 to 4 years. It was now September, 1972, so that would take me right up to the time of the General Chapter! FANTASTIC! I couldn't ask for more! As I sat waiting for Brother Francis to return with the other brother I quickly raced over the summer's events. It was all like a dream, miraculous! But it was *really* happening, right here in front of me! FANTASTIC! There just was no other word!

That evening the three of us drove to Fordham for the prayer meeting. Neither of them had ever been to a prayer meeting so both were interested in experiencing one. I asked the Lord if He wasn't showing off for them that night; we had at least a hundred more people than usual! The singing and praying and sharing was absolutely beautiful. Of course, I'm sure that the fact of my "good news" on the way home from the restaurant somewhat colored my experience of that night's prayer meeting! We came home after the prayer meeting and sat up talking about it until about 2:30 in the morning. Finally I told them that I had to go to bed if I wanted to be able to get up for the 7:00 a.m. Mass in the parish in order to get to work in Manhattan by 9:00 a.m. Mass in the parish and then leave for Ohio after that. The bulk of the rush hour traffic would be cleaned up by then. They liked those plans so we said our goodbyes that night before going to bed. As I hugged Brother Francis good night and goodby I suddenly realized that the prayer of my first core meeting earlier that summer was answered. I was able to hug in love the man I had once hated bitterly!

The apartment had two bedrooms, each with a single bed, so I assigned each of them a bedroom and said I would prepare myself a sleeping place in the living room. That way they could close their doors and would not be disturbed when I left early in the morning. I was making my bed on the living room floor when I heard my name. I looked but they were both in their rooms asleep and even snoring already! But again I heard it, "Patrick," the Voice came clearly, "When are you going to beg forgiveness of your provincial superior for the bitterness and hatred you bore him?"

"Oh no!" I said right out loud. "You can't ask that! You've got no right to ask that. He doesn't even know the bitterness and hate ever existed and besides that *YOU* melted it! Why risk the mended relationship You've just given us? Why stir up the mud in the water again now that it's all settled? No, You can't ask that!" I never even questioned "who" the Voice was; I just knew without asking that it was indeed "the Lord." What surprised me, shocked me, afterwards when I had time to reflect on what happened, was my outright *boldness* in answering *Him* back!!!

"Yes, I can ask it, Patrick, and, in fact, *I am asking it!*" He answered me. *"You don't have any right to be bitter or hateful against any one of your brothers or sisters! I am asking you, Patrick, to ask his forgiveness!"* He said every word very deliberately as if to make sure I didn't miss one of them. Looking back at that whole situation, I'm deeply convinced that our God has a FANTASTIC sense of humor in dealing with us. I played a game, so to speak, with Him that night. "OK," I said, "I told him I wasn't getting him up in the morning, and I'm not! It's now almost 3:00 a.m. and he's snoring away in there; if he's up and ready to come to Mass with me at 7:00 I'll beg his forgiveness on our way to church. If he's not up, I'm off the hook!" I went to bed on the floor and slept like a baby while I'm sure our God "chuckled" all night over what He knew was going to happen in the morning! 'Relief' for me the next morning was waking up exactly one minute before my alarm was set to go off! I quickly pressed the off position, breathed a sign of relief and crept into the bathroom where I cleaned up without a sound! I had my hand on the apartment doorknob and was ready to steal out when I heard 'his' door behind me. I turned, praying desperately that I hadn't really heard it, but there he was, coming toward me fully dressed and ready for church.

"Oh, SHIT!" I said almost right out loud!

"What's the matter?" he asked, "can't I come to Mass with you?"

"Do I have any choice?" I muttered almost inaudibly. We walked out the door and as we started down the steps to the sidewalk, heart in my throat, I began fulfilling my part of the bargain I had made just four hours earlier. "Brother Francis," I began, "you must have wondered what my reaction was when you went to see the bishop last spring?"

"I had to, Pat," he said and wanted to explain more.

"No," I interrupted him, "I don't need any explanation, I don't deserve any explanation, I don't want any explanation." Then I took him with me on a journey through the whole spring and summer from the moment I received the letters, to the bitterness and hate...to the Hoppers...to the first prayer meeting and core meeting invitation...right up to the night before and the conversation with the Lord of some four hours previous. We were standing on the church steps by this time. "Brother Francis," I concluded my story, "the Lord asked me last night to beg your forgiveness but I think I have to go further and do something, believe me, I never dreamed I would ever do: I have to *thank you* for stopping me dead in my tracks last spring! Suppose I *had* gone to the seminary back then according to *my* plans. Sure, I might indeed have become a priest for the handicapped, but would I ever have lived to hear the Lord speak in my heart and dare listen and respond?" We both cried as we hugged each other dearly on those church steps, neither of us caring who watched! I realized than that that core meeting prayer of early that summer was now being answered more deeply that I had ever dreamed it could be!

"Let's go in and celebrate," Brother Francis said at last. I prayed silently as we walked down the center aisle, "A 'kiss of peace' at Mass this morning would be the real 'topping' for this FANTASTIC reconciliation, Lord." The pastor walked out to celebrate the Mass and I remember mentally "kissing my 'kiss of peace' goodbye." He had never offered us a "sign of peace" at the daily Mass before and so there was no reason whatever to expect one that morning! I cried again, that morning though, as he came down to us — as if he had known my prayer — and wished each of us the peace of the Lord and asked us to wish the same to each other! "Lord," I said silently with tears streaming down my cheeks, "whoever said you were a stingy God? You don't give us only the 'meat and potatoes' of life that we absolutely need; you give us the candies and the desserts too!" Today there is no man on earth that I love more dearly than "my " Brother Francis. What a gift of our God!

In December of that same year Brother Francis called and suggested that I speak to the brothers gathered for a Christmas retreat about what had happened in my life. As I knelt in the dark chapel praying for the courage and wisdom to share honestly with my brothers I suddenly felt a reassuring hand on my shoulder. I turned. It was Brother Francis. "You'll do okay," he said confidently. After the talk and tears and applause I was stunned to hear Brother Francis, the provincial superior of our brothers in the United States Province, *beg permission* of the brothers to leave the provincial house in Alfred, Maine, and live with me in New York City for one semester! His humility in asking their permission deeply touched me; his love and respect in wanting to move in with me completely overwhelmed me! All I could think of was the bitterness and hatred I had once borne that man! "Christ has taken over Pat's life," he said to the brothers right in front of me, "and I'd like to find out how and bring that back to others." I've never felt so humble and grateful as that beautiful night.

12

"Free...free to say yes..."

In mid-January, 1973, Brother Francis Blouin, Provincial Superior of the Brothers of Christian Instruction in the United States, moved in to share my East Elmhurst apartment in Queens, New York City. It was absolutely incredible. I had asked the Lord that previous summer that I might learn to love, to be able one day to hug the man I then hated so bitterly; now that man was moving into my tiny, five-room apartment to share life, meals, prayer, sharing, etc. with me! Things had certainly come a long way since that Sunday night core meeting!

As I look back now at the life I was living in mid-January, 1973, I realize even more how 'things had come a long way'! Friday night prayer meetings were now a regular happening at the apartment. Wednesday nights still found me up at Fordham and Sunday nights brought me back up there regularly for the core meetings of the prayer community. Sunday mornings, after the parish Mass, a group of us in the neighborhood gathered for another prayer meeting in a family's apartment a few blocks from mine. For one who had found it hard to believe that people would actually give that one extra night every week to a prayer meeting, things had most certainly 'come a long way' in a very short time!

At work things had 'come a long way' too by mid-January, 1973. I had joined the library's staff in September, 1970, and in December of that same year the city of New York had instituted a 'job freeze,' not permitting the hiring of any more employees during the freeze period for any of the city's agencies. As employees quit, retired, moved, etc. and were not able to be replaced, more and more pressure began to be felt by the remaining employees. For me the pressures were felt in the area of my field work. More and more pressure was being put on me for my participation in the in-house administrative duties of the library operation. Even after a written job description was obtained for my work from the personnel office of the library many of the in-house pressures continued. I found myself at this time actually out new-job hunting for a while. Two FANTASTIC sisters that I had become acquainted with through my work, served the handicapped students of some four dozen parochial schools all over Long Island. How well I recall our dream of an itinerant librarian to help these students find their needed resources. But the idea died even before it could be developed into a job description. Then there was an agency in a diocese of New

Jersey in need of a staff member.

One day I found myself in the 'tubes' beneath the Hudson on my way to Newark New Jersey, for a job interview. It, too, sounded exciting; the grass seemed an awful lot greener than on my present lawn. But that job fell through too before I could touch it. A really exciting, FANTASTIC, beautiful, just-the-right-thing opportunity then rose on the horizon to tease and taunt me. 'National promoter' for a religious organization providing recorded, Brailled, and large-type materials for the blind and physically handicapped throughout the United States and Canada! What a position! I had been invited to speak at a staff meeting of the organization and then the organization's director had talked to me over dinner about the possibility of my joining his staff as that national promoter! That was it! I loved him, his staff, and their work. And what's more, I loved the description of what would be 'my work' that he gave me over dinner! It really sounded just FANTASTIC! Draw up a job description, a budget, etc., I was instructed, and then we'd talk more about the job's possibility!

I did my homework fast; I wasted no time. Several friends came out to dinner to critique my homework and then I typed up the final draft and duplicated it for a round-table discussion with the organization director and whomever he chose to have participate. I read over the papers at my desk before calling for an appointment with the director. I had not even finished reading them when my phone rang. I picked it up and immediately recognized the director's voice. "Brother Pat," he said, "we've done our own homework and I wanted to get to you before you did too much on your end. Pat," he went on as my heart sank lower than the soles of my shoes, "even if you came to us *for nothing,* no salary, we still could not afford the rapid increase in demand for services that you would generate for us. No, I'm afraid," he concluded, "it was a nice dream but I think we're going to have to be content to grow slowly as we have been doing."

I was devastated. I lay down that night and cried! I had wanted so, so, so much to belong to that agency. It still is one of the most beautiful staffs and operations I have ever encountered in all of my years of service to handicapped readers. "God," I cried with my face buried in the pillow that night, "am I going to be condemned to be a wanderer all of my life?" I saw myself those days, 'tolerated' by the library as a member of its staff, spreading the library's services and speaking for them and for dozens of other organizations and service programs in the New York City area, but not really 'belonging' to any one of them! How many times I walked into a family's home, an agency's conference room, a nursing home recreation room...spoke to the family, the staff, etc., and left, closing the door behind me with no need to return. I had helped them, showed them talking-books, etc., signed them up to receive all the materials, and then wasn't needed anymore! A couple of years earlier I had been so excited about doing *my* thing, with *nobody's* help, *all by myself*...and now I wanted so desperately simply to *belong* to somebody, some agency... And I was alone...

In October, 1971, the Library Science Department at St. John's University in Jamaica, Queens, New York City, had invited me out to do a day's program for its students, faculty and alumnae. That 'colloquium' led to a full, three-credit course in the fall semester of the following year. That course brought an invitation for a summer session course in 1973. Catholic University of America in Washington, D.C., meanwhile, whose library school I had graduated from, now wrote and reminded me of this fact and talked about the course they had heard that I had developed for St. John's. Why wouldn't I consider coming down to Washington for a summer session course after the St. John's course in 1973. The evening courses and Saturday colloquium and other programs I had been able to do on my own time, but summer courses would be another story; I would have to request leave from the library to do them. I decided to request 'leave without pay' for the twelve weeks needed for the two summer courses in 1973. In late January, shortly after Brother Francis's arrival in New York, the request was denied by the library. I was quite disappointed. Other requests for talks and programs that had been requested outside the immediate New York City area had also been turned down by my supervisors that year and this only added to my growing discontent with the system.

"Well," I said to Brother Francis the night the request to have time off for teaching was denied, "I guess I'm going to have to write to the universities tomorrow and tell them I can't come."

"Why?" Brother Francis asked surprisingly.

"The library said *No!*" I said simply and showed him the letter from the supervisory personnel office.

"That doesn't say you can't teach," he went on, puzzling me somewhat.

"Do you mean," I asked suddenly getting the theme of his thinking, I hoped,"...do you mean that if I wanted to quit the library and thereby be *free* to teach these courses and do whatever other programs I was asked to do, you'd say *yes?*"

"Yes," he said simply. "I think that's the road ahead. If you stay with the library you keep your own job security but are you necessarily doing what you're called to do? And besides, if you aren't tied to the library then you'll also be free to begin your studies in theology." I couldn't believe my ears! It was wilder than any dream. I would have work but not a 'job!' I would be *free, free to say "yes"* whenever and wherever I was asked to come and speak or help with a program, etc. We both sat there in the living room and I think I got giddy thinking about the freedom it would give me to say yes to the needs I found! We talked about funding and other practical considerations of 'free-lance' work. The university courses would bring in some cash and whatever else was needed, I was sure the Lord would provide! The more we talked the more we were both convinced that it was the best way to go! I couldn't wait to get at my typewriter the next morning. The letter of resignation flowed out onto the paper in front of me like water from the faucet into a cup! I announced my resignation for the end of May of that year. That would give the library three months to find a replacement if they chose to bring one in and I offered to help in the training of that replacement. I couldn't wait for those ninety days to pass by! In the evenings I spent time preparing for my new office and planning for the free-lance work. May 31st was the day!

13

"We love you..."

May 31st, 1973, finally did arrive. As it came closer, however, I found myself torn between excitement and crippling fear. Yes, I would finally be *free,* free to go wherever, whenever, to whomever I was called with no supervisor to check with for permissions, etc. I would have no 'boss' but 'the Lord!' Yes, that was the ultimate, and it was indeed exciting! Several aspects of the fast approaching new life all but paralyzed me with fear, however. Would the calls come? Would I still be needed by people and agencies? Yes, I was kept busy eighty and ninety hours a week now, but would people know where to contact me and would they still want to? Was it all an ego trip and would it fall flat? And, what about the finances? Where would they come from? The apartment's rent was two hundred dollars a month. Where would that come from? Subway tokens and bus fares weren't given away free. Where would the travel expenses come from? How would I live? Was it all an empty dream? I had made the commitment. My letter of resignation had been sent in already and in that letter I had described briefly my 'dream' plans, so it was too late to back out now. Time would tell the answers to all the questions that filled my last few weeks at the library.

On the weekend of March 23-25, 1973, something happened in my life that provided many of the answers to those questions that would plague me two months later, but I wasn't really aware of it at the time. After work that Friday, March 23rd, a couple from Valley Stream, Long Island, picked me up at the apartment and drove me out to St. Josephat's Retreat House in Glen Cove, Long Island. As the car sped along the parkway toward Glen Cove, I sat alone in the back seat, quiet, wondering how I had gotten myself into 'this.' I, a Brother of Christian Instruction with a vow of celibacy and about to begin studies for the priesthood, was now on my way to a retreat house for a 'marriage encounter' weekend! I must be crazy. I thought to myself. What was I doing?

Oh, I had told the couple that had signed me up for the weekend that I wanted to experience the retreat-like weekend in order to see if it was appropriate to recommend to parents of handicapped children or couples who were themselves handicapped. But that wasn't the real reason I was headed for Glen Cove and I knew it. I had seen something in the couple that I was afraid to admit to myself that I didn't have but wanted desperately. They had a freedom to love, not only each other as a couple, but to love *me* and others, too, to love the forty or so kids who came to their home every Saturday night for the Bible study program we had started. They had a freedom to express their love and what baffled me most was their open expression of their *need* for each other, for me, for others. They weren't afraid to ask for my help, my advice, etc.

One of the greatest gifts and pains that I had found in New York City was *aloneness*. I had loved that aloneness when it spelled independence for me, independence from needing help, advice, protection, guidance. New York was *my* town! I loved its subways and buses and taxicabs. With them I could go wherever, whenever I wanted with no need to ask someone else for a ride! With my job in New York I had become the helper, not the helpED, the guide, not the guidED, the protector, not the protectED! I was the professional, the expert. I carefully protected myself from the advice and counsel of my family and the brothers. It was *my* work. New York was *my* home and I loved it all dearly! I could run my own errands, do my own shopping, get to and from work and speaking engagements on my own steam. I needed no one and I prided myself in that finally-achieved independence! A retired neighbor several times offered to drive me to speaking engagements but I always managed to find a polite reason to decline his offer – and preserve my independence. A real day of triumph came for me when the "New York Daily News" did a full story on *my* work in the city, "Brother Martin's Mission to Spread the Recorded Word." I loved it when it came out and quickly I bought out a newsstand so I could mail copies to all the family and the brothers. I wasn't the 'handicapped kid' anymore; I was the expert helping other handicapped kids! I had made it.

My very first Christmas in New York, however, I had seen the pain side of that gift of *aloneness*. I had a week off from work and was really excited about my first visit home and with the brothers since the beginning of my work with the handicapped. I saw myself somewhat as a 'war hero' returning home; after all, I had lived four months in New York City and had *survived!* I polished up my 'war stories', rehearsing the incidents and events of the past four months that I was sure would impress the folks back home, I was sure they'd want to know all about life in the big city and I was prepared to tell them all about it! A crippling blizzard in Maine stopped the 'hero's' flight home, however, and I found myself back in the brothers' residence in mid-Manhattan *alone* for Christmas! The blizzard had closed down all the airports, train stations, and bus terminals in northern New England. There was absolutely no way to get home for the holidays. The brothers I lived with in New York, thinking I had gone home to Maine, had departed for their own homes for the holidays while I was at the airport desperately trying to find 'another way.'

And so, I had returned from the airport to an empty, five-story, brownstone walk-up on West 51st Street in Manhattan for Christmas. *Alone!* I spent Christmas Eve and a good part of Christmas Day listening to *"The Godfather"* on talking book records and wishing I wasn't alone! The house and the empty street below just seemed so huge! I heard every sound except the one I wanted to hear, a human voice, live – not recorded! I didn't have to stay alone that Christmas, except that I didn't know how to tell the few friends I had made in the city that I *needed them!* You don't intrude on people on Christmas! You don't just drop in uninvited! Christmas is a day for families, not outsiders. All sorts of excuses suggested themselves strongly to keep me alone that long day but finally, the aloneness got the best of me and I decided to call a friend of mine from Catholic University days who was now a librarian at Columbia University in New York. He and his wife lived near the university and, at their invitation, I had visited them once or twice before. They were surprised to hear my voice *on Christmas Day;* I regretted calling as soon as I heard them pick up the receiver but it was too late. I said I had just called to wish them a "Merry Christmas" but they played my game FANTASTICALLY! "Aren't you in Maine?" they asked in their surprise, and so, of course, I *had* to tell them the truth. The invitation followed and I excitedly planned the trip to their apartment. I had deliberately said I couldn't make it until four o'clock that afternoon because I didn't want to seem too desperate. After all, I had just called to say "Merry Christmas!" The delay would also give me time to find a shop or florist where I could buy a gift to bring up with me; I couldn't go empty-handed; that just wouldn't be right! Thank the good Lord, in New York City you can *always* find a shop open somewhere no matter what hour of day it is! I found a florist and so a Christmas bouquet came with me to Christmas dinner that year.

At first I saw the pain side of aloneness simply as the necessary price tag for its gift side. The independence I had was well worth a Christmas alone! As the brothers had returned home from their Christmas holidays and work at the library resumed, I quickly forgot even that small price tag for a while. More and more speaking engagements and family appointments brought me to more and more parts of the city and Long Island and the independence tasted sweeter and sweeter. It was really neat being able to figure out the traffic system and getting to where I had to go *on time!* The traffic lights made it so easy to cross streets *alone*. I used to listen for the traffic as I walked up the block toward a cross street; after a while I could usually tell the direction of the traffic and even the types of vehicles approaching before I actually got to the street crossing! I cherished and guarded that gift of independence and aloneness!

Bit by bit, however, cracks began to appear in that cinderblock wall of aloneness that I had built to guarantee and protect my independence. In June of 1972, two big cracks appeared on that wall and steadily widened from that time onward. The first came with the Hopper family on the lower east side of Manhattan and the second, with the Fordham Prayer Community. After my Memorial Day weekend visit to the Hoppers that year, we had decided to try to teach ten-year-old Justine to type on a regular typewriter with her one good hand and virtually no useable sight! The fact that many others had already discounted the project as an impossbile dream made it an even more exciting challenge for me! Thursday evenings after work were selected as the best times for the typing lessons and the Hoppers insisted that since I would be coming from work I should stay for dinner with the family after the class each week. During the course of that one year Justine did indeed learn to type and to operate a reel-to-reel tape recorder with her one good hand and negligible sight but I'm not sure that she received the greater of the gifts from those weekly visits to the Hopper home in Stuyvessant Town, Manhattan. In the course of that year the Hoppers became more than just another family with whom I worked, they became my friends.

I loved visiting families and individuals *if* I had an appointment or reason to be there. I loved a party if I had something to do, a role to play. But I was totally uncomfortable just 'being' there visiting. What should I say? Should I get up and do something, offer to help? What are they thinking about me? Should I bring a gift? And I even felt awkward about how to present the gift if I did bring it. "Oh, it's really nothing!" Visiting friends wasn't a normal part of growing up as kids in our family. There were plenty of us around for games and work and our yard was always full of the neighbors' kids joining in our games. As a brother visiting wasn't the 'in thing' either. Visits home were even limited to three days each year at first. So, I found myself rather uncomfortable about 'just visiting.' Through the gift of their friendship, which went beyond gratitude for what I was doing for their child, the Hoppers taught me slowly the gift of just being 'me' with them, not the helper, the guide, the protector, the professional, but just me. More and more I learned to be comfortable and happy with them whether I was working with Justine, wrestling with Peter on the living room carpet, discussing politics over a drink, or eating lamb that I was sure was FANTASTIC roast beef! As much as I had hated and avoided 'just visiting' people, I now began to look forward to those Thursday evening visits at the Hopper home!

Wednesday evenings in 1972-73 brought the other crack in my cinderblock wall of aloneness and independence. I became part of the Fordham Prayer Community and loved it! For a whole year those Wednesday evening spaces on my calendar were carefully kept clean and free for the Fordham prayer meetings. I loved the prayer meetings themselves and went to Fordham each Wednesday at first simply for that experience of prayer. It was FANTASTIC: it had changed my life and I wanted as much of it as I could get. But something else happened at Fordham almost imperceptibly at first − community, people needing people. My first few times at the prayer meeting I would simply walk in and take a seat and wait for the prayer meeting to begin. Gradually, however, I could not just slip in; people began to know me and would come up and say hello or welcome. And someone even hugged me and said how happy they were that I had come! At first all this greeting didn't even register in my consciousness and sometimes I did question its sincerity. More and more though, I found myself drawn in by it and to it. I'd catch myself wondering as the train approached the Fordham stop whether this one or that one would be there that night. And I even missed people when they weren't there for some reason or other! I almost envied those who could tell me with a word or a hug how good it was to see me or how they missed me if I wasn't there one week; I could respond, somewhat awkwardly, to their expressions of love and caring, but when it came to initiating those expressions I was as clumsy as an elephant in a china closet!

At first I simply dismissed those expressions as empty, insincere or, at the very least, unnecessary. A handshake could do as much as a hug? You didn't need to say "I love you" if you proved it by your actions... But then, I recalled myself standing in front of my dear daddy's casket three years earlier, sick inside as I realized I had never once told that beautiful man "I love you!" Why had it bothered me if it wasn't necessary? And why did it bother me now as I realized I *couldn't say it now?* So many in the prayer community seemed to need my help and my presence so easily and to express their need without apparent difficulty; and I had spent my life trying to need no one, trying to be grown up and independent! It seemed almost unfair that now that I had achieved that dream of independence I wasn't sure I still wanted it! But, it was almost like it was *too late.* How do you turn back the clock? I felt so alone each time I watched someone 'reach out' to welcome or console or reassure another and I realized *I couldn't do that!* Why? I wished I could but it was like the *cream of independence* had soured into the *nightmare of aloneness!* I guess that's why I loved my work so much those early days in New York while hating days off or weekends. My work was a convenient vehicle to put me with people; it was the 'excuse' I needed to be with people. Days off were *alone* days.

In November, 1972, while attending a prayer-meeting-type conference at the Americana Hotel in Manhattan, I met the couple from Valley Stream, Long Island. They came up and talked; the more we talked the more excited they became. Would I come and visit them at their home? I did. And out of those visits came the Saturday evening Bible study sessions for their teenagers and their friends. One Saturday evening in Janaury, 1973, I sat and listened after the Bible study session as they spoke with the parents of one of the kids about a weekend experience they called 'marriage encounter.' They told the other couple that it was a private weekend for the couple, aimed at teaching them 'communication.' Couples, priests and sisters, they said, made the weekend and learned the techniques of communicating on a *feeling* level rather than only on a *mind* level. As they spoke my interest grew. Was this how they had learned to communicate their love for each other, for me, and for others as they did, so beautifully? I asked a few questions and then found myself completing an application blank to attend one of the weekend experiences. They seemed so excited as I handed them the application form all filled in. I never thought anything more of the event for several months.

The Fordham Prayer Community in conjunction with other prayer communities in the metropolitan area frequently sponsored weekend 'retreats' and other such programs in addition to their regular weekly prayer meetings. One such program was a 'healing retreat' scheduled for the weekend of March 16-18, 1973. I had signed up for the weekend retreat as soon as it had been advertised way back in November, 1972. I was eager for the retreat, hoping that the 'grace' I would receive from it would be the ability to *love* as others did, the ability to express the caring, concern and feelings I had inside. Brother Francis, my provincial superior, had moved into the apartment with me, however, in January of 1973 and I knew that he was eager to experience as much as possible of the prayer community during his one semester stay with me. The retreat registration list was filled and a long waiting list had already been filled so there was no chance that he could attend the healing retreat — unless I let him go in my place. "Would you like to go?" I asked him one evening as we prepared supper. Yes, he said he'd love to attend the retreat but he realized it was full. "You'll be here only this semester," I said, "why don't you go in my place and sign me up while you're there for the next one in the fall?" Reluctantly he finally agreed to go in my place. My heart was somewhat heavy that night as I went to bed and realized I had 'given up' the grace I had hoped to get from the retreat experience.

While Brother Francis was away on the retreat weekend a telephone call informed me that my 'marriage encounter weekend' would take place the following weekend at St. Josephat's Retreat House in Glen Cove, Long Island. I was to arrive at the retreat house by 8:00 p.m. on Friday. The couple calling assured me of their prayers for that weekend! I hung up the phone and wondered. What had I gotten myself into? I knew absolutely nothing about this 'marriage encounter' program; I had heard nothing about it except from that couple in Valley Stream and I had promptly forgotten about it after filling in the application form. Now it was two months later and they were calling to say my weekend was *next weekend!*

As the car sped along the parkway that Friday night I sat alone in the back seat, rather quiet, wondering what I had gotten myself into and how I had gotten myself into it! I seriously questioned the possibility that I might be putting myself in an awkward position as far as my celibate vocation was concerned. I had been told by the telephone call that there would be two dozen couples, a priest and myself on that weekend. The chair next to me would be empty. Wasn't I sort of 'tempting myself' against my own celibate way of life? Observing the two dozen or so couples around me that weekend, wouldn't I be tempting myelf to leave my own way of life to embrace what they had in theirs, coupleness and married love? What had I gotten myself into? I didn't dare talk about my doubts and fears as we moved along the highway. The couple up front kept reassuring me that I was going to have a FANTASTIC weekend, almost as if they knew my unspoken feelings.

As the conference room at St. Josephat's began to fill up that evening, I became more and more embarrassed about my being there. As fewer and fewer chairs were left empty the one next to me became more and more conspicuous. A few curious participants asked where my wife was and then were as embarrassed as I for asking. Then, at long last, the weekend began. I sat in the front row so I wouldn't see the others. I really wondered what I had gotten myself into!

The encounter 'team' for the weekend consisted of three couples and the priest. They began the weekend by introducing each other and each one giving his/her spouse's 'most endearing quality.' That was fine as long as they restricted it to the team but when they asked 'us' to introduce ourselves and give 'our spouse's's'

104

most endearing quality *I knew I didn't belong there!!!* I don't remember what I said about the empty chair next to me but somehow I did get through that moment. After the introductions we were handed notebooks and pens and advised to use them freely, that they would be kept private, for ourselves alone, so we could feel free to write whatever came to mind or heart in the books. We should, they went on, write down reactions that came to us during the talks they would give us on the weekend. Then they began their first talk.

"We love you!" the first speaking couple began their talk. I immediately opened my notebook and did as I had been instructed. "We love you," I wrote, *"Bunk!* You don't even know who I am!" Starting off that way, I seriously wondered where this weekend could possibly go! As the first talk ended we were given an assignment: make a list of the six things we liked best about ourselves and then a parallel list of the six things we liked best about our spouse. After writing, each couple would then get together in the privacy of their own room to share their writing and reactions. I opened my book, but had nothing to write. I panicked. Was there *anything* I liked about myself? I was *blind;* I had spent my whole life trying not to be, how could I like *myself?* For 'my spouse', I decided to write about my religious order, the Brother of Christian Instruction. What did I like best about them? Well... well... they had *accepted* me *after I slipped in without their knowing I was blind...* What did I like better about them than other religious communities? Well... well... they had *accepted* me... Needless to say, that first writing time was a real downer for me. I had never been forced to stop and look at myself that way and now that I did I didn't see anything that I liked! "Boy, you sound like 'Sunday night' already", the team priest said as he came in to share with me after writing his own reflections. I shared with him my panic at finding *nothing* that I liked about myself...

Starting that low, that far down, the weekend could only get better! And it did! I watched the team couples and the team priest as they shared their talks. I was deeply moved by their sincerity and their honesty in sharing with us, and the sincerity and dedication of their lives. I was so moved that they had no 'superiors' watching over them and yet they lived such beautiful lives. I looked at my own life in the mirror of theirs and got sick! How shallow my life had been, seeking my own 'normalcy', my own importance, my own thing in life, and here they were, so open, so dedicated, and so sincere for each other, for their children, and for us! Saturday night of the weekend I slipped away from the group and found my way down to the retreat house's chapel. All was dark as I entered the empty chapel. Only the Sanctuary candle gave its light to the room. I turned on no lights. I knelt and simply gazed at the Tabernacle in the dim light of the candle. My heart was sick as I knelt there. "Father", I prayed more earnestly that I had ever prayed before, "why can't I be as sincere and dedicated in my life as a brother as they are in theirs?" As I prayed it was as if I were in a theater and the movie had suddenly begun before me. There on the screen of that vision my thirteen years of religious life as a brother passed before my eyes. I saw every retreat I had made as a brother — at least six days a year, eight days some years! I could make out the retreat directors. I saw the lists of FANTASTIC resolutions taken at the end of each retreat, resolutions to change my life and really *live* the life I professed to be living, resolutions that were all ineffective in my life because they were all forgotten as soon as I left the retreat, and got back into the routines of life as a Brother! I saw all the monthly days of recollection and prayer during those same years, days that should have deepened my life but days that were also quickly forgotten once over. I got sicker as the 'movie' continued. Finally, I cried. "Lord, is this going to be just another retreat weekend like the rest? Is it going to be a nice fervent high now and then quickly forgotten once I get back home? If it is, I don't want it! Forget it! Lord, I want my life to change because of this weekend. I want to be just as sincere and dedicated in my life as a brother as fathers and mothers! Lord," I went on, "if my life is to change and really become the life of *their brother,* not *a* brother, Your people's *brother,* then I need a change in my life that will be a constant reminder of this weekend! Will you give me some physical change in my life, some change, Lord, that whenever I see it I will remember this weekend and my calling to be Your people's *brother?* Please, Lord, help me. I'm tired of living a shallow, empty, routine life. Convert my heart, please!" **Our deepest ultimate longing is to be a gift to someone; our biggest fear is that we're not.** I prayed so hard that night to learn how to be that gift for others!

I found my way back to my room long after most of the couples had retired for the night. I wasn't fully conscious of it at the time, I realized it only later, but a peace had stolen over me after my prayer. I slept FANTASTICALLY that night and the rest of the weekend moved onward beautifully. As much as I had feared that empty chair next to me, I can honestly say that it never once, that weekend, was a threat to my celibacy or my way of life. Instead of that, it was precisely the couples' beautiful love for each other that was the chief inspiration for me to become fully who I was called to be. The talks and sharings made me cry and laugh and I did both freely all weekend. The team priest informed me at the end of the weekend that I was their 'thermometer' — "we're doing ok, Pat's crying again!" The program moved so quickly and so fully that it was over almost before anyone realized it! There wasn't time to stop and analyze what was going on or what was happening to you. Each talk and reflection time, built on those that had preceded it and so the effects did also. At the end you knew for certain that you had grown but it seemed impossible to put your finger on when or how or why! It was just incredible — there were virtually no 'public' sharing sessions at all; husbands and wives shared with each other in the total privacy of their rooms after the talks and yet, by the end of that weekend you felt like you had known everyone on the weekend all your life. It was only when I finally got home that Sunday night that I realized that I knew absolutely nothing about anyone on that weekend!

"Sure," I said, "I'd love to!" The team priest, overhearing the invitation and its response, commented to my drivers, "if you're bringing him to a 'renewal' tonight you'd better tie cinderblocks to his feet! I've got a sore neck from following him around the ceiling all weekend!"

We went to the renewal meeting that night. It was FANTASTIC! I walked in, quite unaware, hugging people like it was going out of style! As I moved in I came to a short man, wearing a yellow pastel shirt, open-collared, with a plain brown sports jacket. As he approached he somewhat gingerly put out his hand to shake mine, and as he did I saw myself. A voice inside said simply, "Patrick, you see that man? That was *you!* Last weekend you gave up your grace of healing to let Brother Francis go on the retreat. Last night you asked for a sign, a change in your life that would remind you of this weekend. You've got your sign, Patrick, your healing! Go out and hug your world! Let it know how loveable it is in My eyes and each time you tell someone you love them, each time you hug them, remember this weekend and *live* the *brother's* life I have called you to! *Be My peoples' brother!"* I shivered violently as the awareness of the answered prayer came over me. Gently, I took the man's hand, pulled him close and told him I loved him! I now knew what the team had meant that very first night of the weekend when they had said so simply "We love you!" and I had written *"bunk!"* How wrong I was! The awkwardness and shyness to love and be loved were all gone. It was phenomenal! FANTASTIC! And I have *never* forgotten *that* weekend!

The Marriage Encounter weekend has had far-reaching effects on my whole life, effects that I have gratefully noticed and effects noted gratefully by others! Part of my work routine at that time was visiting and telling stories monthly at some three dozen nursing homes in the New York City, Long Island area. I visited one of the homes a week or two after the encounter weekend, told my short story as usual and opened the floor for questions and/or comments. Was I ever surprised as one little lady stood up from her wheelchair and said forthrightly, "Something's happened to you! You're different this month from what you've ever been! It's like a glow, a warmth! What happened?" I had been going to that home for almost four years. I cried now as I realized through her beautiful, touching words that up to that time I had been sharing stories with them but this morning I had shared *me...* I told them the story of the Marriage Encounter weekend. "Too bad we couldn't have one of them here," she commented at the end of my description.

A big area of change and deepening in my life because of the Marriage Encounter experience was my prayer life. I used to get literally angry whenever one of the priests in our local parish celebrated Mass in the morning. He literally *ran* through the celebration and I found it difficult even to follow the prayers which were said so fast. I used to get so angry whenever I'd see him coming out for the daily Mass. The morning after my Marriage Encounter weekend he came out for Mass but, because I was still so "high" from the weekend, there was no anger in me. At the 'consecration' when the bread and wine become the Body and Blood of Christ, I noticed I was crying. That 'voice' was there again, saying "Patrick, all those times you were so angry, did you forget that I was still here? I am here at slow Masses and fast Masses. I am here." It was so beautiful.

After each talk on the weekend the couples were asked to write a 'love letter' to each other about the topic discussed. Since I had no spouse to write to, I decided to write my 'love letters' on the weekend to God. On coming home I decided it would be good to continue the 'love letter to God' practice on a daily basis. The letters, I realized, had forced me to take in the talks, think about them, internalize them and do something with them in my life. They had produced such an effect on the weekend that I could only imagine what the practice might do for my life it I were to continue it at home on a daily basis. It was really hard getting used to the love letter format at first. After all, I was a religious with vows of poverty, celibacy and obedience; love letters weren't exactly in that ball park! My prayers had always been 'manly' prayers, book prayers, prayers from the head and not so much from the heart. Thanks to the intensity of the weekend and guidance of the team priest who shared and understood my life style, I learned to write a 'love letter' and I grew because of it. The daily practice at home gave discipline and structure to my otherwise very undisciplined prayer life and I grew now because of that. Each day I would choose a scriptural passage or an event of the day to write about in my love letter to God. I would simply open the letter, "Dear Father," and then proceed to tell Him what the passage or event did to me, how it made me feel, how it challenged me to grow... The daily practice quickly became a burden and I was most tempted many, many times to discontinue it as silly or unnecessary. I pictured myself as a ninety-year-old brother still writing daily love letters to God and the thought turned me off completely. But, each time I was tempted not to sit and write, I'd remember the weekend and what it did for my life. I'd pick up the notebook and pen and write again.

The daily love letters had been continuing for some eight or nine months in 1973, most of them routine love letters to God done for the sake of not stopping the practice. But then one night, I believe it was in December, I sat down to write routinely, wondering as usual if this was really doing anything at all for my life, when all of a sudden I discovered exactly what it was doing. I began to write as usual, "Dear Father," when that 'Voice' inside me said "Write 'Dear Daddy'." I was dumb-founded, to say the least. No one calls God 'Daddy,' I thought to myself with at least slight disgust at the very thought! But the thought wouldn't go away. "Write 'Dear Daddy'," I decided that would make an interesting love letter; I'd write "Dear Daddy" and then tell Him exactly how I felt about calling Him 'Daddy.' And so I began,

"Dear Daddy,

Calling you 'Daddy' makes me feel childish, silly, mushy, sentimental and quite embarrassed, like if, as a child, I were to call my mom by her first name instead of calling her "Mom." At the very least, 'Daddy', it makes me feel quite presumptuous: Who do I think I am to presume such a close relationship with You, our God, as to call You 'Daddy?'..."

But I stopped writing after that question. I was sitting on the edge of my bed where I wrote my love letter each night, but now my pen wasn't writing at all. In fact, I had dropped the pen and just sat there listening as He interrupted the love letter. "Why, Patrick", He was saying, "why are you afraid to call Me 'Daddy?' What does the word 'Father' do to Our relationship, Patrick? Doesn't it protect you from Me? Patrick, doesn't the word 'Father' keep our relationship nice and safe and formal where you can invite Me in with a 'Sign of the Cross' and turn Me off with an 'Amen?' Isn't that it, Patrick? Doesn't the word 'Father' keep our relationship nice and safe and formal, like you sit Me – in a well starched suit and tie – in your living room stuffed chair sipping tea from your most delicate china, while you sit – in casuals – on a stool in the kitchen drinking coke out of a can. Patrick, I don't want to be a word in your vocabulary. I want to be *your Daddy!* I want to run with you when life is hectic, walk beside you when life is lonely and perplexing, support you and comfort you when life is unfair and hurts you, cry with you when it does to you what it did to My Son, walk gingerly with you when life's challenges are scarey or awesome, laugh at you and with you when you insist on 'doing it your own way' and then you find out that I was right...Patrick, please let Me be your Daddy!"

I was crying as He finished His plea. I had not expected anything more that night than I had gotten from the love letters the many nights before. But now I felt the warm, salty tears flowing down my cheeks and I felt good. I sank to my knees in reverence beside my bed and sobbed, "Daddy, I really feel like your kid tonight!" I've got one physical sign of affection that my memory treasures dearly from my earthly father, God rest him. When Dad was proud of one of his kids we got a stroke on the head with his big carpenter's hand, a stroke that you could hear across the street, a stroke that we looked for at moments like graduation. It was a stroke that said without words, "This is my kid, world, and you'd better respect him and keep off his toes!" Now, four years after his death, as I knelt beside my bed in the Jackson Heights apartment and told our God how very much I felt like His kid, my tears flowed harder and hotter as I felt that old, familiar 'stroke on the head!' It was like our 'Daddy' was saying, "Yeah, Patrick, and I really feel like your Daddy tonight!"

I shudder every time I recall that 'Daddy story' of my life and wonder where I would be today if I had never dared to accept His call that night to call Him "Daddy!" The daily love letters have brought my whole prayer life from a life of words to a life of relationship with our God!

In addition to changing or deepening my relationship with God, the Marriage Encounter experience also affected deeply my whole relationship with people in my life. It dealt an all but fatal blow – not instantaneously but over a period of time – to that cinderblock wall of aloneness and independence! Prior to my weekend I had heard virtually nothing about the program except from that couple in Valley Stream, Long Island. Shortly after the weekend in late March I saw an announcement in the local parish's Sunday bulletin, telling of an 'information night' about marriage encounter to be held in the parish hall one Sunday in May. Excitedly I walked to the church that Sunday evening to attend the information night and hoping to meet local people who had shared the experience. A couple greeted me at the door. "How many in the parish have made a weekend already?" I asked. "Seven couples and a brother," they responded, "but we've never met the Brother. We don't know who he is." "Well here he is!" I said with laughter and a big hug. I ended up talking about the weekend that night after the program for those who came to *learn* about the program. As usual, I received much, much more that I gave that night. I gave a talk; I received a community, a family! I met all of the families of the area who had experienced the Marriage Encounter Weekend and discovered, much to my joy, that they all lived within a few blocks of my apartment! The wall of aloneness and independence crumbled under the weight of this FANTASTIC blow! Their lives, too, had been deeply affected by that weekend experience and the continuation of their "dialogue" at home and that drew us closer. As I left the library that May to begin my free lance work with the handicapped, I now found that I was not alone in it after all; they were very much a part of it. The love and interest of these families in my work very often gave me needed support as I began it rather timidly those early days in June, 1973. It was very often their offered rides — which I now learned to need and accept — which made it possible for me to get to families and agencies in need. It was also quite often their interest and involvement that uncovered families with handicapped members who needed a brother. And it was also very often that their generous gifts made my work among the handicapped both possible and fruitful.

14

"Why didn't you ask us...?"

I knew next to nothing about the Marriage Encounter program in September, 1972, when permission was granted for me to begin my studies in preparation for the priesthood, and I still knew next to nothing about it in February, 1973, when the decision was made to leave the New York Public Library in May in order to freelance my work with the handicapped, and yet, the families involved in the encounter program were to play a most important role in both aspects of my life! As I look back at it now, I find it difficult to believe it wasn't 'planned' by 'someone!'

Once the decision to leave the library had been made, I immediately set to work investigating theology programs for my preparation for ordination. I discovered what seemed like a FANTASTIC program at the Immaculate Conception Seminary in Huntington, Long Island, and what made it even more FANTASTIC was that I was accepted to do my studies there! I planned to enroll there, find out my course schedule and then mould my freelance work around that schedule for the next couple of years. The seminary was too far from the train station for walking so I knew I couldn't live at the seminary itself. To do that would be to take away the possibility of any work with the handicapped persons during those semesters of study. I followed up several leads but came up with no housing possibilities whatever. Several religious communities were sending their seminary students to Huntington but each informed me upon inquiry that their residences were full and so no living or commuting arrangements were possible with them. The seminary was not on the normal traffic route so it was equally impossible to arrange rides with workers passing by. After several weeks of searching, I really began to wonder and even got somewhat discouraged about the whole situation. My dialogue love letters to the Father spilled out the feelings of discouragement and disappointment and wonder with each 'dead end' I came upon that summer. When it looked like I might never find a place to stay during my time of studies, I received a note in the mail one morning from a teaching sister who had made an encounter weekend at about the same time I had. Her letter began with the passage from the Bible, "In my Father's house there are many rooms..." She went on in her beautiful letter to talk about her struggle to trust more fully in God in her life. That evening I shared her letter with some of the encountered couples of the area and its effect on me! The couples were touched deeply by the timeliness of the letter and the coincidence of its theme but we ended up spending most of the evening talking about my plight. "Why didn't you ask us to help you find a place?" they asked almost indignantly. "We know a lot of families out that way and we'd really love to be able to help you in any way that we can...but we can't unless you ask..." That was but the beginning of a valuable lesson I was to learn on 'needing people.'

Another 'needing-people' lesson came in early June, just after I left the Library for the Blind and Physically Handicapped. I was asked to speak at a luncheon for retired telephone workers on Long Island. I gave my talk, demonstrated some of the available equipment and resources for handicapped persons and then began answering questions from the audience. At the end of the question period one of the men of the group came up and handed me a wad of bills and said something about their appreciating my coming and speaking with them. I was embarrassed. I said I could not accept the money; they were retired and, I was sure, could use the money more than I could. Besides, I told them, I didn't want to take from them, I had come, rather, to give to them! A lady in the front row got to her feet, asked for the floor, and then turned half toward me and half toward her fellow retired telephone workers. "Brother Pat," she began, "we've all listened and were quite moved by your story and your work. We're all green with envy wishing we could be a part of it, but the only way we can is if you let us help in this, the only way we can! You give a lot to a lot of people," she concluded powerfully, **"but half of giving is letting others give to you!"** With a lesson eloquently taught and, I hoped, well learned, I apologized for my attitude and accepted their gift and their involvement in my work. Slowly I was learning.

While teaching my first summer course at St. John's University in Jamaica, New York, that July, I discovered that the university's theology department had a program of studies leading to a master's degree for students preparing for ordination to the priesthood. It was almost too good to be true. The university was only fifteen minutes or so from the apartment in Jackson Heights where I was now living. If I were accepted to complete my studies there I wouldn't even have to move at all! A university rule prohibiting teachers on the university staff from also being enrolled as students was waived and so I was registered and a program of studies was set up to begin with the fall semester, 1973! I was on the road to ordination and I could hardly believe it! It was exciting to be able to respond to a group of senior citizens whose luncheon speaker I was, that, yes, I was about to begin studies for the priesthood and would thereby one day be able to serve the handicapped as a priest! The lady who had asked the question about my becoming a priest seemed almost as excited as I was with my answer!

My summer teaching at St. John's and Catholic University brought in about twelve hundred dollars. By the time I had left the library at the end of May, I had about eight hundred dollars in the bank account. Other donations for talks, etc. also swelled the 'kitty' somewhat. By fall, financially at least, things looked quite good as my freelance work and studies began. A Marriage-Encountered couple from the area made the picture look even better in late August with their gift of my first semester's tuition for studies at St. John's, eleven hundred dollars! I cried as they handed me the check with a most touching note about my being a part of their 'community.' Another couple sent up a desk, a file cabinet, etc. for my new 'office' at the apartment to help the new work get started. A Lutheran Church in the area donated a mimeograph machine they weren't using and the Hoppers and their friends provided two typewriters for the work. It was absolutely unbelievable as I watched it all fall together. Many, many times I gazed around the apartment, survey-ing the abundant gifts that had equipped the new center of my work for the handicapped, and cried a silent prayer of thanksgiving to the Father for the gift of all the coincidences that had led me to make that Marriage Encounter weekend! I had never dreamed, there is no way I could have dreamed, how that single weekend would change my life!

The fall semester of 1973 began. Tuition, books, and other fees were paid on time. Rent and utilities were paid each month, that fall, on schedule. Food and transportation and office supplies and program materials were also paid for as needed...and the 'kitty' got smaller and smaller. Finally, one Friday afternoon in December, 1973, I sat down and did what I had been afraid to do for several weeks – I balanced my accounts, and they *didn't* balance! I had about four hundred dollars left in the bank. The next month's rent, telephone, utilities, and next semester's tuition added up to fifteen hundred dollars! Panic was my response! All kinds of thoughts came crowding in on me. One of my sisters, when she had learned about my new way of life in New York, had written that fall and said, "Gee, I guess I'll move to New York and bum off the people, too!" Now I wondered if she wasn't right. How many had commented about my need for 'security'..."God helps those who help themselves," they had quoted Ben Franklin as if he were scrip-tural! Maybe they were right? I had no idea where the needed eleven hundred dollars was going to come from. Maybe it was foolish to think that God would provide the needed monies for my work with the handicapped and my studies for the priesthood? Maybe I should get out and get a job to support myself and my studies and do my apostolic work on the side??? Doubts and questions came at me from all sides as I looked at my rather unbalanced accounts and wondered. Maybe I had no right to expect that God would provide so radically for my financial needs that way.

With these doubts and questions on my mind, I began to prepare for that Friday night's prayer meeting at the apartment. Alone in prayer, I opened the Bible and read at random, from the Book of Job, "Even if the whole river should overflow on him, why should he worry?" I shuddered and wondered about the 'coincidence' of the reading. The house was filled by the time our weekly prayer meeting began. I shared nothing about my worries at first. The prayer meeting had hardly begun, however, when a woman opened her Bible and read from Paul's Letter to the Colossians, "Focus your attention on higher things and let Him take care of you!" A moment later someone else read from the Twenty-third Psalm, "The Lord is my Shepherd, I shall not want!" The entire prayer meeting focused on *trust* in God. I couldn't believe it as I sat there and listened to individuals who could have known absolutely nothing of my day's worries and cares, praying and sharing passages on trust!

At the end of the prayer meeting I laughingly shared my day with the others attending the prayer meeting and then we all united and prayed for a greater trust. I slept peacefully that night and woke up the next morning with a song in my heart. Yes, I was sure "He would provide" somehow! The bills weren't due yet and when they were due, I told myself, I was sure He would provide! The mailman brought me a foot-long tube that morning. I examined the brown wrapped tube before opening it. It was addressed with a black flare pen, simply "Brother Pat, 3020 92nd Street, Jackson Heights, N.Y." There was no postal zip code and no return address. The postmark read "Bradenton, Florida." I wondered as I laboriously sought to open the very well wrapped tube. I knew no one, and still know no one, in Bradenton, Florida. Strange. I thought to myself as I finally succeeded in opening the tube. A long 'prayer scroll' rolled out from the opened tube...a half dozen or so sheets of typing paper joined together with masking tape, a cardboard coat hanger rod at each end of the five-foot scroll. A blue and black flare pen had been used to print a most beautiful Christian prayer on the long scroll. There were no clues whatever as to the author or sender. This long scroll was rolled up from both ends toward the center and the rolled-up prayer was wrapped in a sheet of paper on which was written, "Dear Brother, Roses are red, violets are blue; prayers will help, money will too!" There was no signature but a twenty-dollar bill was attached with Scotch tape! As I beheld the two 'scrolls', I didn't know whether to laugh or cry. On the one hand what was twenty dollars against the eleven hundred I had to come up with? But then, it was almost as if 'He' was speaking in my heart again: "Patrick, just as you don't know where that twenty came from *don't worry where the rest in going to come from!* You asked Me to be your provider, let Me! Get out and do the work I've sent you to do and let Me worry about the bills!" I resolved to do just that and did my best to keep to that resolution but, I must admit, it was tough not to at least wonder how He was going to do it. December finished and the eleven hundred still had not come in and I still had no clues as to how it was going to come in!

Way back in June, 1973, after a talk to senior citizens in Jamaica, New York, one of the seniors had gotten as excited as I was about my approaching studies for the priesthood. That September I had received a letter from her sister-in-law who had been told all about me after the June meeting. The letter informed me that the family had a chalice and paten for Mass that they wanted to give to *me* as a gift for when I would finally be ordained a priest! I could hardly believe it; I had only just begun my studies and already I had a chalice and paten for Mass! FANTASTIC! That gift was a very special gift from our God, I am sure, to hold me through the long, long road ahead. At times when it looked like ordination was all but out of the picture, I would take out the gift, look at it, and *know* in the depths of my heart that He wouldn't have provided it if it were not to be used one day! The letter stated that the two sisters-in-law wished to take me out to lunch some day to present the gift. That some day finally came in January, 1974, just before second semester studies were due to begin. The lunch with the two ladies was delightful and the chalice and paten brought a surprise flood of tears to my eyes. They were gorgeous. I couldn't believe they were *mine.*

I had shared the chalice and paten story with friends in Hicksville, Long Island, and, at their request, I took the train from Jamaica to Hicksville after the lunch that January afternoon. They wanted to see the chalice and paten; they seemed almost as excited about it as I was; how could I not bring it out for them to see? George and Ruth Hatalsky had been the 'Prayer Couple' for my Marriage Encounter weekend the previous March. On Sunday morning of that weekend I had been handed a small card that read "We are praying and sacrificing for you this weekend, George & Ruth Hatalsky." Each couple on the weekend had received a similar card from a couple who had dedicated their prayers and sacrifices for them that weekend. The 'prayer couple' card deeply moved me that Sunday morning. It was hard to believe that somebody, whose name I could hardly pronounce, was praying and sacrificing for *me* when I had never met them! Incredible! It was just another unbelievable facet of that FANTASTIC weekend that changed my life! On Tuesday, after that weekend, I had decided to call this George and Ruth Hatalsky, and thank them for the prayers and sacrifices that, I was sure, had helped me to have such a FANTASTIC weekend. As Ruth invited me to come out to dinner the following Sunday, George stood in the background wringing his fists and muttering "What do I want with a 'man of the cloth' here? Why did you invite him over? What do we have in common? What are we going to talk about...?" I accepted the invitation, knowing none of George's reservations. I took the train out to Hicksville that March Sunday afternoon at about 3:00 since they had said to come early." Only when I arrived did I find out that dinner was at *noon* at the Hatalsky home, not at *night!* "I hope you like dried-up turkey!", George said as I walked in! But, somehow, with all the awkwardness of its beginnings, a FANTASTIC friendship was formed that day, a friendship with the whole family that persists to this day. As I arrived back at the apartment that Sunday night the phone was ringing. "Hello," I said and then heard George and Ruth's voices at the other end. "We're willing if you are," they said with laughter ringing in their voices. "I'm willing," I said, "but what for?" "Adopting!" they said together. And it was a very real adoption! Their home on Long Island became 'my' home. They were there with me through thick and thin all the way to the priesthood and to this day. Ruth's mother, Mrs. Gertrude Soper, a widow, also from Hicksville, quickly became my personal recorder for all of my seminary studies! I would pick up my needed textbooks in several shopping bags each semester and she would proceed to tranform them into 'talking books' for me! She recorded an average of fourteen ninety-minute cassettes a week during the next four semesters! Without her help, I could not have carried the full load of theology studies and continued my work with the handicapped at the same time! I still remind her today that she deserved the degree as much as I did!

I was quite excited as I boarded the Long Island Railroad bound for Hicksville to show off the beautiful chalice and paten this January afternoon in 1974. They were all as genuinely excited about the gift as I was! After supper we all sat around looking at it from time to time and talking about what it will be like to be able to celebrate the Mass for the handicapped! We had sat for some time when another couple rang the doorbell at the Hatalsky's and then came in. I had met them through George and Ruth so it was no surprise to see them walk in. We sat for a few minutes and then George cleared his throat and began to speak. I knew something was up but I wasn't quite sure what it was. "Patrick," he began, "we all know the way you're living and working and we love it. You've done a lot for us in Marriage Encounter here in Hicksville," he went on, "and so we decided we'd like to help you out a bit in your life and work. This check is from all of us in this area." He then handed me a check for eleven hundred dollars! I was speechless, incredulous! That was the amount I needed exactly! I cried and laughed, laughed and cried. I hugged them and we all cried together! 'He' had truly provided, through the generosity and love of His FANTASTIC, beautiful people! Several semesters later George and Ruth paid yet another semester's tuition for theology studies with funds they had worked hard to save for a vacation! I, who had prided myself in my aloneness and independence, in my not needing anyone, didn't know quite how to handle all of this love and generosity and sacrifice on my behalf. Month after month, semester after semester, as the funds were needed they were there. Through the generosity of audiences, families, and the brothers my work and studies moved ahead on schedule. but, even more than my work and my studies, my *growing up* was also happening quite on schedule those months and years in New York City. I who had fought so hard and succeeded so well in growing up to need no one was now, unknowingly of course, growing up to need people! My dream of independence had most assuredly soured into the nightmare of aloneness. The fear and pride that had locked me into that nightmarish world were now, however, slowly being replaced by trust as I began taking the tiniest baby steps toward the vision, **"People who need people are the luckiest people in the world!"**

'Needing' and 'trusting' became more and more common elements of my life in New York those mid years of the 1970's. In the summer of 1975, I was asked to give a series of talks in the province of Ontario, Canada. "I'll be there on Wednesday," I said and purchased the ticket for the flight. It *did* cross my mind as I handed the ticket agent my credit card that the bill would have to be paid when the mailman delivered it. And, *I did* wonder just how 'He' would take care of this one, but I had learned to trust a little bit better that indeed *He would take care of it!*

"Hello! I'm at the airport!" I sang into the telephone that Wednesday morning as the couple in Sault Ste. Marie who had requested that I come answered their phone. "You can't be!" was their prompt reply. "Where *are* you?" "I'm at the airport!" I came back. "I just got off the plane. I'm not kidding!" "Patrick," they replied, there are no planes that come in at this hour!" "I beg your pardon," I said, tired of playing around, "I just got off the plane!" A pause was finally followed by the question "Where *are* you? Which airport?" "I'm in Toronto," I said, and a hearty laugh preceded my instructions. "Hop the next plane to 'the Sault'!" "The next plane?" I questioned, "how far am I from 'the Sault'?" "About 500 miles!" they laughed, "we'll see you this afternoon!" "Oh well. I never claimed to be good in Canadian geography!" I had landed in Toronto, Ontario, and had just presumed that Sault Ste. Marie, Ontario, couldn't be "that far away!" My travels have done much these past thirteen years to broaden my knowledge and understanding of many subjects not the least of which is geography!

My plan was to spend seven days in the Sault Ste. Marie area and then to return home to New York. The Sault area talks, however, gave birth to requests from Sudbury and Toronto families for similar talks in their areas. Obligingly I decided to stay in Canada an extra three days. My last talk in the Sault area was at a family picnic. For all of the talks and arrangements for the trip money was never discussed, but after this picnic talk an envelope was handed me by one of the families 'in appreciation'... The envelope made me cry as its pennies, nickles and dimes and colored Canadian bills fell on the table in front of me. None of the families I had addressed were rich and I had expected no monetary gift from them. When their offering was counted it went forty dollars over the cost of my plane ticket. That night in grateful prayer I asked an extra question of the Lord, "What's the extra forty for?" I had come to know by then that He does indeed take care of my every *today* but He wasn't in the habit of giving me *tomorrow's* needs today. He didn't usually build up a bank reserve for some probable need of the future. None of today's needs ever went unmet; trust meant waiting till tomorrow to look at its needs. So now I looked at this extra forty and wondered... My wonderings didn't last too long, however, as I confirmed my new flight plan with airline agent on the phone. As she confirmed the needed stops in Sudbury and Toronto she finished with "Of course, that will cost you extra, sir." "How much extra?" I asked, sure of her answer even before asking the question. "Forty dollars," she said...

Dear Brother,

I'll say this for you, Patrick, you had a lot of nerve... I believe the street slang for it would be "guts." Where did you ever get the notion that you should be a teacher? Not a teacher of helter-skelter teenagers... Patrick, you really took a chance...and all to be normal.

But then you kept on taking chances, didn't you? I struggle with the idea of your being happy about being on your own in New York City... I've never been there, but I hear it is a good place to stay away from... I suppose though, you had someone in your corner, taking care of you. You must have really worked Him overtime.

I finally came to the place in your story where the 'real' Patrick started to show himself... that call to be a priest for the handicapped. Really blew your mind, didn't it, Patrick?

I believe that at that time, as I am now, I would have been drawn very close to you... would have laughed with you and probably would have done a lot of crying along with you. But, that wasn't the way things were with me at that time, I imagine that your problems would have been just that, your problems... I just could never have gotten involved. And, besides, you were not even the remotest figment of my imagination at that time. I wish that our courses had crossed then... maybe I would have grown much more that I have... perhaps they would call me the FANTASTIC spirit of the handicapped.

It took you an awful long time to learn that you really needed people, that you had to have trust in them, that you had to love them and let them, above all, love you. Patrick, I surely do believe that at that time in your life, you were very dense or else your blindness was just not relegated to your eyesight. But, you learned, as I did... the hard way.

Do you know what I did, when I read that you had definitely made up your mind that you wanted to be a priest, no matter what... I shouted out in my loudest voice, the one that nobody can hear, "Go for it, Patrick."

I always knew that you were human, had all the human traits and faults. We spirits are very 'with it' when it comes to summing up the good and bad points of humans... we don't do as well on ourselves. I know the anger and bitterness you must have felt at Brother Francis... but, do you know, Patrick, I truly believe that he was thinking of your best interests as he saw them. I've met him... although he didn't know it... he is a remarkable man, don't you agree?

Next chapters look very interesting... I must read on to see what new characters will step forth from the pages. Being that it seems to center around my area, it should be very good reading.

With the peace and love of the great I AM

The Spirit of the Handicapped

15

"A new nation I will give to..."

"Everything's packed!" I hollered out the front door to the two men who were helping me move to Norwich, Connecticut, on December 4, 1975. Even as we closed the door of the house behind us, climbed into the pick-up truck that would bring me to my new "home base" and took the ramp onto the highway that led us away from New York City, I found it all but impossible to believe I was leaving the city. It had all happened so suddenly, it seemed, and yet, as I look back over the years and months that preceded the move, I see it was not a sudden break but rather the gradual unfolding of 'His Plan' in my life.

In May, 1975, having finished my last semester of theology studies at St. John's University in Jamaica, New York City, I had gone down to Washington to teach my annual course at Catholic University's Library School. While there I had spent a weekend with the Connolly's, a beautiful family whose daughter was autistic. At Mass in the family's parish church that Sunday morning, we had met a couple from Groton, Connecticut. They had experienced the Marriage Encounter weekend and so our conversation quite naturally drifted to the up-coming Marriage Encounter International Convention to be held at St. John's University in New York at the end of June. No, the Buechler's from Groton, Connecticut, said, they couldn't attend the convention since they had registered too late to get housing. "You can stay at my apartment," I said. "register again and come on down! I'll keep space for you *on my floor!*" They seemed excited about the prospect but mentioned friends of theirs who also were interested in the convention but had a similar housing problem. Tell them to come, too, I said, reminding them to bring plenty of pillows and sleeping bags. I was then informed that their friends had a 3-month old baby who'd be coming along. An apartment with 2 single beds — two couples, a 3-month old baby, and a brother? It should be fun! It was! I hadn't realized, however, as I 'booked' these families for the floor space in my apartment, that the local Marriage Encounter couples in New York City had just presumed that I'd love to have some of the out-of-towners stay with me for the convention, and so they had booked a couple and a priest from Washington state for the *same floor space!* Now, when I returned from Washington I discovered that in my tiny, 2 single-bed apartment, I was to house three couples, a priest, a 3-month old baby, and myself for that convention! It was FANTASTIC! Since the Connecticut couples were staying at my apartment they just 'naturally' decided to attend my talks at the convention, and, just as naturally, they dragged an awful lot of other Connecticut couples to those same talks. We had wall-to-wall people at the apartment; to say we were 'close' is to greatly understate the case! It was downright dangerous to even think of getting up during the night to find the bathroom! We lodged the 3-month old baby beneath the dining room table — for safety's sake!

In July of that same year, several weeks after the convention, I received an invitation to speak at the first state-wide convention for Marriage Encounter in Connecticut. The state convention would be held in September, I was told in the letter. Couples who had attended the international convention had been polled as to possible speakers for their state convention and thus it was that those who had been dragged to my talks had suggested my name as one of those 'possible speakers.' I booked the date for late September, 1975, and prepared to attend the convention with no further thoughts. The couples I had 'hosted' for the international convention now wrote asking to be allowed to return the favor, so to speak. They lived several hours drive from the convention site so I suggested that I might come and visit after the convention if that was okay with them. The convention went without hassle and I went on to Groton for a couple of days. 'A couple of days' stretched into some two and half weeks! I found myself speaking to various encounter groups every evening, to school classes and nursing home gatherings and agency staffs during the days. Requests for speaking just kept coming in. One priest from the local diocese heard me speak several times during those two and a half weeks and began to wonder just who this 'brother' was with time on his hands to be so available for speaking. He called my provincial headquarters in Maine and spoke to the brother serving as Brother Francis's secretary. The brother told him all he wanted to know and then went on to inform the priest that my studies were now completed for ordination to the priesthood and that I was awaiting our General Chapter's decision in March of 1976 concerning the brothers and the priesthood. Speaking with the bishop of the diocese a day or so later the priest told him about the brother he had heard speak. He told the bishop all that the provincial's secretary had told him and when he mentioned the priesthood the bishop told him to tell the brother that if he needed a diocese he, the bishop, would be happy to talk with him.

I could hardly believe my ears that morning in early October, 1975, when that priest called me and told me of his conversation with the bishop. Were the pieces of a puzzle perhaps fitting together? I didn't know. I was somewhat scared. New York City had been home for me for a half dozen years. There I had all the public transportation I needed. Three weeks before this phone call I hadn't even known the Norwich Diocese existed! It seems like a very tiny diocese compared to the metropolitan area dioceses. Did it have any public transportation at all? And then there was my work which often took me for talks and programs all over the country and even into Canada. Could I tie myself to a tiny diocese like this seemed to be!

On the other hand, I had finished my studies – as far as I could go without a sponsoring bishop – in June, 1975. I was now in a 'holding pattern' waiting to see what our General Chapter would decide concerning the possible ordination of a brother in the order. If the decision was affirmative then there'd be no problem; I'd be ordained a 'brother priest.' If the decision was negative, then I would have to either forget the whole idea of serving the handicapped as a priest or else leave the order and apply for acceptance in some diocese of other religious order. I had already approached personnel of several of the metropolitan-area dioceses concerning the latter option but had found no enthusiastic response whatever. Now, I had a bishop inviting me? Could this be the handiwork of our God? I didn't know. I was afraid of the move and yet I was afraid to summarily dismiss it.

I decided to make a 'Directed Retreat', an eight day 'walk with the Lord' under the guidance of a priest, at Gonzaga Renewal Center in Monroe, New York. I wanted to clear my head so I could make the right decision. I didn't want the priest-director to tell me what decision to make; I didn't even tell him about the momentous decision that lay in front of me. I simply told him at the outset of my 8 day stay at the retreat house that I wanted to come closer to God during that stay. Every day I would meet with him for an hour or so and I would share 'where I was' the previous day – spiritually, emotionally, etc. From my sharing he would draw out scripture passages for me to read and pray over during the following day and thereby he guided me on my 8 day walk with the Lord. After telling him a bit about myself in our first session together he suggested that I might begin my walk with the Lord by reading and praying over Isaiah 55:6-9. As we read the several verses together right there in his office I began to cry – "A new nation I will give you," he read, "a people you have never known, you will lead!..." For six days he gave me similar passages. Finally, on the sixth day, he asked me "Are you contemplating a move?" I broke down and shared the whole story of the Norwich Diocese with him. When I finished he said, "Have no fear; go to Norwich."

I didn't know whether to be nervous or scared that early November afternoon when that priest picked me up for my appointment with the bishop. I wasn't even sure what I was there for. The general chapter of the brothers still had not met and wouldn't meet for several more months. The bishop hadn't offered me a job in the diocese. Why was I going to see him? We arrived in Norwich a bit early so the priest brought me in to see the cathedral church of the diocese. As we knelt before the Altar of the Blessed Sacrament, I found myself praying that one day I would be ordained a priest in that cathedral! I don't even remember the walk from the church to the bishop's office. I was immediately taken in by his warm, enthusiastic personality. I was there but a few moments and all my fears and wonderings had changed to excitement! Bishop Daniel Patrick Reilly, formerly from Providence, Rhode Island, had been named Bishop of Norwich only a couple of months earlier. The families I had met and shared with those past few months had talked excitedly about 'their new bishop.' Now I knew why! He asked me a few questions and I shared bits and pieces of my story and my dream of serving the handicapped as a priest. We talked about the brothers' community I belonged to and he totally amazed me by naming brothers of that community that he had met! As our meeting seemed to be drawing to a close he said that after the general chapter of the brothers made the decision concerning ordination he would be happy to meet and talk with me again concerning my own ordination to the priesthood! I could hardly believe I was hearing those words. I felt so confirmed at that instant on my journey to serve my brothers and sisters as a priest! It was absolutely FANTASTIC! I looked at the bishop and just marveled that I was sitting and chatting with the *bishop!* In all my years of training and service as a brother I had hardly ever met a bishop, let alone sat and chatted with one! I then responded to his 'closing statement,' "Bishop Reilly, I feel like I'm 'using' you. I need a bishop for ordination so I come to you... Is there anything I can do for you and your diocese? My life and work are with the handicapped. Can I help in that area?" The bishop's face glowed as he spoke. He told me that just that morning Brother Martin O'Brien, Director of Religious Education in the diocese, had come in and spoken to him about the need in the diocese for someone to work directly with the handicapped! We talked a bit more about programs and possibilities then he suggested I talk with Brother Martin and also with the diocesan Superintendent of Schools. I spent that afternoon visiting the two offices suggested and meeting more people than I could name.

Things seemed to be falling into place faster than I could dream them! It was incredible. I had invited a couple from Groton, Connecticut, to come and stay at my New York City apartment for a Marriage Encounter convention weekend and now here I was, interviewing for a position of service in their diocese! Unreal! FANTASTIC! With the interviews completed I returned to New York and continued business as usual for the next couple of weeks. I had a number of talks to give in East Rockaway, Long Island, as well as an 'awareness program' for the parochial school there so those couple of weeks *flew by!* It was November 24th. I was on my way to Manhattan. On my way into the city from Long Island, I stopped at the home where I was living to check my answering service. Even that was strange — I had moved out of the Jackson Heights apartment in August after living there for three years! Rather than renew the lease for another year or so I had decided to terminate the lease and accepted living quarters with a family in Woodside, Queens. They had a two-family home but had not wished to rent the lower street level apartment. I had known the family, Les and Sally McCurdy, for about a year through the Marriage Encounter. Their offer of the downstairs living quarters was particularly opportune...things were still uncertain concerning ordination so I didn't want to tie myself to a living arrangement that might have to change. The lease was up on the apartment so it just seemed like a good move. The new residence wasn't far from my Jackson Heights address so I would be able to continue local activities and services and friendships. My new home with the McCurdy's was close to both buses and subways so that was another plus.

And so, I had moved in late August, 1975. Jack Butler drove me to Woodside from East Rockaway this late November afternoon and came in with me while I checked the answering service. I couldn't believe the message that the tape delivered. It was from Norwich, Connecticut, and it said simply that the bishop had approved everything and I was hired to work in the diocese with the handicapped. I started to cry. Jack just held me and I couldn't even explain why I was crying. I had yearned for so long to be a part of the Church with my ministry with the handicapped. I had worked for five years as a volunteer in the diocese where I had lived. I had even thought of this diocese as a possibility for ordination if the general chapter of the brothers had decided against ordination within the community, but when I had inquired about that possibility my inquiries had met with silence. That very fall of 1975 Brother Francis had suggested I open a long dreamed-of 'information center' for the handicapped, a center that would help them find the materials and services they needed in life. The diocese had responded that the center was not needed. I had cried when that decision had been made. Now, standing in front of the little black box that taped my telephone messages, that decision and all the other 'coincidental?' events of that past summer suddenly seemed to fit together, to form a pattern, a road map that led to Norwich, Connecticut. If I hadn't met that Groton, Connecticut, couple in Washington... If they and others hadn't stayed at my apartment and come to my talks... If I hadn't given up the apartment in August... If the local diocese had not said "no" to the information center dream... If that priest in Connecticut had not called to get my credentials... If Bishop Reilly had not come to the Diocese of Norwich that summer... More and more 'if's' raced across my memory screen... It was all like a dream, a dream coming true! I just cried.

"Mom," I said on the telephone that night,: I'm moving to Connecticut!" "My prayers have been answered," she said and then she cried! "What do you mean?" I said, "what prayers?"

"Patrick," she said, still sobbing, "I never wanted to say anything to you; I didn't want to influence you; but I've been scared to death for you ever since you moved to New York a half dozen years ago! I never wanted you to move out to please me but *I've prayed!* I've prayed God to protect you every single day for these past half dozen years and I've prayed Him to move you out of there one day. And now,... my prayers have been answered at last!" And she cried. I never loved my dear mother as much as I loved her that night! And, oh, how dearly I felt her love!

I called Brother Martin O'Brien in Norwich the very next morning to say that as I saw it I should be able to move up by January, 1976. Oh no, he said, we need you now! The bishop had approved my appointment effective immediately! "What do I do?" I asked. "I've got programs scheduled all over the country and others here in the New York-Long Island area. I've got to give people some sort of notice..." Come on up as soon as you can was his response. He said I could continue much of my work from my Norwich 'home base'. Just move up and get started as soon as I could!

How can one thing be both exciting and terribly hurting at the very same time? My last ten or so days in New York were perhaps the most difficult of my half dozen years there! For me, it was exciting, a dream was unfolding right before my very eyes... but that dream meant leaving families and friends I had grown very close to the past couple of years. As we said our good-bye's I thanked God that I would be only a couple of hours away by train.

Yes, it really had all happened so suddenly! It was like putting a puzzle together and now you're coming to the end... one piece fits in and because of it fifteen others fall right into place! Our Daddy's plan seemed so clear that day as we packed up the two pickup trucks that had come down from Connecticut to pick up all my things and move them and me to the Diocese of Norwich. As the two pickup trucks moved along Interstate 95 North, we often sat for long spells in total silence as I traced our Daddy's loving through all the events of my life, all the torn and twisted, rough and broken, hope-filled and exciting roads that were now leading most assuredly to Norwich, Connecticut. "I'm sorry," I'd say when I realized I'd been 'away' for quite some time. "That's okay," Jay or Marty would say, "we know right where you are! We too have often been there!" Marty Sullivan and Jay Fleck, two men I had met through the Marriage Encounter groups in Connecticut a month or so before, had now taken time off from their work, borrowed pickup trucks, and had driven down to New York to help me move to their diocese.

We arrived in Norwich – finally – that evening, December 4, at about 5:30. The pickup trucks had been systematically packed so it was easy enough to distinquish 'office baggage' from 'residence baggage.' Trucks unloaded, we then drove to one of the families for dinner that night. Strangely, I don't recall too many details of those first few days, weeks, months? in the diocese. I'm sure it was somewhat of a 'culture shock' moving to a primarily rural diocese from the New York City metropolitan area. The Norwich Diocese comprises the four eastern counties of the State of Connecticut, bordering on the Atlantic Ocean and the State of Rhode Island on the east, Massachusetts on the north, and the Connecticut River forms almost all of the western and southern boundary of the diocese with the exception of a few towns. The largest cities of the diocese would be Norwich, New London, Middletown, ... with populations barely reaching 40,000! Some of the larger towns and cities have limited bus transportation systems but there is little or nothing connecting one with another. It was quite immediately evident that walking and/or volunteer drivers would be my means of transportation in the area. For the convenience of transportation I was given a room at St. Mary's Rectory, across the parking lot from the building where my office would be. Again, because of transportation, I used that room rarely during the two years that it served as my official residence. I found myself more and more stay-ing in the homes of the handicapped themselves in the various areas of the diocese where I happened to be traveling. Some homes became regular 'inns' for me. One of those 'inns' in Jewett City always brings back smiles whenever it comes to mind. I'd call the

Laliberte's and tell them 'Vacuum my bed; I'm coming in tonight!" When I arrived, my favorite spot on their living room floor was all set up – often with balloons and other such 'extras' beneath the pillow or mattress! Staying in the homes this way not only saved me much transportation but also brought me and the ministry very close to those the Bishop had intended it to serve.

The original concept of the office seems to have been a 'Special Religious Education Office.' It was set up as a part of the Office of Religious Education under the direction of Brother Martin O'Brien and it was assumed that most of those served by the new office would be handicapped children. I spent my first weeks in my new office moving in and unpacking, getting to know people and resources of the area, and, finally learning *Geography!* In New York City I could schedule several talks in several different boroughs of the city on the same day! Now, I had to learn what towns were relatively close to each other and that if I had a program in Middletown on one day I'd better not schedule one in Putnam on the same day!!!!

With the aid of the diocese's Office of Communications, the natural interest of the area's news media, and a quickly filled calendar of speaking engagements, the office grew rather quickly. It was only several months old when Brother Martin O'Brien came to me one day and suggested that we make it a separate office rather than a part of the Religious Education Office. "You're going to end up doing much more than strictly special religious education," he said. Time has already verified the wisdom of his decision. The Office of Special Religious Education grew very quickly into the Office of Ministries for the Handicapped. The growth was so rapid, first of all, because, except for a few parish programs here and there in the diocese, nothing was really being done in this area of service prior to the Bishop's establishment of the office in December of 1975. The need, the hunger for the service is very much attested to by the rapid growth of the ministry in the diocese. But, the ministry owes its rapid growth primarily, I am sure, to the freedom given it by the Bishop of the diocese. I will never forget my meeting with Bishop Reilly in April or May of 1976. Brother Francis had flown in from Rome and we had discussed the priesthood issue with Bishop Reilly. When the matter was settled Bishop Reilly sat back in his chair, puffed on his cigar, winked at Brother Francis across the table and said, "I've got to tell you a story." He then proceeded to tell Brother Francis about our first meeting and his invitation for me to come to the diocese. "I had my own ideas," he went on, "about this new office and how I thought it should be set up. Pat moved in at the beginning of December, never came to see me but got immediately to work. I watched what he did – which wasn't at all what I had envisioned – but I didn't touch it!" Wow! I cried that night as I thought about the tremendous gift of freedom I had indeed been given in the Diocese of Norwich! He had never once called and said "I want it done this way or that..." He'd listen when we'd meet and I'd tell him all that was going on. He always seemed more excited about the new ministry that I was! The Office of Ministries for the Handicapped was, then allowed to grow in response to the needs of those it was founded to serve. Contrary to expectations, it was not the needs of the handicapped children that presented themselves overwhelmingly but rather the needs of handicapped adults! Some families with handicapped children did indeed come forward to be heard but the vast majority of those who presented their needs were adults and teenagers who themselves were disabled in some way. A social/discussion group was formed to meet regularly at a nearby school in Norwich. Parish talks, parents' meetings, family visits... all voiced the same need – the need for the handicapped to be a part of the Church. It was exciting, almost unreally so, to be without rigid structures and format in the office and so, free to respond to the needs that were discovered during those first days, weeks, months, years of the ministry. The Office of Ministries for the Handicapped took its beginning goal as simply bringing the Church to those who could not come to it and determined not to duplicate what other agencies were already doing on behalf of the handicapped. The ministry's first year was proclaimed as a time for looking, listening, and learning – looking to find the handicapped, who they are, where they live in the diocese, etc.; listening to *their* needs, not the needs others think they have or the needs they 'should' have, etc.; and learning what is already available in the area to meet those needs! It would then become the ministry's goal to try and meet the unmet needs discovered.

That was one exciting year for me. As fearful as I had been of coming to a tiny, rural diocese, that tiny, rural diocese very quickly became *home* for me. Transportation never seemed to be a major problem. "You find out how to get there and I'll get you there," volunteer after volunteer would tell me! I very quickly learned route numbers, landmarks, shortcuts to use and shortcuts to avoid! Before celebrating my first anniversary in the diocese, Connecticut had truly become my *home!*

In March of 1976 the long awaited General Chapter of the Brothers of Christian Instruction convened in Rome with 'the priesthood' slated as one of its topics for discussion. Brother Francis promised to write as soon as some definite action had taken place on the topic. I couldn't wait to hear from him! And, finally, his letter arrived. He said the issue had been discussed for a full week on the chapter floor and that it was a very touchy issue. Many felt that it was essential to the very nature of being a brother that he not be a priest; just as many felt that the needs of the Church today demanded the ordination of some of the men. A concensus could not be arrived at, and so, the issue had been tabled until the next General Chapter, 1982, with the assignment given to research the area more fully before that chapter. After briefly describing the chapter's actions, Brother Francis went on to say that he would be returning to the States very soon and at that time he would come to see me.

He was true to his word of some four years earlier. He came to Norwich and we discussed that evening the chapter's decision and its application to my life and work with the handicapped. "You've waited long enough," he said, "I can't ask you to wait another six years." I prayed intensely that night but I think the decision was already made. Norwich had become home for me and now, if Bishop Reilly were willing, I would become one of its priests. We met with the bishop the following morning and it was agreed I could request the special 'indult' from Rome to leave the Brothers of Christian Instruction to be free to be ordained a diocesan priest, a priest for the handicapped! By June 15, 1976, the papers had all been processed and they were in my hands. If I signed them they became official and I was no longer a Brother of Christian Instruction. In one of the most peaceful prayer hours I had every known I signed the papers that June morning. It was a strange experience. The papers stated that I was no longer a brother, that my vows of poverty, chastity and obedience were now null, and yet, as I signed the papers I felt a strange conviction inside that I was renewing, not nullifying, the vows that had been my life for twelve years! I delivered the papers that day to the Bishop's office with a written request that I be accepted as a candidate for ordination to the priesthood in his diocese.

Several weeks later I was called to the bishop's office where I received the news that *yes* I was accepted as a candidate for Holy Orders! I couldn't believe it. The dream was now almost five years old! Was it really going to come true! Ordination day now seemed almost tastably close! If I had known then that ordination would not take place for more than two full years, I would have been totally discouraged with the dream. How merciful our Daddy is in hiding our tomorrows from us! Records of my studies were obtained and studied and a final semester of studies was set up to immediately precede ordination. Every Tuesday for the fifteen weeks of that fall semester, 1976, I flew back and forth from the New London Airport to LaGuardia Airport, 15 minutes from St. John's University, where, it was decided, I would complete my preparations for ordination. Pilgrim Airlines' green and orange planes became a familiar site for me that fall. In light and in darkness, in good weather and in not so good weather, I flew down to New York, attended my three classes, and flew back home that night! This rather precarious arrangement was my choice. Instead of closing the ministry's newly opened office for a semester of studies, I was permitted to commute to classes every week! As I look back on it now, I don't know how it all came out right! The Marriage Encounter couples were FANTASTIC! One drove me to the airport each Tuesday morning and another picked me up when my *midnight* flight arrived! They recorded my textbooks that semester and helped in more ways than I can name so that the ministry office could remain open and serving, and my studies could be completed at the same time! In addition to the three university courses I also took two other courses tutorially in the diocese, meeting each week with a priest for the lesson. Christmas of 1976 was one happy Christmas! Studies were completed; grades were in; ordination was even closer! On March 18, 1977, in the bishop's private chapel, I was officially accepted as a Candidate for the Sacrament of Holy Orders. That was my thirty-third birthday but it seemed more like my *first!!!*

16

"He was born this way that the works of God might show through him..."

As I write these pages, reflecting all the while on my own story, I shiver with goosebumps as I survey the part that that Marriage Encounter has played in my entire life! At one point several years ago a few of my brothers and sisters thought I had left the handicapped to get involved with the Marriage Encounter movement. As I look at it now, I see how it's actually the opposite of what they thought. That weekend and my subsequent involvement with the couples and religious and priests who are involved with it actually saved my vocation to the handicapped! How well I recall praying more earnestly that ever before on Saturday night of that weekend in March of 1973 that it would not be 'just another high experience' but that my life would really *change* because of that weekend! Nine and half years later I'm still writing those daily letters to 'Daddy.' letters that have melted my own stony heart and made me sensitive and open to my people and their needs! It was the couples who paid most of my way through the seminary to be a priest. It was they and their loved ones who recorded my textbooks and needed articles making it possible for me to study and continue my work with the handicapped at the same time. How often their calls and rides brought me to one disabled person or another that they had met! And, most excitingly, it was they who 'brought me' to Connecticut, to Bishop Reilly, to the Diocese of Norwich, to my 'home!' Ever since that beautiful weekend in my life I have dreamed of giving it to other handicapped persons as it was given to me. In the fall of 1976 that dream came true more wildly than I had ever imagined it could!

That summer my courses at St. John's University and Catholic University were canceled because of scheduled hernia surgery. Ten days before the surgery, however, the hernia 'disappeared!' "Do you still want to operate?" I asked the doctor as he finished his examination. No way, he said. I'm sure it's there and will probably reappear. If it does, come back and see me. We'll take care of it then. "God bless you, Doctor!" I said getting up from the examining table. "No, it's not 'me' He's blessed," he said! "Have a good summer!" A good summer I did have. My teaching at the two library schools had already been canceled so my summer was wide open. Earlier I had declined an invitation from the Croteau family to spend a week at Cape Cod with them because of my teaching schedule there was no way I would have a week off at the time they were going. Hearing about the 'hernia miracle,' Rudy and Marge called immediately. "That invitation for the Cape is still on," they said. "FANTASTIC!" I responded. "Can I bring my typewriter and work on a book while I'm there?" (Some people just don't know how to take a vacation.) People had been at me since the mid-1960's to write this book and several times I had actually made a start at it but I had never come up with a completed manuscript. This summer, truly a *gift from God,* could be just the opportunity to produce that manuscript! A seven chapter, 50 to 60 page book was actually completed during that July week at the Cape! I sent it to a friend in New York who works in a major publishing house. She had several editors read and comment on the manuscript and then returned it to me with the advice to work on it and complete it. I had only touched the surface of the story. I never picked it up again that summer.

In September the hernia came back. I called the specialist and two days later underwent the needed surgery. Recuperating at home in the rectory, my eyes fell on the manuscript on my book case. Picking it up I began to read...and wonder... The whole thing had flowed together so smoothly and so quickly... Seven chapters in five days! And then it hit like a bolt of lightning – *a weekend for the handicapped!* In those seven chapters I had the outline for seven sessions of a weekend helping persons with disabilities to dare to look at themselves in terms of their 'giftedness' instead of their handicaps! A wild dream? Maybe, but it came true! Within two hours lying on my bed I had called and gotten commitments from seven handicapped persons that I knew. All of them said they'd be excited to work on the first 'Persons Are Gifts Weekend!' From the chapters I prepared a question outline for each talk of the weekend. Each 'team member' answered the questions from his/her own life story. The weekend would simply be their sharing – as catalysts – followed by reflection times and then group discussion times. It was worth a try and, who knows, it might even give to others what that Marriage Encounter weekend had given to me!

The manuscript had been entitled FANTASTIC! I AM A GIFT!, a title drawn from a retreat experience of the previous fall. On the last day of that eight day directed retreat that I had made before deciding to come to Norwich my retreat director had said "Pat, I'm giving you only one passage to pray over today" (instead of the four or five that he had been giving me each day prior to that). "I think you're ready for this," he went on. "It will be tough but I think you'll be able to handle it. If you need me you can come in to see me but otherwise pray a lot over the passage." The passage he gave me was John, Chapter 9, the story of the man born blind. By that day on the retreat I was literally basking in the abundant sunshine of God's love for me so I started out into the woods that gorgeous October morning with my Bible under my arm and my notebook in my hand. The leaves rustled as I shuffled through them; the sky was absolutely cloudless! I sat on a rock and began to read.

"Jesus and his disciples were walking on the road. His disciples saw a man who was blind from birth. 'Master,' they said, 'who sinned this man or his parents that he should have been born this way?'... Jesus calls the man over, spits on the ground and makes mud and covers the man's eyes. He then tells the man to go off and wash. The man goes off, washes, and comes back seeing!"

As I read the passage I got more and more excited. Nowhere in the passage does it even say the man asked to be cured! The miracle was Jesus's love; it was His initiative! I was so excited as I realized it and then the question hit, as with the force of a mighty wind... "You poor misinformed *fool!* Do you really believe God loves you? If He does why doesn't He cure *your* eyes? Or, maybe He can't??? Is that it, Patrick, maybe He can't! I mean, what father who had a cure for blindness would run around curing everybody else's eyes except the one He loved? Could you really say He 'loved' him?..." The questions came hard and fast one right on top of the other giving me no time whatever to even think about responding. I found myself plunged almost literally into *hell* with doubts and questions and confusion... And I had no answers to the truckload of questions that had been so suddenly hurled at me.

I found my way back to the A-framed chapel on the mountain-top and I just sat there, alone, in front of the Blessed Sacrament, for some three and a half hours! I hated the director for having given me that passage to read! I had been flying high for days... now this. I was confused, filled with doubts and anger, I was ashamed... all at the same time. Do you know what it is to clench your eyes so tight that no light whatever gets in, and then pray with all the faith you can muster, and then open your eyes to find out you're still as blind as you were when you closed them? Maybe I really don't have any faith? Doubts, doubts, more doubts.. sheer hell for three and a half hours sitting in front of the Blessed Sacrament.

And then, all of a sudden when I had all but despaired of any peace ever coming back, my retreat director's words of some eight days earlier rang clearly inside my head. "Patrick," he said on the very night I had arrived at the retreat house, "during this 'walk' you're going to hear many voices; **'by their fruits you shall know them.' The Spirit of God, the Voice of God, brings with it charity, joy, peace, patience, long suffering, mildness... It is the spirit, the voice of the tempter, not the Voice of God,"** he emphasized, **"that brings with it confusion, doubt, anger, shame, guilt..."** Eight days ago he had spoken them; how clearly they rang true now! I got to my knees and prayed the simplest, truest *Act of Faith* that I had ever prayed in my life, I am sure. "God," I said with tears of anger and confusion and fear and doubt still plaguing my cheeks, "don't ask me to understand because *I can't understand*. But, God, I do believe without understanding! I do believe that you do love me. I do believe that you *can* cure my eyes if you want to. And I do believe that you love me whether you do cure them or not! I don't understand, God, but I do believe." And as I finished that utterly simple prayer of faith my eyes fell on the open Bible in front of me. I had read the passage at least fifty or a hundred times that morning, I decided to read it just once more.

"Jesus and His disciples were walking on the road. His disciples saw a man who was blind from birth. 'Master,' they said, 'who sinned, this man or his parents, that he should have been born this way?'..."

I had read that passage dozens of times those three and a half hours but *never once* had Jesus's answer hit me. Now as I read I could hardly believe what I read! Oh, I knew it practically by heart, but it now seemed to 'settle into place!' "Neither this man nor his parents sinned! *He was born this way that the works of God might show through him!"* Wow! I suddenly looked at my life, my whole life since the meningitis as a kid... and I cried tears of faith and love as I saw where I was today and wondered where indeed I might be — in jail somewhere? — were it not for the *gift* of my blindness!!! How many people I had been privileged to touch and help the past half dozen years alone! Would I have met even *one* of them without the *gift* of my blindness? For years, almost two dozen years, I had begged God to cure my eyes so I could serve Him. Now, I breathed a sigh of relief that He had answered that prayer in His way and not in my way!!!

It was that retreat experience that really started me thinking about the possible 'giftedness' of my handicapping conditions. We learn so quickly in education, in upbringing, in rehabilitation programs to hate who we are and work hard at becoming someone else! You're blind? Then try to live as though you could see; deaf? live as though you heard; crippled? do everything a 'walkable' can do!... Has anyone ever challenged you to dare look at the giftedness of your handicapping condition? Have you ever dared ask yourself "What can I do for my world *with my blindness* that I couldn't do if I weren't legally blind?" Would the world ever have heard of Helen Keller if she had not had the *gifts* of deafness and blindness. Oh sure, those gifts carry a pretty price tag... but doesn't every good gift? What can I do for my world as a legally blind person, a blind priest, that I could not do if I were not blind? That question haunted, inspired, motivated me for months and years after that retreat experience. Maybe 'get rid of it' isn't the only answer to the question of suffering in our world???

The Persons are Gifts Weekend took its entire theme and direction from that retreat experience as did that summer produced manuscript. The object of the weekend program became simply 'helping persons to discover and believe in their own, unique giftedness *as they are,* not as they'd like to be or as they think they should be, but *as they are."* Some forty disabled teens and adults made that first *Persons are Gifts Weekend* in early November, 1976. Since then a dozen more weekends have been given to hundreds of persons in the Norwich Diocese and the weekend has also traveled to more than a dozen other dioceses in the United States and Canada!

The 'giftedness' theme wasn't really just a sudden inspiration from that gem of a retreat in October, 1975. It was rather, I am sure, drawn from a lot of the experiences of my life where the Lord's redeeming hand bringing good from my tragedies and weaknesses had been so powerfully evident. The retreat experience with John, Chapter 9, seemed to give voice to the awareness that had been growing within me through all of these other experiences. After that October retreat I began to find myself looking for that redeeming hand in the various moments of brokenness of life around me; and I began to find it!

That theme of giftedness affected not only the ministry's retreat weekend for the handicapped; it colored the entire ministry. Gradually the ministry's goals evolved into a three-fold set around the theme of *giftedness:* First, helping handicapped persons to discover and believe in the *gift* that they are and the *gifts* that they have for their world, their society, their families, their church — even the gifts of their handicapping conditions — helping them to dare dream of what they can do for their world with these conditions that they could not do if they did not have them; secondly, helping families, friends, professionals, parishes, congregations, and society at large to begin to believe in the *gifts* that persons with handicapping conditions have to offer — helping society to stop looking at the handicapped individual only in terms of 'what are we going to have to do for him/her?' and to dare discover how society inself can be better if the handicapped individual is a part of it! We see thousands of headlines each year that read "...ORGANIZATION THROWS CHRISTMAS PARTY FOR THE HANDICAPPED." I'm still looking for the one that reads *"HANDICAPPED THROW*

PARTY FOR SOCIETY–" For this to happen our society has to learn to believe in and *need* the gifts that persons with disabilities have to offer, the unique gifts of each person. As long as our society continues educationally, religiously, recreationally, socially, etc. to group persons with disabilities according to those disabilities 'so we can better serve them' the gifts of those individual persons will continue to be lost behind the mask of blindness, retardation, paralysis, stroke, deafness... The third goal of the ministry complements the first two: it's helping handicapped persons, their families, friends, etc. to find the materials, resources, and especially attitudes that will enable them to live the normal, giving lives that our world, our church, our family needs from each of us.

The ministry's goals were first stated formally in the fall of 1976, but again, they were a statement of what already was rather than what would be. From the very beginning of the *Office of Ministries for the Handicapped* the programs requested were along the lines of these goals. Public awareness programs in schools, churches, organizations of all types, industries and businesses, etc., grew quickly in popularity and demand. The *Persons Are Gifts Weekends,* days of recollection on the theme of giftedness, and even week-long 'Parish Missions' on the theme of the gift of brokenness in our lives have become more and more wide-spread. Requests for awareness talks, weekends, missions, etc. have come from as far away as Alberta, Canada, and South Dakota, Florida, Michigan, Ohio, Pennsylvania and Vermont! Today when I think back about my 'fear of being tied to a little, tiny diocese' I chuckle as I see again that 'redeeming hand of the Lord!'

17

"Dear Brother..."

As the ministry grew that first year of its history more and more programs were initiated, more and more people began to participate in its activities, and more and more volunteers became its life's blood! In April of 1976, the ministry's first issue of *Caring & Sharing,* an informational and inspirational newsletter, went out to 256 persons just barely five months after the ministry was founded! Today that same newsletter, now in its fifth volume, goes out to more than 2500 readers!

It quickly became evident in the spring of 1976 that the ministry would very soon outgrow its office in the diocesan office building at 201 Hickory Street, in Norwich, where it had been since the founding day a few months earlier. Bishop Reilly suggested in early summer of 1976 that I begin a search for a permanent center. Several agencies and organizations serving the handicapped of eastern Connecticut had cited the need for office space as one of their own crucial needs. Rents were high and accessible office space that disabled persons could use was scarce. Our center, it was envisioned then, could serve not only our needs but the needs of these organizations as well. In the fall of 1976 a sixteen-member board was called together and given the double task of finding the center and raising the funds needed to purchase that center. The board set to work immediately taking into account a wise caution from Bishop Reilly when he had addressed the group at one of its first meetings. "we don't want a center that will be a noose around Brother Pat's neck." He was wiser than all of us put together. As I ponder his statement now, some five and half years later, I wonder if he couldn't see into the future that night! Several sites were inspected and plans for fundraising were initiated. A name for the ministry's proposed new center was one of the group's first contributions – *God's Gift House* it would be called, taking into account the goals that had become the very heart of the ministry. Finally, in December, 1976, the best of all the sites inspected was settled upon and plans to raise the purchase and operating price were studied seriously. Two Christmas gifts that year, tearfully, made real the center that up to now, was but a dream. "We want to help make your dream come true," Jack and Carol Beauregard, of Norwich, told me just before Christmas, "and so we want to give you for your new center what we would have spent on each other for Christmas this year!" I cried as we hugged for a long time. Tears ran freely during that entire drive for the center. The second gift turned them on again that Christmas. I spent an evening with the Croteaus, the family I had gone to the Cape with that summer. After supper that night their two kids, Eddy and Lynn, came up with a note for me. "This is our gift for your dream center," the note read, and in the envelope were coins totaling seventy cents!

The proposed new center came with a price tag of one hunded and thirty-five thousand dollars! It was figured that an extra twenty-five thousand should be raised for minor renovations and first-year operating costs. This was big business! For me, who had gone several years without even a salary, depending upon the good Lord through the generosity of His people for my life and my studies and my work, this was B I G business! But somehow even that price tag of $160,000 didn't scare us! Perhaps we were too naive or simple to be scared. We set about the task immediately of collecting the needed cash. The one stipulation I made with the group was that whatever center we chose to purchase we would have to pay cash for it; I could not live with a huge mortgage on the ministry, I said. How I wish we had stayed with that simple principle!

We tried most of the normal fundraising ideas to collect the needed funds for our dream center. We went to the diocesan-wide organizations and state-wide organizations but, except for a few small token offerings, our pleas for help fell on deaf ears — with one beautiful exception. In May, 1976, I had been asked to speak at a 'Communion Breakfast' of the local circle of the Daughters of Isabella in Mystic, Connecticut. I gave my address, talking about our ministry and its dreams and about the need of handicapped persons in our church. Mrs. Claire P. Little, who held an international office with the Daughters of Isabella, was seated next to me at the table. "Why," she asked me privately at the conclusion of my talk, "are groups like the Daughters of Isabella dieing out in the church today?"

"Probably," I said nonchalantly, (surprised by my own boldness!) "because they aren't needed anymore..." That's all she needed to hear. "What do you mean, they aren't needed anymore?" "If the church needed them," I came back, "would she let them die?" "Well, what do we do about it?" she asked persistently. "Get involved in the very life blood of the church," I said. "Don't worry about your own existence but rather about the existence and welfare of the church and the church will not let you die. People will see you as a vital force, involved in the needs of the church, making a difference in the church, and they will flock to join you." "Well," she said thoughtfully, "how can we get involved in the needs of your ministry?" We talked about what circles could do to recruit the handicapped women as members and then, somehow, we got into a discussion of the dream of our center that was already forming. "We'll see what we can do to help," she said as we ended our conversation. The Daughters of Isabella are the only group that 'adopted' our dream as their dream and worked their hearts out to make it a dream come true! Local chapters or councils of other organizations did make some offerings toward the dream but the Daughters were the only statewide group that simply made our cause their own and dedicated their fundraising efforts for the year to our drive and to that cause. By themselves those valiant ladies raised more than half the purchase price of the center that we ultimately bought! Their first gift toward the dream, a check for $1,000.00, came as the fundraising board was first forming in the fall of 1976. Claire Little was asked, and accepted, to serve on that board and did much to keep the dream of the center alive in all thirty two circles of the Daughters in the State of Connecticut.

In order to raise the needed $160,000.00 quickly and realistically in a rural, economically not-too-well-off area, a 'Dollar-Bill Campaign' was envisioned as the major fund raiser. It would be kicked off at a 'Prayer Breakfast' officially opening the drive on February 5, 1977. Each of the sixteen board members was asked to bring to that breakfast ten friends or neighbors, etc. The public was invited also. At the breakfast each person would be asked to donate just *one dollar* toward the dream with the assurance that that was all they would have to donate throughout the campaign! Each of them would then be asked to return home and ask ten of their friends, acquaintances, etc., to each donate just *one dollar* and also get ten of their neighbors to do the same. I don't recall how many 'generations' of that one dollar request were needed but it looked exciting. No one would be burdened with too big of a request and even those who had very little of this world's goods could feel part of the new center. The publicity for the event went out in plenty of time. Gorgeous banners depicting the themes of the ministry and its program were created. The food for the prayer breakfast was ordered and the program and speakers were set up. The only thing we couldn't control was the weather and it did a number on us. We all held our breath for a week before the kick-off breakfast, listening to every weather report and hoping against all hope that 'they'd be wrong again!' They weren't. That Saturday morning, February 5, 1977, just happened to be about the worst blizzard of that winter! Several dozen persons, most of them already deeply involved in the dream, showed up at Our Lady of Lourdes Church in Gales Ferry, Connecticut. Bishop Reilly and our other speakers were there but the crowd we had prayed for were wisely 'at home' safe and secure from the blizzard! The program went ahead on schedule, but since those we had hoped would take the dollar bill campaign home with them were not present, we did not ask for the dollar donation but merely described the new center proposal and 'officially launched' the fundraising for it. As the day's guests were leaving, one elderly blind lady stuck a crumpled up bill in a priest's hand and said, "Give this to Brother Pat for his dream!" The "widow's mite?" Maybe. A sign of things to come? Definitely!

The publicity of the Dollar Bill Campaign did start some mail-delivered contributions. Anne Marie Canova, our board treasurer, faithfully deposited and kept track of them but progress was very slow. As an effort to spark new interest in the campaign the board came up with the idea of a *birthday party dance* for *me*, 'help make Brother Pat's Dream Come True For His Birthday!' The auditorium was donated. The food was brought in. There was almost no expense to the event. It would certainly be an excellent money-maker! The only thing we couldn't control that March, Saturday night was *the weather!* Pea-soup-thick fog rolled in all over eastern Connecticut that night and all but killed the affair!

The board was persistent, however. About a half dozen of the sixteen member committee refused to give up. It was at this time that things seemed to make one drastic turn for the better. When Jack and Carol Beauregard, who had given their touching Christmas gift toward the dream, went out to invite their 'ten friends, neighbors, etc.' to help on the dollar-bill campaign, they had asked a Norwich eye doctor, Dr. Norman Israelite, and his wife to be part of their 'ten.' The Israelites, looking at the proposed $135,000.00 center, decided to help in the way they best could — they offered us another building, on Main Street in downtown Norwich, for what the family owed on the mortgage, twenty-thousand dollars!!! The building was FANTASTIC! It comprised some nine thousand square feet of space, was immediately accessible off the Main Street sidewalk, and was on the local bus routes. It would take some renovations but the amount saved on the purchase alone made it an offer we could not refuse! *GOD'S GIFT HOUSE* would be in downtown Norwich!

With the goal of the fundraising campaign now FAN-TASTICALLY lowered, we decided it was time for another real plea for public support in the drive. An art contest for the building's logos would bring great publicity and the prizes could be awarded in the ministry's present office which would greatly impress the public with our need for a center! Any student, grades seven through twelve in public and/or parochial schools in the diocese, was permitted to enter as many drawings as he or she chose. The winning entry would be the one that most clearly spoke the ministry's three goals and the center's name. Seventy-seven entries were registered in the art contest. A winner and first and second runner-up were chosen and a date for the awarding of the prizes and unveiling of the building's logos was announced. Mid April was chosen as the safest time for this event, as far as *the weather* was concerned! The only thing we didn't count on was the horrendous thunderstorm that broke out that night. Trees were uprooted in the area, power lines dropped, and almost nobody showed up for the event! The one newspaper photographer who did show up arrived after the presentations had been made!

The board's stalwart half dozen workers refused to be beaten even by this third onslaught from *the weather!* They retreated, looked at the figures thus far, and came up with another idea... a 'Drop-in-the-Bucket Campaign!' Kentucky Fried Chicken was approached and agreed to supply all of the needed 'buckets and covers.' *Electric Boat,* a major employer of the area, agreed to print the needed posters. Some thirty volunteers were recruited to prepare each downtown and shopping area of the diocese for the campaign. Police and municipality permissions had to be obtained and in addition to securing these, each volunteer had to recruit his/her own team to 'man' the collecting station for the shopping period – Friday night and all day Saturday, the first weekend of June! Printed leaflets about the new center and the ministry's programs and goals and activities would be handed out and donations would be accepted as 'drops in the bucket.' The slogan for the day was "Your drop in the bucket will help..." It always amazed me that no matter how crushing the previous defeat had been, excitement ran high for the next 'try.' This bucket campaign was no exception. But it too was foiled like the others. Two nights before the campaign date, I called the thirty volunteer site coordinators only to find out that at least a dozen and a half of them had canceled out! We were left with about ten collecting spots in the entire diocese. As I got off the phone with the last coordinator, I was angry – mad is probably the correct word!

I was staying at the Canova's home that night and I went into the room where I was sleeping, closed the door, and proceeded to let the Lord know that I was mad! "I'm only trying to do *your* work," I bellowed! "You *could* help if You wanted to! A snowstorm! Pea-soup Fog! A thunder storm! and now just plain disinterestedness! I've done all I can do. Look, have we not done our darndest for every single event? We're only tying to do *your* work! There's nothing in it for us! When are You going to do *your* part?" I don't think I've ever been so angry at Him in my whole life! But, I wasn't prepared for the response I got from Him. I heard the words as clearly as I hear these typewriter keys right now. "Well, get out of the way and let Me do My own work!" I was stunned! Was He saying that perhaps we had done *too much*? that perhaps if we had spent as much effort with Him at the helm maybe we would have succeeded? I opened the scriptures almost not daring to read whatever I opened to. It was John 21. Peter says to the others that day after the Resurrection, "I'm going fishing!" The others join him on the Sea of Tiberias. They were fishermen who had earned their livelihood at the trade, who had cared for their families with their catches. But, that night, with all their skills they caught absolutely nothing! In the morning, however, the moment Jesus appears on the scene the nets are filled to breaking point! The message needed no explaining. I went to sleep that night begging forgiveness for 'trying to do His work.' I thought back to the many lessons of those freelance years before coming to the diocese and now everything seemed to settle into place. The next night we had scheduled a 'pep rally' to put spirit into the campaign. Instead, we had a prayer rally and turned the entire drive over to the Lord! Those that wanted to went ahead with the campaign on the weekend and the very few of them that there were brought in several thousand dollars! The rest of us took a pilgrimage that day to the shrine of Our Lady of LaSallette in Ipswich, Massachusetts. We spent the day praying for the center and all who had given so much to make it a dream come true.

All of a sudden things began to happen. Donations for talks I had given months previous suddenly came in — twelve hundred dollars! A school in Elmsford, looking for a cause to unite its student body, decided to sponsor a bike-a-thon on the Bronx River Parkway on a Sunday afternoon 'to help Brother Pat in his work!' I had spoken at a communion breakfast in that area of *New York* a year or so earlier! Their check for fifteen hundred dollars pushed us over the top of our goal on June 17, 1977, just about two weeks after we surrendered the whole project to the Lord!!!

"You'll need a custodian/watchman for the center, Pat," Bishop Reilly had said to me that spring when he and I had gone to look at the Israelite's offered place. "Do you mind if I offer the job to my brother?" I asked him. "He's handicapped himself; he has a learning disability of sorts, but has done custodial work all his life. He's been working with the Brothers in Alfred, Maine, for fifteen years now and has tried to join them four times. When they said no this last time, he asked me to keep my eyes open for a parish down here that might need a custodian. I'd love to have him here with me."

The Bishop agreed that if Gerry were willing it would be great. I was really excited that night when I called home and asked Gerry if he wanted a job! He didn't jump at the offer right away. He wanted to 'check it out.' In April he came down for our second *Persons are Gifts Weekend* and made a hit with everyone on the retreat! The family home in Sanford had been all but destroyed when frozen pipes burst when the town's power went out in the winter of 1975. Mom had had the whole place remodeled but it was not 'home' as she had once known it. The touches of Dad were gone and so she had decided to sell the house that spring of 1977. Gerry decided to make his move at the same time. June 17th of that year was a big day for all of us. Our drive for *God's Gift House* went over the goal; Mom sold the house on that day; and Gerry finished up his work at Denis Hall Jr. High where he had worked for fifteen years. Mom gave us a lot of the furniture from the house for the new center but the greatest gift of all was that crucifix they had all gathered in front of for me when the meningitis had struck! That crucifix hangs in my chapel today and is a constant reminder to me of the love of my family and the love of our God!

My youngest sister, Anita, and her husband, Al, took their vacation that June to drive up from Florida to aid Mom in the packing and sorting and mailing. Gerry came from Alfred, six miles away, and I came up from Connecticut. It was a beautiful gift to watch Mom go through everything, talk about the memories, and then decide which box it was going into. It was like she executed her own 'last will and testament.' She mailed parcels all over the country, keepsakes and memories that she knew would be specially precious to each of us, her kids. My sister, Patricia and her husband Jerry had invited Mom to come and live with them so Jerry drove up with a friend from Washington, D.C., where they lived, to help her pack and transport whatever she decided to keep for herself. That was a week of tears and laughter, a week of hastily thrown together meals and meals eaten out because dishes were packed already. But it was a week with Mom that I will treasure all of my life, a week with several of my brothers and sisters and in-laws that will be forever a gift! As of June 24, 1977, our home in Maine was no more. Mom and Dad had lived in Maine all their lives; they had raised all of us in Maine. One by one each of us had left the state except for two of my sisters, Lorraine, who lives in Portland, and Annette, the oldest of us, who lives with her husband, Fern, in Presque Isle. There was somewhat of an emptiness in each of us as we closed the house door in Sanford for the last time that June afternoon in 1977. We all stayed at a motel that night and then all went our separate ways in the morning.

Mom flew to Washington to avoid the long car trip; Jerry and his friend drove to Washington with all of Mom's things and the things she had put aside for Pat and Jerry; Al and Gerry drove the U-Haul truck loaded with Gerry's goods and all the furniture Mom had given us for the center; and Anita and I and their children followed the U-Haul in her car. After they dropped us off in Norwich, Anita and Al continued on to Washington and then to Florida.

Gerry's first job in Norwich was packing up our office at 201 Hickory Street and preparing for the move to our downtown center. The papers were signed on July 5, 1977, and we moved immediately to the center! The keys were turned over to us at the bank as we delivered the check and the mortgage papers were marked *paid in full!* That very afternoon we went over to the center for a sign raising ceremony! Gerry led the way as we explored every nook and cranny of 'our' center!

It took all that summer and hundreds of pairs of volunteer hands to get the center cleaned up and renovated for Dedication Day, September 24, 1977! That whole summer is still very much 'a dream' for me. I thought very much those days of the tiny center that I almost opened in New York! I wouldn't be here now and all this wouldn't be happening, I used to think if that center had been allowed to open! It was absolutely incredible the number of people who just 'showed up' those days and nights, with their own pails, mops, rags, tools, and even a coffee pot and goodies, to help in the preparations for opening day! The volunteer hours of wood-working, painting, varnishing, cleaning, carpeting, packing and unpacking...could never be calculated! The city's building codes all had to be satisfied before the building could be opened to the public; the work that went into meeting those codes was unreal! No ads went in the papers soliciting volunteer help. The volunteers just came! They were the dozens of encounter families I had already met in the diocese and they were the hundreds of friends of the ministry that already were an integral part of our programs and services! Even interested passersby stopped in, found out what was going on, and joined the volunteer army of workers!

But, the 'general' of that volunteer army was, I guess, the greatest proof of our Daddy's love for us that summer! It wasn't easy for Gerry to leave Maine, to leave Denis Hall where he had worked for fifteen years even though his dream of joining the brothers he had worked with had been discouraged. It was a big move to uproot and take a new job in a strange place where he really knew no one except his own brother – which doesn't have to be a plus!!! When he first arrived in Norwich he spent the summer living with one or another friend of mine, never permanently unpacking his things until that September when we moved into an apartment together, a few minutes' walk from the center. But, what a gift he was that summer. "Gerry, where's this? or that?" "I need this?" He was the loving 'general' of our volunteer army and he kept us all happy and working. That year would have been all but impossible for me without Gerry. How well I remember those long nights we spent together at the center waiting for the carpenter, the plumbers, the electricians... the meals together at the local diner... the walks to and from the center together each day. I had always known Gerry was a custodian but I guess I had never known all that a custodian does until that summer when Gerry came down to our center! I think of the things he did and I know I would have gone out of my mind if he hadn't been there. I'd look at the mess in one room or another and then turn to Gerry. "I don't know how or with what," I'd say, "do you?" "Watch this!" he'd say... and it would get done! Each of us has our gifts... *painting* is *not* one of mine. I'd watch Gerry and he made it look so easy but why, when I tried, did I manage to get more on me than anywhere else? We must have gone through a hundred gallons of paint, varnish and sealer that summer. It totally fascinated me to see him 'go at it!' The center was almost ready for Dedication Day when Gerry and I went over to visit one of our FANTASTIC volunteer families, the James. "Sit down! You gotta hear this!" Dotty said that night after supper. "Read it to him, Don." Don, her husband, handed me about ten looseleaf sheets of paper, written in red ink, I think. "I don't know what you want to do with this," he said. "I just got the urge to write and I couldn't stop till this was done. I'm not sure what should be done with it; it's yours." And then he began to read.

Dear Brother,

I do not feel as though I know you well enough to call you Pat, although you know me very well. I might say that you know me intimately, inside and out. You have studied me very closely for a period of time, so, perhaps, being that you know me so well, I could presume to address you as 'Patrick.' I can surmise, Patrick, that you are wondering who I am. Well, I will not keep you in suspense one moment longer. I am the Spirit of the building at 323 Main Street, Norwich, Connecticut. You seem surprised, Patrick. Didn't you know that buildings have spirits? You have, I imagine, heard it said, that a building has 'character,' that it is cold or has warmth. Why not a spirit? I can also tell you that it is very possible to look at a building and be able to tell all about its spirit. There are happy spirits, depressed spirits, and very dejected spirits. The use or production, the warmth or coldness, the repair or disrepair of a building have much to do with the well-being of its spirit.

I can confess to you now that when I first saw you and you first saw me I was a very depressed spirit of a building in a casual state of disrepair and emptiness. I can remember very distinctly the first time we met. You came with a group of people, your association, on a sort of 'inspection' tour. It tweeked my interest a little, but it had happened before and nothing had happened. My floors remained silent and dusty and empty. My windows, my eyes to your world, were still dirty and rain-streaked. People came to look. They came to examine, poke and prod, but nothing ever happened. But there was something in your manner, Patrick, a strength in your tone of voice, a real conviction as you spoke to the others, and, as I was drawn to you I began to get interested, enough to notice that you were blind! Do you know what my reaction to that was, Patrick? I thought to myself, 'Good, he won't be able to see all my defects!' And as I heard your exclamation of joy — I remember that you said I was 'FANTASTIC!' and 'Beautiful!' — I laughed so hard it was a wonder I didn't shake down those loose ceiling tiles on the first floor. And then I heard something about a gift house. I snorted and howled with glee! 'Poor foolish human! Poor blind man! He would open a gift house in this neighborhood? If he wasn't already blind, they would steal him blind!' I roared with laughter at my own joke, so hard that the water pipes rattled in my basement!

That was when I heard it again, only this time I heard it all. And you said God's Gift House... And I was silent. Who was this 'God?' Was it you, Patrick? Was it one of those people with you? I didn't have an answer but the questions I was asking myself made me much more attentive to your conversation.

I was appalled at the words I heard...handicapped... blind...deaf...wheel chairs...canes...seeing-eye dogs... It went on and on. My mind reeled. What on earth were you talking about? You weren't going to make me a useful, productive building again! You were going to fill me with jabbering, groping, stumbling half-people. I vaguely remember wishing that some catastrophe would befall me so that I could suddenly collapse.

Because, Patrick, you see, I knew all about the handicapped. I knew who and what they were. I had seen the man without legs who had sat in my doorway and sold pencils. He had cursed people when they didn't buy them; he had cursed them when they did! I remember the drunken blind man who had slept in my hallway

148

and had left his peculiar odor behind him when he had moved on. I remembered those and I had seen others, ... enough so that I knew that I wanted nothing to do with the handicapped!

Then, you and your friends were gone and the thought occured to me, Patrick, that nothing would happen. Nothing would change. Nothing ever did. You would lose interest and go on your way. I would continue to erode, continue to die as the rest of my part of the city was dying. I almost made myself content with the thought. But, still it nagged at me. What if?

Weeks went by, or maybe it was months. My walls had calendars but they were all of years past. So let me just say that a period of time went by. Nothing happened. You didn't come back. No brigade of workmen appeared to renovate me. No hoard of handicapped suddenly appeared. I relaxed and continued to die.

One day a rumor came down the block, passed from building to building. Did you know that we building spirits have a grapevine? It starts at one of the buildings near the center of the city, a bank, I think, and it spreads like a spider's web. As the rumor had it Patrick, I had been sold. It would only be a short time until I would be known as God's Gift House. Immediately I became full of fear and many thoughts raced through my mind in an uncontrolable panic! Gradually I became quiet and settled down into a very depressed state. That particular afternoon is very vivid in my mind. The sun was sending its last weak rays through one of my rain-streaked dirty windows. The city was quietly settling into a twilight time of day. And then all time stopped.

In that instant there was a dull rumble in my basement. It grew louder and louder until it became a thousand times louder than the thunder of a sudden summer storm. The dust danced on my floors and bits of plaster and paint flaked off of my walls. The rumble ceased as quickly as it had started. I was aware of a presence within my walls, not just in one room or on one floor. It was everywhere at once.

I cried out fearfully, I guess, to ask if anyone was there. A voice that boomed like thunder and yet whispered like an evening breeze permeated the atmosphere. "I AM." it said.

"Who, What? Where?" I asked those questions almost afraid of the answer I might receive. The voice answered each question the same, "I AM."

I was silent, and for a time so was the voice. Then the dust swirled in the sunlight and the lighting fixtures swayed as the whispering rush of words resounded through my rooms.

"Little building, why are you so fretful? Why do you shudder and quiver? What do you fear?" For some reason that I do not understand, Patrick, I felt that I could empty my soul to this voice. Do you know why I was able to do that? I realize that I went on and on for some time. I ranted about the thought that no one wanted to return me to my former productivity. I raved about my feelings, my very negative feelings, about the handicapped. Patrick, I even cursed, yes, I cursed you and your associates for what you were doing to me. I was very distraught and I cried. My windows became more streaked, but now they were tear-streaked.

The voice boomed and stopped my tirade short. "Stop your crying, you fearful, fretful, ignorant little shell of a building. I will tell you something. I will show you something that you will see and learn in the months to come! The voice paused... It was as if it was trying to find the words that I would understand.

"Your fear of not being wanted," the voice continued, "that is a fear of ignorance. Look out on the world through your glass eyes and see what has transpired over these many months passed!" Through my windows appeared a myriad of scenes... couples standing at the doors of buildings as people came out... the couples had cans in their hands... they gave the people a small piece of paper... and many of the people put something into the cans... The scene changed and I saw many places at one time... people standing in front of my stores... places that were not in my neighborhood... these people had paper buckets in their hands and wore signs that read 'God's Gift House, An Open Door'... They too were handing out slips of paper to the people passing by... Some of those passersby stopped, read the signs and put something into the buckets... The scene in my windows changed again... People were dancing, laughing, enjoying themselves immensely. You were there, Patrick. They gave you an envelope and you looked very pleased... Again the scene blurred, shifted and changed... I saw children riding bicycles... They wore signs... I strained to read what the signs said... As I read 'We ride to help God's Gift House' tears flowed freely down my stained windows... A picture flashed suddenly in front of me... It was very different... many women banded together, working all over the state for a common cause... There were signs and banners everywhere... The signs made me realize that I was that common cause!... As the scene faded I could make out one of the banners that read simply 'The Daughters of Isabella'... Who are they, Patrick? Do you know them?... The scenes were changing ever faster... always, people doing

150

something, collecting something... always, a sign or placard denoting 'God's Gift House'... In these flashing scenes I could see the names of many places in the background — places with names like New York, Maine, Virginia, Maryland, Texas... Places that I had never heard of or had any idea of their location...

"Little building," the voice said as the scenes continued, "these are just some of the many people who wanted you. Many more pleaded, cajoled, and begged for pennies, nickels, quarters, and dollars, or whatever, because they wanted you." There was a deep silence as though the voice was letting what it had said sink into my senses.

Then, there was another whirlwind rush of sound throughout the building and the voice continued in its loud, yet muffled, whisper, "Your feelings about the handicapped are neither right nor wrong; it is just that you have a misconception of them from what you have seen. Look again through your eyes of glass and see the handicapped as you will see them, as you will know them, as you will love them."

Again the scenes appeared in my windows, vivid and clear, constantly changing... I saw a black man in an electric go-cart, a smile on his face and happiness in his voice as he talked to a passerby... I saw a cherubic blind girl, smiling and talking as she walked along with you, Patrick... I saw something else in that flashing scene too. There appeared to be an aura, a light of love shining about both of you... In the changing window scenes there was now a group of handicapped boys with two or three older boys or men... From their happy, bouncy conversation I realized that they were part of a basketball team that had just won their last game of the season! They had won over a team of non-handicapped players. I suddenly felt like cheering for them but I had a lump of guilt in my throat that suppressed it. The window flashed more and more scenes and it came to me that the handicapped were no different from other people; they knew the same joys, suffered the same hurts... They were whole people, just made a little different.

The rushing wind and the whispering voice interrupted my thoughts. "Now, you see, little building, how you are wanted and how beautiful my handicapped children are. You see how wrong you were. Now let me show you how productive you will be, how an ever growing warmth and love will emanate from your open door."

151

What happened, Patrick, was not scenes in my windows. It was happening all around me. My rooms were filled with people, handicapped and non-handicapped. An aire of brotherhood and love filled my whole being. Happiness reigned supreme within my walls. Everyone was busy at something they called the newsletter. You were there, Patrick, and again I could see, and yes, even feel, that aura of love that surrounded the handicapped and the people who seemed to be your helpers and associates. I suddenly felt so warm, so wonderfull; I guess I must have glowed!

The thought came to my mind, 'If it could only be this way!' The voice read my thoughts and broke into my reverie "THIS IS THE WAY IT SHALL BE. I HAVE SAID SO."

The air moved violently and the dust swirled around and around in the sun's rays. The vision was gone. My rooms were empty again. The rumble within my walls began to fade. Hesitantly I said, "Don't go. Please, don't go! Stay a little longer." The whisper was very faint, "I am always here. I have always been here. I will always be here." I had a question that I wanted to ask the voice. I blurted it out almost knowing what the answer would be as I asked, "Are you Patrick's God?" The whisper, fading away like the receding waves in the sea, came back to me softly, "I am... I Am... I AM!"

Time began to move again, Patrick, rapidly now. It was only a few days and you showed up again. There was a large group of people with you, including a smiling man, a happy-faced, big man who seemed to be very important to everyone except himself. He seemed to be your employer, or maybe, he was just someone with grave authority. I remember that people called him 'Bishop.' I don't ever remember hearing his name. I had a strong feeling that he had much to do with my becoming what I was to be. And then I saw my name, Patrick, I saw my sign that some wonderful boys had made. How proud I felt! How wonderful it would be to wear that sign 'God's Gift House-An Open Door' above my eyes to the world! Cheerful, clear eyes, now, Patrick, for some of your associates have washed away the tear streaks, the rain spatters, and grime of inactivity.

As I write this, Patrick, many things are happening to me. Many people have been in and out of my door. I am being renovated not only physically but spiritually. I can hardly wait, Patrick, for the beautiful day when you open my doors to the world. I quiver with the anticipation of the rolling and whirring of the first wheelchair, the first clump, clump of someone on crutches, the first tap, tap of a blind person's cane. I eagerly await those happy, joyous people who will fill my rooms with love. It is my hope that I shall always be able to engulf them in my warmth while I drink in their happiness.

I pray that I shall be able to be of use, be needed, when they have problems or tears. I know that I shall, Patrick, because the voice said "I am here always!" I know that He will make it all possible.

Some day in the future I will write to you again, Patrick. I know that it will only be a short note for I expect that I shall be too busy, too happy spreading my warmth and feeling their love. May God... May your God, Patrick... No, may OUR God protect us all and by His will we shall become more and more a gift to His people, His very special people, the handicapped.

> *The Spirit of God's Gift House*
> *Written lovingly by Donald P. James, Sr.*

When I finished crying after he had finished reading, I said, "That's got to be published and given away to the world!"

"It's yours to do with as you see fit," he said. The letter was published and given as the very special gift to all who attended the Dedication Day Celebration. More than 13,000 copies of the letter have been distributed in the past four years since it was written. The "Spirit of God's Gift House" not only spoke to me but, very evidently to thousands of others as well; it not only voiced much of my own heart's throbbing but also the feelings, hopes, fears, and dreams of thousands of others! When that letter was read by Don himself at the Mass of Dedication on September 24th, not only the spirit's glass eyes teared! The 600 or so who attended the opening-day celebrations mixed plenty of tears with those of their center's spirit. *The weather* on Dedication Day was exactly as expected; it was "true to form" as it had been throughout the drive's events. The only difference now was that *the weather* couldn't make any difference! It poured torrential rains all day on September 24th, but nobody cared! For us the sun was out all day! The Bishop was there along with many priests and religious of the diocese and over 600 of the new center's 'friends!' Tornadoes couldn't have kept them away! There was an aire of victory, of conquest, but especially of gratitude throughout the day's celebrations. At the offering of the Mass, Claire Little walked up bearing more gifts from our beloved Daughters of Isabella — checks totaling more than $1,800.00 that had been raised even after the center's goal had been reached!

Claire Little and her beloved 'sisters' never lost interest in our center; we weren't abandoned at birth. She was forever calling to ask how things were going with the ministry. What were our needs now. She was truly a God-given gift to us. In February, 1978, just five months after the center's dedication, we learned the tragic news that Claire P. Little had cancer of the liver; doctors gave her six months to live.

Even this could not daunt Claire Little, however. When it was decided to dedicate the center's downtown chapel in her honor and in gratitude for the loving support of the Daughters of Isabella, Connecticut State Circle, Claire and her "sisters" quickly took over the job of raising the funds and finding the volunteer workers to complete the project! An additional four thousand dollars was raised by them to complete the memorial chapel which today serves the needs of the downtown poor and handicapped with daily Mass and other services! Claire, from her hospital bed, helped pick out the carpeting, paneling, etc. for the new chapel. When Claire P. Little died in early 1979, the Daughters of Isabella lost a devoted 'sister' and the Office of Ministries for the Handicapped of the Diocese of Norwich lost one of its most dedicated friends and patrons. When Claire Little died the ministry was barely four years old but it was thanks to her and the many like her, who gave life itself to the young office that its short history was as full and as far reaching as it was! Talking about all the events and high points of those short but fast-moving years for me is like slipping into a dream. It's hard to believe it all *did happen!*

18

"He loves me..."

In the late spring of 1977, as the dream of the center began to look more and more like a 'possible dream,' another, older, dream seemed also on the verge of becoming a 'dream come true.' On March 18th of that year, my thirty-third birthday, Bishop Reilly had officially accepted me as a 'Candidate for the Sacrament of Holy Orders' in a small ceremony in the chapel of his residence. Studies were completed, acceptance was now official, the road to final ordination seemed wide open! It was decided that I would be ordained a 'Deacon,' the last major step prior to ordination in the priesthood, on May 20th, and priestly ordination would probably come in the fall. I must have been absolutely terrible to live with that spring! The drive for the center was moving even though often sabotaged by the weather; we had our second *Persons are Gifts Weekend* that spring at Easter; my brother, Gerry, was planning to move down and join us in the ministry; and now, plans for ordination were finally taking shape! I was in heaven! It was FANTASTIC!

In April, I went on another "directed retreat," this time in Portland, Maine, to prepare for my ordination to the diaconate. At the beginning of that beautiful week, my retreat director asked what special grace I would like from the retreat. "Well," I said, "I'd really like a *picture of God* this retreat." He looked at me sort of questioningly so I went on to explain. "A young man falls in love, he asks his love for a picture so he can show his world 'this is the girl who's brought meaning into my life!' Well," I concluded, "I'd like to have a picture of the God who loves me, a picture of 'my Daddy,' so I can show the whole world, *'this is the God Who loves me'!*" "I've got a feeling," he said, "that you're going to get that picture!"

There was a park about a mile or so from the priest's residence where I was making my week-long retreat so every day I would take my Bible under-arm and would head out for a long walk through the park. The retreat experience always made me feel tremendously *free,* free enough even to *sing right out loud!* I heard once that you should always sing loud when you sing — if you've got a good voice you sing loud to praise God for it; if you've got a bad voice you sing loud to get even! Well, most of the time I sing to 'get even!'

It was the sixth day of the retreat, I believe, and, as usual, I was walking in the park — singing at the top of my lungs. I'm sure the park's regular visitors had already commented 'here comes that wacky priest again!' But, all of a sudden, I stopped *dead* in my tracks! How do you sing a song you've never heard before? I mean, I can't read music at all. Oh, I could probably figure out the notes from 'F-A-C-E' and 'Every Good Boy Does Fine'... but I really don't know music. I tell people I've got a hard time carrying a tune in a basket, let alone writing original songs! But, there I was, singing away as if it was a long-ago learned favorite.

I ran back to my room at the retreat house, almost faster than my legs would carry me! I dug out my 'Dear Daddy'... notebook and opened to a clean page. In fifteen minutes I wrote down six verses of a song *I had never heard before!* Not being too trusting, I then took out my trusty tape recorder and proceeded to sing the song into the mic so I wouldn't forget its melody! (Incidentally, I've never forgotten that melody and I've never had to go back to that tape!) That night, when I went in to see my retreat director, I brought the tape recorder and announced, "God sent audio-visual aids tonight!" and then, without comment, I pressed the 'Play' key of the recorder. We both listened with tears. When the song was finished he said to me, "Patrick, what did you ask God for at the beginning of this retreat?" I was dumbfounded! "Oh my Lord," I said, "I asked Him for a picture and I can just see Him looking at me and saying, 'The poor dummy, has he forgotten that he's blind? If I give him a picture he won't even be able to see it!' So, in his own, inimitable, creative love, He gave me a picture that I could *hear!*"

He loves me. He loves me.
He loves me as I am, oh yes, He loves me!
Yes, He loved me yesterday, and yes, He'll love me still tomorrow,
For He loves me just today the way I am!

He loves me. He loves me!
And all He asks is that I let Him love me,
Let Him love me as He chooses, with not thoughts for wins or loses,
Let Him love me as I am is all He asks!

He knows me. He knows me!
Better than I know myself, oh yes, He knows me!
Who I was the other day and who I will become tomorrow,
But He loves me just the same the way I am!

He calls me. He calls me!
He calls me as I am to spread His love!
Knowing well who I have been, who I will be, who I am,
Yet He calls me just the same to spread His love!

He frees me. He frees me!
He frees me to say yes whenever He calls me!
Showing me His own compassion, love and care and understanding,
He frees me to say my "yes" when He calls me!

He loves me, He loves me!
He loves me as I am, oh yes, He loves me!
Finding me wherever I am He gently guides me by the hand,
For He loves me as I am, oh, He loves me!
For He loves me as I am, oh, He loves me!

Gradually, over the years of my life, I had come more and more to see our God's love for me. That 'daddy night' in late 1973 is still vivid in my memory like it was last night! I've seen, tasted, felt... the countless blessings He's heaped on me — when I least deserved even one of them... and on my family and on my work. Even more, I had gradually begun to see His love bringing good out of the evils, the tragedies, the sufferings that befell those He loved. That had become the whole theme of the ministry in Norwich and all over the country wherever I was called. But, never, had I actually seen it put into words — and music — that way! I had asked Him for a picture — the audacity of asking God for a picture! And He had responded with a picture that the blind man asking could hear! And in that picture He had described Himself in terms of His love for me, for us, His kids! Wow! Needless to say I *flew* home from that retreat. I was ready for anything! Or was I?

Invitations for ordination to the diaconate went out about a month before the scheduled ceremonies! I couldn't believe it when I saw my name in print with the two other men who also were to be ordained deacons that Friday evening, May 20, 1977. In addition to the invitations, the ceremony was also announced in the ministry's newsletter whose circulation was now about one thousand! That would be a glorious night!

Just ten days before the diaconate ordination, I was standing by my desk in my Hickory Street office when the telephone rang. "Pat," the Chancellor of the Diocese said when I picked up the phone, "will you stay in your office for a few minutes? I've got to talk to you. I'll be right over." He hung up and I wondered... he was driving across town to see me? Oh well, maybe he was coming to set dates for the other 'minor orders,' steps prior to the ordination to deacon. Fr. Thomas Bride, the Diocesan Chancellor, had done his utmost to prepare me for ordination. He had even prepared tapes of the ceremonies and the theology behind each one for me so I could listen to them and be better prepared for each step on the way to the priesthood. Now I wondered what this visit would bring. I didn't have to wait long, but it seemed like hours. The front door of the Hickory Street office building opened and I knew it was him. He came right into my office, closed the door behind himself, walked over to me, threw his arms around me and cried, as he said, "Pat, we've got to cancel your ordination."

I was stunned. But... the invitations had all gone out... I thought all was definite now. "We thought so, too," Father Bride explained. And then, very quickly he went on to tell me how the bishop had sent all of my papers to the 'Priestly Formation Committee' of the national conference of bishops in Washington because of my legal blindness. Legal blindness had always been an impediment to Holy Orders because of the dangers of spilling the sacred species, etc. It had seemed an insurmountable barrier in my teen years when I had first contemplated becoming a priest. But now? I had not expected any problem at all. The commission apparently had looked over my papers and, seeing my years of education and service as a religious teaching brother and my years of service already as a worker with the handicapped, had passed favorably toward ordination. They had apparently either overlooked the point of blindness being an impediment or not considered it applicable in this case. With their 'green light' for ordination in hand Bishop Reilly had decided to move ahead on my road to the priesthood, knowing, I am sure, how long I had waited already. It was apparently the 'Apostolic Delegate to Rome' who had picked up the point and asked that the ordination process be held up until the matter of the legal blindness could be looked into. "Bishop Reilly had hoped," Father Bride continued, "to clear up the whole matter before May 20th without saying a word to you; the next morning we would have told you, 'Pat, you almost didn't get ordained last night!' and then we would have explained all that had happened. Bishop Reilly has already made several long trips to try and work it all out but now it doesn't look like he'll have any results in time, so we have no choice, Pat, but to cancel and hope that we can reschedule at some later time... if it comes through favorably, but right now we can't even talk about that."

I was numb. Father Bride's compassion certainly made the blow easier to take, but it was still a blow. "Father Bride," I asked with a sudden aire of panic, "What about all those who've been invited? All those who've waited for this day as long as I have and who are now making plans to be here for the 20th?" Somebody had to tell them and it seemed immediately clear that that someone had to be *me*. Yes, I was sure if the bishop wrote a letter a lot of people would merely respond 'that's the church again! How's Pat feeling?'

And I didn't want that. The last thing in the whole world I wanted was for someone else's heart to be crippled with bitterness and hate as my own heart had once been! Immediately the scenes of those weeks of bitterness, resentment, and downright hatred for Brother Francis flashed through my mind. I knew, too, the hurt and despair I had gone through in New York when a local diocese there had said 'no' to the center and to my serving there. I didn't want those chains for anyone else, "Father Bride," I said, "how do I stop them from getting bitter because of this?" "Only you can, Pat," he said with true compassion. "We'll help in every way that we possibly can."

I was utterly amazed as Father Bride left my office that May 10, 1977. I had just gotten the news that my dream had been canceled and I wasn't bitter! It was a weird combination of disappointment, disbelief and wonder about what's next, mixed with a kind of joy as my own reaction to the news. It was like, "I don't believe it... I've really *grown up!*" My road to the priesthood had often been pock-marked with surprise obstacles and every time my own heart would grow stony and bitter. But this time it didn't. I'm certain that the genuine compassion of my bishop and Father Bride and so many of the other priests of the diocese on hearing the news had a lot to do with the staving off of bitterness and resentment in my heart. The absolutely beautiful love and compassion of all the priests, sisters, brothers and lay people who had been involved with the work was also a healing gift at the right time! One couple in New York drove all the way to Connecticut as soon as they got the news — just 'to be with Pat.' The priest who taught me my 'how to celebrate' course in preparation for ordination immediately drove clear across the diocese to be with me. There was no end to the compassionate support that brought me through that hour. The task ahead of me was how do I extend that same compassionate support to the thousands who had been invited to the celebration that was now canceled. How would I break the news to them in such a way that bitterness and resentment would not be their response?

In Matthew's Gospel Jesus tells His followers not to worry what they are to say or how they are to say it when they are called to testify to His name. He says that His Father will send the Spirit and the Spirit will do the speaking. I believe. The letter that flowed out from my typewriter that very night just baffled *me!* It read,

My dear Brothers and Sisters,

This is probably the most difficult letter I have had to write in

my life. My ordination to the diaconate, which was scheduled for Friday evening, May 20th, cannot take place at this time.

The very theme of my work with the handicapped in the Diocese of Norwich has come to be 'the giftness' of each person and each situation in life. God loves us, I have often said, and therefore He wishes, and is able, to bring good out of everything that comes into our life. Our faith in the love of our Father really shines out as a witness to our world when in the midst of adversity, illness, disruption of cherished plans, etc., we can still look into His face and say through our tears, 'Daddy, I know that You love me and that from this, too, You will bring a gift! Help my faith.'

We have another gift — a gift that right now somewhat excites me as I try to discover exactly what it is! May 20th was to be our FANTASTIC day, the day of my ordination as a deacon — one of the final steps before ordination to priesthood. Because of cannonical considerations and the unexpected need for a dispensation from the Holy See, that diaconate ordination to the diocesan clergy cannot take place on May 20th.

My brothers and sisters, I ask you most sincerely to rejoice with me in faith at this moment of trial. All of you have shared this road to ordination with me, and you know well that this is not the first delay that we have experienced along that road, but, let us look at and remember well the gifts that have indeed come through each of these delays! Had my original plans for ordination gone smoothly some five years ago as I then wished, I would not be here in your diocese among you now! I would not have come to know and love my Provincial Superior, Brother Francis, of the Brothers of Christian Instruction, as I do now so dearly! I wonder if I would have ever made the beautiful, moving, growth-giving Marriage Encounter experience through which I have come to know and love and share with so very many of you! It was several of the trials that fell across this same path that led me to my first 'directed retreat' — and two more since that one — and helped me so excitedly to discover the very giftness of my own handicapping condition just before coming here to the Norwich Diocese in 1975. I would never have known the support and love of our own dear Bishop Reilly and the priests of the diocese! That support from the bishop sustains me in this hour.

My brothers and sisters, our plans and hopes for one day have indeed been postponed for a time. What gift will our Father bring from this moment? Will you please join with me in renewing our faith in His love and concern for us? This truly can be a great time of growth, love, peace and joy for all of us!

In union of love and prayer, I remain,

Your brother,
Patrick"

The next morning I brought a rough draft of the above letter to Father Bride who helped me add to it and prepare the final copy. Did the Chancery Office (the Diocesan Administration Office) close down for the day? I don't think so but everyone available there joined in the project of getting the letters duplicated, the one thousand envelopes addressed and stamped, the letters folded and inserted and mailed *all in a single day!* I think all of the secretarial staff at the chancery office worked on the project! The compassion, love and support pouring in from all over were themselves our Daddy's gifts from that hour of trial. I don't ever remember feeling so loved and supported as at that hour!

There was one person on my mailing list that I didn't want to find out about the ordination cancellation by mail – Mom, dear Mom. The letters were mailed Tuesday night, just one day after I had gotten the news! I planned to travel to Maine on Thursday to visit Mom and break the news to her personally, but love does funny things at times. My phone rang Wednesday morning and when I answered it, it was Mom. Mom is very frugal with her meager social security income; she doesn't make long distance calls; she's the world's greatest letter writer! But that morning there she was on the phone. I almost didn't recognize her voice. "Patrick, is anything wrong? Is everything ok?" she asked before I could say a word! "Why?" I asked, trying to stall. Patrick, I couldn't sleep all Monday night" I had you on my mind all night and all day yesterday! Something's the matter. What is it?" Love does such things! Monday was the day I got the news; apparently she did, too!

Mom's call made my trip to Maine, later that week, more of a pleasure trip than an errand of sad tidings. Because she knew about the cancellation we 'went on from there' and enjoyed each other's company for the weekend! The 'Letter of Faith', as it came to be called by many, did everything that I hoped it would, prayed it would. The responses told of how the letter had helped them through their own trials at the very moment they received it. Couples contemplating marriage break-up wrote how the letter had been handed to them by 'a friend of a friend of a friend' and how the letter had given them the courage to try again! Even one letter came from a man 'behind bars' who said that my letter had been brought to him by 'a friend of a friend...' and it had changed his own outlook. I cried an awful lot as I read and reread many of those responses, realizing already the gifts our Daddy was bringing for so many from that little moment of darkness!

Because I was not to be ordained on May 20th, I was able to say 'yes' when the New York Telephone Company requested that I keynote an assembly of its "Telephone Pioneers of America" in Cooperstown, New York, on May 19th. The request had come earlier but I had thought it an impossibility because it was just too close. The Pioneers, who do voluntary work with the handicapped all over the United States and Canada, had offered to charter a plane to bring me there, let me give my address, and then bring me back in time for ordination! Now, however, I was able to come without their rearranging the conference schedule for me at all. I even welcomed the opportunity to be busy on that day! Because of that talk, I was invited several weeks later to address another Pioneer gathering, this time in New York City. Partly because of that talk a woman is now working as a 'lay missionary' among the Indians on a reservation in South Dakota! She literally 'left all' to follow His call. Would I ever have met Marge Werner if my ordination had gone as scheduled? Would I ever have gone to South Dakota — as I did this past December — to give a Mission of Brokenness in Our Lives to the Indians she now works with? I often look back to those days of 1977 and I wonder how life would be different if they had been different! I praise God dearly for the way they were; I thank Him most sincerely that I, for the first time in my life, was able to praise Him when I didn't know exactly what the gift was!

My work continued on as usual — that is, if it ever is usual! That was the summer we purchased God's Gift House so I didn't really have much time to be depressed or even to question! He kept me rather busy, the best thing for me, I am sure! Summer moved into fall. The center was dedicated and work moved steadily forward. The weekend of December 10, 1977, I was asked to speak about the ministry at all the weekend Masses at St. Mary's Parish in New London, Connecticut, about twenty minutes drive from Norwich. I stood in the sacristy that evening waiting for the Saturday night Mass to begin. Father Thomas Bride walked in, walked right up to me, took my hands in his and proclaimed, "Pat, your Calvary is over! We've got the green light from Rome!" I don't know who was more excited about the news, the bishop, Father Bride, myself, Mom, or all those who heard about it so quickly! It was FANTASTIC! Ordination to diaconate was scheduled immediately for Saturday, February 25th — just far enough away to give people time to plan to get there! What a Christmas gift it was to bring to Mom. My brother, Gerry, and I flew to Florida for the holidays where Mom was visiting my youngest sister, Anita, and her family. What a care free, almost slapstick time we had those days together! Anita's husband, Al, is a real joker and when he and Gerry get together there's no telling what's coming up next! It was a *real vacation*, a Christmas I will never forget!

Ordination to diaconate, February 25, 1978, took place during one of the worst winters eastern Connecticut had known in years! But, ordination day was bright, sunny, and gorgeous even though six foot snowbanks lined all the streets! Because the cathedral of the diocese was being renovated for the diocese's twenty-fifth anniversary celebrations that summer, the ordination to diaconate was held at SS. Peter and Paul Church in Norwich. Strangely — or is it expected — I remember very little about the day. It was just FANTASTIC that it had arrived! The pristhood for the handicapped was truly now touchably close!

Those months following my ordination to the diaconate were, if I have to be honest, as long as the seven or eight years that had preceded them in my wait for the dream of the priesthood for the handicapped to be a dream come true. In June of that year the men who were ordained deacons the previous year were called to the pristhood. I was excited for them that morning but excited, too, knowing that somehow mine would be next on the calendar! That morning as I arrived at the cathedral and went to the sacristy to dress for the celebration, Father Bride came over to me and handed me a small white envelope. I *knew what it was — it had to be my ordination date!* I said, "Thanks, Father!" and tried not to look too excited but I immediately looked for a corner where I could be alone so I could open it up and know the date! I must have been like a young fiance, all excited because the date for the wedding was finally being set! I was right. All the note said was *Ordination Date-October 7, 1978!!!* It didn't have to say anymore! It couldn't have said anymore! I could hardly contain myself! How do you get excited for others when you've just gotten news like that! I watched their ordination ceremony that morning keenly, knowing that in less than four months I would be going through it! It was just unreal! I couldn't wait to get home and call Mom and everyone to let them know! FANTASTIC!

My work with the handicapped continued normally after my ordination as a deacon. On weekends, when the ministry didn't have a program, I was assigned as a deacon to St. Catherine of Siena Parish, in Preston, a small town just outside of Norwich. As a

163

deacon I was able to read the Gospel passages at Mass, preach the sermons, distribute communion, and help out in other ways during the services. The diaconate tradition in the church dates way back to the Apostles of Jesus. Shortly after Jesus's Resurrection they chose the first seven deacons to help take care of the temporal needs of the people in order to free the apostles for the preaching of the Word. Today, most men who are scheduled to be ordained priests for a diocese will spend their last year before ordination to priesthood as ordained deacons in one parish or another of the diocese. In keeping with the tradition of the apostolic church, the practice of ordaining some men as 'permanent deacons' has also been revived today. My duties at St. Catherine's were very limited because I remained full-time with the ministry of the handicapped.

One of the many gifts that came from waiting that extra year for ordination was our renovated Cathedral of St. Patrick in Norwich where my ordination to priesthood was to take place. The Diocese of Norwich was established in 1953, and so, as prepartions were underway for the silver jubilee celebrations, renovation and refurbishing of the diocesan cathedral were included as part of those preparations. And, as part of that renovation, accessibility for handicapped persons was included. A beautiful ramp was added to the church's structure – not in the back or on the side where it doesn't show, but right in the very front of the Cathedral itself, taking off from the landing at the floor level of the church and arching its way down to the Broadway sidewalk! It's beautifully landscaped to fit in with the church's over-all decor – and it's used by practically *everyone!* The ramp was completed for the diocesan jubilee celebrations in early August, so it was also there for my ordination! More than several hundred handicapped persons were thereby permitted to attend the ordination celebrations, as well as all cathedral celebrations now, without major difficulties! What a FANTASTIC gift!

Surprisingly I didn't seem to get nervous or excited as ordination day drew near. The invitations were printed and sent out. The returns started coming in. Plans for receptions and First Mass were put together... and the ministry went on as well. I started to get excited as I noticed those who stated on the returns that they *were definitely coming!* People from all over Connecticut, from New York, Pennsylvania, Maine, Massachusetts, and a host of other states as well as *Canada!* It was like a "This is Your Life" program – each return brought with it the memories that had made us one and now would bring us together again! But, I was still pretty calm right up to the afternoon before the ceremonies. At 3:00 p.m. I had to go for practice and that did it! Everything broke loose inside me! So it really was going to take place this time! There were no more road blocks, no more surprises, no more delays. I couldn't sleep that night at all! As my brothers and sisters began to arrive with all the friends from out of town things really began to get exciting!

Seven of my brothers and sisters traveled from all over to be with me for this dream-come-true day! Martha left her husband and kids in Tucson, Arizona, to come for the ordination; Patricia came from Washington, D.C. with her little daughter, Jennifer, leaving her husband, Jerry, to watch their two boys at home; Lorraine drove down from Portland, Maine, and Marie came up with my great Aunt Marie from Stamford, Connecticut; my brother, Paul, and his wife, Karen, and their boys came from Enfield, Connecticut, for the whole weekend of celebrations. Paul is but a year older than I so we grew up very close to each other. He and his wife did one of the readings at my First Mass that Sunday afternoon. Gerry, of course, was all ready and was the life of our staff. If he wasn't chasing someone around with a bug on a piece of paper he might well be standing behind a door to scare you as you came in! He had a corny line for everything you came out with. Both those we worked with and those we worked for came to love Gerry deeply during the years he worked as part of our ministry! Anita, my youngest sister, really wanted to come for the ordination celebrations. She and Patricia, who is a couple of years older than she, and Paul and Martha and Lorraine and I had all spent many of our 'older' growing-up years together; our battles had been many, our scars few, and our laughs and deep joys more than we could ever count. Albert, a year or so older than Lorraine, had left for the high school seminary in 1953 while most of us were quite small; he finished his high school and a year of college there and then decided to enter the Air Force. Stationed in South Dakota, he met and married his wife, Mary. A joy of my travels to Marge Werner's Indian mission was getting to spend that New Year's Day with their FANTASTIC family and friends in Aberdeen, South Dakota! My brother, Philip, was in high school when I was sick with the meningitis in 1953. He was FANTASTIC with radios, televisions – anything electronic! He was the one who so often drove me to the doctors offices for shots, examinations, etc, when Daddy's work wouldn't let him leave. Phil today is a priest in the Archdiocese of Santa Fe, New Mexico. The witness of his faith and perseverance often held me up through the delays and potholes on my road to ordination. He entered the seminary after some eight years in the Air Force and several years in other work! His own road to ordination was often obstacled with delays and surprises. His perserverance to ordination in October, 1979, was a gift of inspiration to me. Theresa and Germaine, my older sisters, were both married and settled with their families in Louisiana and Oklahoma respectively. We younger kids had grown up with several of their own children; we loved being called 'uncle' and 'aunt' by them, who were almost the same age as we were! Willis, the oldest boy of the 14 living children in the family, had participated in the invasion of Normandy at the end of World War II and had fought in the front lines in Korea. He had spent most of his years in the Army overseas. He had come home from Korea on emergency leave when it didn't look good for me in 1953. He was now married and settled with his wife in Titusville, Florida. Annette was the oldest of the kids in the family. When we lived in northern Maine during our growing up years she had always lived not too far from home with her husband, Fernand, and their children. Several of us grew up very close to her older children who were about our own age. Annette has kept her home in northern Maine, the only one of the family to have settled up there. Most of the older ones in the family, because of distances to travel, expenses, and their own family commitments could not make it for my ordination celebrations. Anita, living in Florida at Egland Air Force Base with her husband, Al, and their three children, really wanted to come but they had made the long trip to Maine the previous summer to help Mom pack up and move when she had sold the house. Financially, there was no way that she and Al could swing another trip north this year. But, she *did* come! The base chaplan and several friends in the parish on base heard of her plight and presented her the money with the roundtrip tickets to Connecticut! What a FANTASTIC gift of love!

It was most literally a *riot* having the eight of us together with our dear Mom for the weekend! Mom had flown up that August when the ministry had dedicated another house which I will talk more about later. It was her first visit to the area in the summer and she had fallen in love with it. She had been up with my sister, Patricia, when we had dedicated *God's Gift House* the previous September and had returned in February for my ordination as a deacon. She had lived with Pat and Jerry in Washington for a full year by this time and had felt at home with their three kids. Pat and Jerry had adopted Andy, their first child when they were in Texas. It was with them that Mom had stayed after Dad's death in 1969. Wanting a brother for Andy who is handicapped, they had adopted Julian from an orphanage in Delhi, India. Jennifer was adopted several years after Julian and became the 'heart stealer' of the family! As much as she had loved it with them in Washington, however, Mom had missed her independence and the joy of having her own 'few little rooms.' That was what she had prayed for that summer, "Lord, help me to find just three little rooms somewhere." While visiting in Connecticut in August 1978, I had taken her to visit a friend of mine in a senior citizen apartment complex in Norwich. She liked the friend but *loved the apartment!* It was *three little rooms!* She had placed her name on the waiting list 'just in case' that August. She flew up to Connecticut a few days before ordination in order to be well rested when it came time for the days of celebration. Two days before my ordination, I got a call from the local housing authority — "Father Pat," they said, "we've got an ordination gift for you — an apartment for your mother! She can move in as of October 18th!" Mom has been in her 'three little rooms' ever since that day in October, almost four years ago. She's made loads of friends and comes and goes more than I do! It's funny, because several times I've had the opportunity to get her a bigger or a nicer apartment but she always responds. "You'll have to move me with a bulldozer! I'm at home here! This is what I prayed for and it's what the good Lord gave me!"

It was really special having so many of the family there for this most special day of my life and all the cards and letters from those who couldn't come added even more to the excitement. Mom had invited them all to 'chip in' for an ordination gift from the whole family — a Mass kit! She knew that most of my priestly services would be 'on the road' among those who could not come to church and so her dream was to give me the 'porta church' that I could carry with me wherever I go! She had the paten, the communion plate, engraved underneath with the names of all of my brothers and sisters and the chalice, the communion cup, engraved on its base in memory of Dad and her. Each time I raise them at Mass it's like I'm lifting up my whole family to our Lord!

But, I've jumped a bit ahead of myself, I'm not ordained yet! As I left the rehearsal Friday afternoon, the day before ordination, Father Bride, who had conducted the rehearsal, said to me "Pat, don't come here until just ten minutes before the celebration tomorrow morning and when you arrive come right into the sacristy! If you get lost out here in the church with all those people we'll never get started!" We laughed together and I walked out on air. It was really about to happen!

Saturday, October 7, 1978, even *the weather* finally cooperated and rejoiced with us! The sky that morning was a brilliant blue, unmarred by a single cloud! The fall foliage was at the very peak of its New England colors! I remember saying to God as we drove to the cathedral that morning! "Boy, you're really showing off this time! With people coming from more than two dozen states and from Canada you're really putting on a show!" It was FANTASTIC!

I walked Mom into the church to her place. I was too nervous and excited to notice all who were there but someone called me over to one side and there I saw the Joys from Sault Ste. Marie, Ontario, over eleven hundred miles away! Friends of mine, the Merciers, had 'smuggled' them there without my even knowing they were coming! That started me off. Several television cameras were already set up and newspaper reporters and photographers were in every corner. Bishop Reilly was as warm and excited as he could be as I walked into the sacristy as I had been told. "Pat," he said, "this is not only a big day for you and your family; it's doing much for our Church!" The handicapped were there by the hundreds. It was just unbelieveable the aire of celebration and emotion that packed the church. I believe it was the Hartford, Connecticut, daily paper that had 'done its homework' in that research had found this to be the first ordination of a legally blind person in the New England states and the third in the nation. There was cause for celebration! Close to a hundred priests from all over the diocese formed the processional line as the big moment began. The priest who had directed my 'He loves Me' retreat a year and a half earlier was there from Maine; several priest friends from New York came; and as the processional march began another priest, Father Jack McKenna who had taught me at the seminary at St. John's University, New York, ran up and joined us! As we entered the church and I realized for the first time how full it was, I suddenly got really *nervous!*

At the beginning of the actual ordination ceremony, the Bishop calls for public approval of the ordination of the candidate and eveyone rose and applauded. Father Bride and Father Brown, my guardian angels through the whole ceremony, signaled for me to stand and face the people and as I did the applause went wild. I turned white. It was almost like I was in another world. "I didn't think you were going to make it at that point," the Bishop said to me after all was over! "I wondered, too!" I said. The actual ordaining gesture is when the bishop lays his hands on the head of the one being ordained. That laying-on-of-hands brought such peace and calmness to me that I had never experienced before. After that it was as if the nervousness had left me. I savored every aspect of the whole ceremony. What a feeling of brotherhood there was when at the close of the ordaining ceremony itself all of the hundred or so priests present filed by to hug and welcome me to the priesthood! It was like the dam burst when at the end of that long line of priests *Brother Francis* appeared and hugged me for dear life! How he got into that line that was only for the priests I will never know, but what a thrilling moment it was for the both of us! It was awesome to stand by the bishop during the solemn prayers of the Mass and co-celebrate the Mass with him! My eyes were clouded with tears as I took my place at the head of the main aisle and began giving communion to those who had waited for this day as long as I did! But one of the most touching moments of that whole day − of my whole life − was just before the closing of the entire celebration when Bishop Reilly, my beloved bishop without whom this day would probably never have come, came over, knelt on the floor in front of me, and as our eyes met he asked me for my first priestly blessing! All I remember as I laid my hands on his head was the prayer that filled my heart at that moment − *"Lord bless him a millionfold for the many blessings he has given me!"* After the Bishop, my own dear Mom, and then each of my family who were present were escorted up so I could give them my priestly blessing. What a privilege to look into the face of the mother who gave me life, who prayed for that life when it seemed so threatened, who worked, prayed, worried, and anxiously watched as she saw that life mature to this day... what a privilege now to be able to pray our God's choicest blessings on her! And then, another gift! To see there in front of me the brothers and sisters who had believed in my life when even the doctors had doubted, had taught me to walk when it was said I would probably never walk, had laughed, worked, played, fought, and prayed with me... what a gift to be able as a priest, their brother priest, to beg our God to bless them as they had blessed me!

The rest of ordination day for me is like little scenes from a movie − with no continuity − just dozens of scenes of love − the 'First Blessings' line that formed and went for what seemed like hours downstairs at the cathedral; the huge tent with hundreds of guests eating and many of them meeting each other for the first time; tours with friends and family of our now one year old center; the piles of gifts and cards; Steve and Pat Smith singing the song, "He's a Man, Lord," that they had written as my ordination gift; my four sisters Anita, Patricia, Martha and Lorraine physically taking me by the shoulders and leading me to the kitchen where they *made me sit and eat!*

Sunday morning was scheduled beautifully as a quiet morning just for the family, a family breakfast! We laughed more and passed around more stories of childhood than any one of us alone could remember. From Mom's reactions it seemed clear that many of the incidents she was hearing *for the first time!* The whole morning just passed too quickly and already it was time for the next part of the weekend's ceremonies − my *first Mass!* I had given hundreds, thousands?, of talks to large and small audiences all over the country. I am not a nervous speaker by nature, but that afternoon I could identify with those who become tongue-tied and panic-stricken before any sort of public performance! My knees quite literally *knocked* all during the Mass. Since I read letter-by-letter, I had to practically memorize all of the prayers and readings that were mine to do that day. I had horrible, nightmarish visions of my mind going *blank* and my not being able to find my place or read at all from the books! Father Dennis Jarre, who had taught me the 'how to celebrate' course and who had driven all across the diocese to see me the day my ordination had been canceled a year and a half earlier, did the homily and sermon, at my first Mass. The day before, Bishop Reilly in his closing remarks, had gotten the one thousand people packed in the cathedral to yell out my 'favorite word' FANTASTIC, as he had struggled to find 'the right word' to describe the day! Now, Father Dennis took the word apart and I cried as he applied its meaning to my life and work — "to make real what is unreal," he defined it, "and that's what Pat does in the lives of the broken, in all of our lives."

I could go on forever talking about that FANTASTIC weekend. My second Mass was celebrated in Sacred Heart Church, in a little town in the northeastern part of the diocese, Wauregan, where we had recently opened a residence for the handicapped. The Mass was follwed by the ordination banquet at the Yankee Greyhound *dog track!!!* It was the closest, available and totally accessible for the handicapped, restaurant — and it was donated for the day! Richard Mercier, First Selectman of the town, whose sister is physically disabled and a dear friend, was Master of Ceremonies for the banquet. A local singing group, the Mass Production, provided music for the festivity and a 'roasting' provided the laughter and tears *at my expense!* It was fun.

That Sunday night most of the guests and family had left and I finally found myself alone. I lay down on my bed, still too much in a dream world to sleep. All of a sudden as I lay there the bed began to shake as I began to shake, quite literally, with the realization that it had happened — *I am a priest, a priest for the handicapped!* "You're a dreamer, Patrick," Sister Estherine Bruno had said to me one day about six years earlier, "but what scares me about you is that all of your dreams come true!" I had laughed then; I didn't now. Instead I cried as I thanked God for the gift of that dream-come-true!

19

"Who needs Mary?"

"Are you going to assign me 'parish duties'?" I asked Bishop Reilly a week before my ordination in 1978. "No," he had responded, "I'm ordaining you for your ministry not to take you away from it! Bring the church to those who can't come to it!" Wow! Most of my daily Masses are now celebrated for groups of the handicapped, for organizations of and for the handicapped, and in the institutions and homes of the handicapped themselves. I've been ordained almost four years as I write these pages and still I get all teary eyed as I begin Mass and recall that it really is *me*. It wasn't just a dream; it wasn't 'my dream'... It was His calling... expressed by my bishop in his calling me to ordination... 'ratified' by the people in their applause on that beautiful day. I can still hear Bishop Reilly in his closing talk saying "'Father Pat, no, we'll never be able to call him that; he's been 'Brother Pat' to us for too long now. But, in a sense," he went on, "you can always call him 'Brother Pat' for that's what he is; as your priest he belongs to you, you know!" I will never forget those words. When I had signed the papers, officially leaving the Brothers of Christian Instruction to go on for the priesthood to serve my people, I had felt instead that morning that I was 'renewing' my vows of brotherhood, not doing away with them. The only difference was, I guess, that now those I served were my brothers and sisters; I was *their* brother and that's what I now seem called to be even as their priest.

One month to the day after ordination, I found myself in Sault Ste. Marie, Ontario, again! I had made my first trip back there in April, 1978, three years after that first flight up in the summer of 1975. At this springtime visit many of the handicapped of the area had talked about taking a bus to Connecticut for our next *Persons are Gifts Weekend*. I had told them then that if they had that many that wanted to made the weekend, find a parish that would host a weekend and I would come back to put one on for them right there in Sault Ste. Marie! Father Ray Farrell, then Pastor of Blessed Sacrament Parish in 'the Sault' offered his parish as that 'host parish' and so, with one of his parish families, Joe and Annette Kilty, coordinating all the nitty gritties, and the Joys, Richard and Lois, coordinating the presenting team, the retreat weekend for the handicapped of Sault Ste. Marie fell together and was scheduled for the second weekend of November, 1978. Some eighty to eighty-five persons made the weekend. It was my very first retreat as a priest and that made the whole experience at least doubly exciting! I flew to the Sault a week ahead of time, spending the first weekend speaking in another parish in the city, St. Jerome's, and then working with the local team for the weekend during the week prior to the actual *Persons are Gifts Weekend.* Several more 'from back home' joined us to add to the team and the weekend began on schedule Friday night. There's no words that can describe how I felt as I administered the Sacrament of the Annointing of the Sick for the first time or as I heard confessions, the Sacrament of Reconciliation, and was able to gently, lovingly welcome broken people 'home' after long years away! Those same feelings are still there each time I humbly hold up the bread and the wine and say "This is My Body... This is My blood!"

The *Persons are Gifts Weekend,* the first one ever done outside our own diocese in Connecticut, was as FANTASTIC as those back home! Watching people come to discover that maybe... yes, of course, their handicapping conditions indeed could be *gifts* is like watching the majestic waters of Niagara Falls or coming around a bend and beholding the wonders of His mountains! Sunday night, the weekend over and everyone gone home, I knelt beside my bed and cried tears of deep joy as I thanked our Daddy for the gift He had given so many of us that weekend. I was staying at the home of Joe and Annette Kilty that night and we had stayed up for hours reminiscing about the various high points and touching moments of the weekend. As I now knelt alone by the bed in the room where I was sleeping that night, I was suddenly aware that *I wasn't alone.* There standing right in front of me was *The Cross of Jesus.* It was as real as life, as if I were seeing it that first Good Friday almost 2,000 years ago! Jesus was still alive on the cross. I looked at Him and then my eyes fell on Mary standing to one side, next to the cross. On the other side was *not* John, the beloved disciple as in the Gospel account, but *me.* I saw Jesus look at Mary and say "Behold your child," and then He turned to me and said, "Behold your mother." And I cringed...

Mary had had no part in my life for years... I hadn't let her. I had shut her out. "Who needs Mary? You can go directly to Jesus. Why all this Mary stuff?" Way back in December, 1963, as a young novice brother with the Brothers of Christian Instruction in Alfred, Maine, we were preparing to make the traditional 'Consecration of Mary' of St. Louis de Montfort. I remember well the day I went up to Brother Master's room and said, "Do we have to make a consecration to Mary? Can't I write my own consecration to Jesus?" Brother David Touchette, Master of Novices, never scolded me or argued with me. He just said, "Okay, if you prefer." The Rosary

Devotion to the Blessed Virgin Mary was a regular part of the brothers' daily prayer. I 'said' it with them whenever we said it together and either raced through it or said it not at all when it was eventually made a private devotion. Eventually the rosary became simply a sting of beads with a crucifix attached that I carried in my left back pocket – as a 'good luck charm?' For the next fifteen years I left little or no place for Mary in my life. After all, you really didn't *need* her. 'Wasn't too much emphasis placed on her anyway?' And then there were my friends and the people I worked with who might not believe in or even make fun of such silly devotions. It was just 'safer' not to have 'her' around. But, Mary never left me out. Mysteriously in little ways – and some of them not so little – she was always there. Vow days and big celebrations with the brothers were almost always on one of her feast days. And then, in Jackson Heights, N.Y., when we opened the apartment and had our weekly prayer meetings for the people of the area, the first prayer meeting was held on the very first available Friday night after I had moved into the apartment; that just 'happened' to be the feast of *Our Lady of Sorrows* and so the apartment was called by the people 'Our Lady of Sorrows House of Prayer.' In June of 1978, when Bishop Reilly sent me the note naming my ordination date, I had nothing to say whatever about the date he chose. He made the choice. It just 'happened' to be October 7, the feast of *The Most Holy Rosary.* Two days before ordination, I went to Worcester, Massachusetts, for a day of prayer that I heard was going on there; I figured it would be a gift, a quiet time, before this great day. The whole theme of the day was *Mary* and *The Rosary.* That was all well and good; I really didn't hear any 'messages' or notice anything special about all these 'coincidences.' The first *Persons are Gifts Weekend* done outside the Diocese of Norwich was a month after my ordination, as I have said, in the Diocese of Sault Ste. Marie, translated *St. Mary's Rapids* or *Falls.* The whole diocese is specially dedicated to our Lady. And it was there, at the end of that retreat, that I saw and heard Jesus on His cross! "Behold your Mother!"

I cringed as I heard myself saying "Who needs her? Why can't we go directly to you, Jesus? Why all this Mary stuff? Pious devotion, nonsense..." as I had said for fifteen years! Only now, I saw exactly *who* I had been saying it to. I knew all too well the love of Jesus for me. I had seen countless times that He had redeemed my blunders and my brokenness with His merciful, gentle love. And He, Who loved me so much and so tenderly, had offered me His Mother and I had said *"no, thanks, Jesus!"* Oh, I hadn't said it in those words; but didn't my life say exactly that? The 'vision' disappeared as quickly as it had appeared and I found myself stunned, silent... until I realized all that had happened. I found myself praying like I had never prayed in my life. "Please, Jesus," I begged Him, "give me just one more chance to accept Mary as my Mother, to 'take her into my home' as your beloved disciple, John, did. Please, Jesus!" And I was sure I was going to die that night, that I'd probably never get the chance to take Mary into my home and heart. I had rejected the gift He had offered. I cried myself to sleep that night begging for that 'one more chance.'

When I awoke in the morning my head and my stomach told the story of my crying most of the night; I was sick! The priest who had hosted the *Persons are Gifts Weekend* came over for breakfast and we sat around the Kilty's table sharing the highlights of the beautiful weekend. I took all I could take and then I said, "Listen, guys, I'm sick! I'm going to the bathroom and when I come out will you *please* pray over me. If I don't feel any better than this tomorrow there's no way I can board the plane for home tomorrow morning!" I came out of the bathroom feeling no better than when I had gone in. They were all gathered in the living room; a large stuffed chair had been pulled out to the center. "Sit right here," Annette Kilty said, and as I sat down they all gathered around me. Father Ray Farrell stood somewhat apart, if my memory serves me right, and raised his hands as if over the whole group of us. Then everyone began to pray in subdued tones. I couldn't believe it when I heard Father Ray begin his prayer.

None of them in the group there knew of my lack of devotion to Mary through those fifteen years; in fact, very few people I worked with knew anything about it. I just never brought 'her' up. Father Ray, I know for certain, knew nothing about it.

It's said of St. John Vianney, the patron of parish priests, that he 'could read your heart'... that if you went to confession to him but concealed something he would ask you about it and help you to leave the Sacrament with the greatest of peace. Well, I had read about that 'gift' but had never experienced it in anyone until this morning in Sault Ste. Marie, Ontario! As Father Ray Farrell began to pray, his prayer was to Mary. In his prayer he begged Mary to forgive me for all the times that I had rejected her and shut her out of my life. He asked her to come and be my mother, and at one point in his prayer, he said to one of the women present "Hug him as Mary would hug him." And I cried... And I cried... At the end of his prayer, seeing my tears he gave me the sacramental absolution. What a gift! I had been given the chance I begged for the very night before! I just couldn't get over how deeply loved I must be! How much our God loves us... No matter how we reject Him; No matter how we reject His gifts; No matter how long we're away... He's waiting just to hug and forgive us the moment we turn around and 'come home' and when we do come 'home' He helps us to clean up our 'whole' act!!!! I thought of all the very close mements of love He had given me in my short life − the conversion moment with Brother Francis; the 'Daddy' story; the 'John Chapter 9 Story of the Man born Blind,' the 'He loves Me Story,' and Ordination itself, and now *Mary*... He just never stops loving His kids!

I don't know how long Father Ray prayed that morning; I'm not sure exactly how long the prayer session lasted buy *no one* thought to pray a single word for my head or my stomach and *neither one of them got better!* When they finished that out-of-this-world prayer I had a tremendous peace in my heart but my head and my stomach were as sick as when they began! I had to go to the hospital that afternoon to pray with the chronically ill. One of the sisters there had asked that I make the stop to pray with those who hadn't been able to leave the hospital to attend our *Persons are Gifts Weekend*. I had promised to come Monday afternoon, the day before our scheduled flight back to Connecticut. Now I made up my mind that I would go down but when I finished praying with the patients if I wasn't feeling any better than I was right then, I was going to 'check in!' I arrived at the hospital on time that afternoon, feeling no better at all, and sister was waiting for me. She brought me to every patient in the chronically-ill ward one at a time. With each patient I would simply lay my hands on the patient's head for a short time in silence and then I'd pray a bit and conclude with a blessing. I love to pray spontaneously, to let my prayer just flow from my heart, but that day, with every single patient, the only prayer that would come out of my mouth was...

Hail Mary, full of grace, the Lord is with You,
Blessed are You among women
And blessed is the fruit of Your womb, Jesus!
Holy Mary, Mother of God, pray for us sinners
Now and at the hour of our death! Amen!

Patient after patient, that simple 'Ave Maria' and my blessing were the only words that would come out of my mouth. "And now, would you pray over me?" sister asked as we had evidently reached the last patient. When I finished the same simple prayer over her *another tear* escaped my eyes because I realized that as I had prayed for them I had gotten better! Mary had truly 'come home' to me! On December 8, 1978, fifteen years to the day after I had first asked "Why do we have to make a consecration to Mary?" I made that exact same Consecration of St. Louis de Montfort of the Blessed Virgin Mary. A lot of people still ask me "Why Mary?" only now I'm not ashamed to talk about my mother; I simply say "Why? Because Jesus chose to give her to us before He died and who am I to argue with Him about the gifts He chooses for me?" I love our Mother. When most of the big macho disciples had abandoned the Lord on Good Friday she stayed right with Him, the Gospels tell us. Who better can teach us to walk like Him on our roads of brokenness than she who walked His with Him? She is truly the Mother of the Broken, our Mother, *my* Mother.

One of the great gifts that I received from Mary not long after receiving the gift of her in my life was the 'gift of my oldest sister!' Because there's like two dozen years between the oldest and the youngest in the family, we younger ones never got to know our older brothers and sisters as kids but only as adults. They were *'always'* adults as far as our experience went and it often seemed to us that in their eyes we were always kids! When you add to this picture the fact that the meningitis pretty well wiped out the first nine and a half years of my life as far as memory is concerned and then six years later I left to enter the Brothers' prep school, that doesn't leave me too much of a chance to really get to know any of my brothers and sisters very well except those right around my own age if they happened to be at home those six years. I don't remember Annette, Theresa, or Germaine not married! Willis was 'always' in the Army as far as my experienced memory goes! When Daddy had died in 1969 and Willis came home he had to ask which one of his brothers I was! He had seen me as a child right after the meningitis; now I was twenty five years old! Theresa and her husband, George, were stationed at the Air Force Base near our home in Limestone, Maine, during my late grammar school days; I remember visiting them in their base housing and loving it. I never really got to know Germaine until my year in Washington, D.C., getting my master's degree in library science. They, Germaine and her husband, Ted, and their six kids, 'just happened' to get transferred from Goose Bay, Labrador to Andrews Air Force Base, Washington, D.C., the same year so we got to spend many weekends together! Lorraine has lived and worked in Portland, Maine, area since the mid-1960's so during my teaching days at Denis Hall I got to spend more time with her when we were at home for visits together. During my university teaching days at St. John's in New York and Catholic U. in Washington in the early 1970's, Patricia and her husband, Jerry, were stationed by the Air Force in Washington, D.C., so whenever my course at Catholic University was scheduled I got to spend enjoyable times with them! When I moved to New York in 1970, Marie was only a hop, skip and a jump away in Stamford so I got to get to know and love her dearly through our too-few visits together! When Phil was ordained, in addition to getting to spend some time with him, Martha and Andy and their kids came from Arizona, Germaine and Ted and one of their's, Brian drove out from Oklahoma, and we all stayed at Anita and Al's who had moved to Albuquerque from Florida a year or so earlier! When I moved to the Diocese of Norwich in 1975, Paul and Karen and their boys were already in Enfield, Connecticut, in the neighboring diocese, so I've gotten to spend some time (but you've got to say that 'some time' very fast; with my travels, I'm sure at times they wonder if I've dropped off the face of the earth)! Last year, when my programs on 'brokenness in our lives' brought me out to South Dakota, I got to see Albert and Mary and their FANTASTIC family after some twelve years!!! What a visit that was! And, of course, since Gerry was working at Denis Hall we became pretty close during my studies and teaching years in Alfred and now, for the past five years we're happily together in Connecticut! But that covers everyone in the family — except Annette — and it was our mother, Mary, who drew us close in the fall of 1979.

I was invited back to northern Maine to celebrate a wedding Mass for my cousin Sylvia's daughter in the same town where Annette and Fern lived. Annette had always been more like a mother than a big sister for me as far as I could remember. When she and Fern came home to visit we 'little ones' played with her kids and she was one of the 'adults' visiting with Mom and Dad and the other 'adult children' in the family! We never really had gotten a chance to just sit and gab as brother and sister, as two adults, two people, until that fall. Fern, Annette's husband, is a truck driver for *Coles Express,* driving all over the northeastern part of the country, I guess. I remember as kids whenever we saw one of the Coles' orange cab trucks approaching we'd be sure it was Fern! The night I arrived at their house in September, 1979, Fern had to work so that left Annette and I home alone, since all of their kids are now grown-up and settled on their own. I don't remember how we got started but I think Annette asked me a question about Mary and I surprised myelf by telling her pretty much of the foregoing story of 'Mary in my life. When I finished, she asked me if I knew anything about the Marion Movement of Priests in the world. I confessed I was ignorant of it and she began telling me the whole story. It wasn't so much what we shared, I guess, that night but *that* we shared what brought us very close together for the fisrt time that I can recall. It was such a precious gift! It was like having someone next door for years but never discovering who they were till some accident brought us together and we wished it had happened years earlier! Mary gave me the gift of my sister that night, a gift I shall always be grateful for! And Annette reinforced that FANTASTIC gift of Mary in my life, a reinforced gift that I was to cling to not too many months later as I watched the beautiful blossom of our ministry dream suddenly droop and all but die!

20

"A wild canary..."

"Pat, I think it's time to start over again", Bishop Reilly said compassionately in late June of 1980, as the two of us sat alone in the conference room at the Chancery Office in Norwich. We had taken a hard look, an honest look at where the ministry had come and both of us had come to realize that we were far afield of the goal, the dream, that had been the ministry's almost from its beginning. The ministry had grown big physically — it had five centers in the diocese at one point! It was beginning to do much to 'care' for the handicapped. The main center, God's Gift House, was there in Norwich to provide for their needs, to give them programs, etc. and several group homes were in the process of being set up. But there were problems, basically twofold problems, already appearing by late 1979 and all through the first half of 1980. In the midst of this excited growth structurally, the ministry actually seemed to be dying! Financially, the first big problem area, the ministry was just plain *broke!* "Pat, we have no money," Bishop Reilly had said to me when we had first talked about the ministry in the fall of 1975, "but I really believe the Lord wants this ministry so if you're willing to work with these conditions, let's get it started." And so, we had opened the ministry office under the presumption that if it truly was 'His work' He would indeed provide for it. Provide for it, He did! Donations began coming in to the new ministry almost as soon as it was begun. In March, just three months after the ministry had been founded, a friend called one Sunday morning and said "Did you read the Obituary Column this morning?" "No," I said, "with my vision I don't read any part of the newspaper very often." "Well," he came back, "you better read it this morning... your name is in it!" "Harvey," I said, "you're crazy!" I was sure he was pulling my leg. He insisted so I went and picked up the morning paper and turned to the Obituary Column. There, in bold print, was the headline *Memorial gifts to aid Brother Martin's work.* The strange thing was that I didn't recognize the name of the woman who had died. The notice stated that "Cecelia Lambert" had died and it was asked that in lieu of flowers, donations be made to aid *my work???* An address and telephone number were given so I called the family as soon as I could. Yes, Mrs. Lambert's daughter, Cathy (Lambert) Russi, told me, the article was correct. The Lamberts were cousins, I believe, to the Kellys, a family I knew very well. Two of their sons were handicapped and Mrs. Lambert had been very close to them.

Because of this, the family had decided to aid the new ministry in her memory! They aided that new ministry much more than simply with the many financial gifts that came in; George, Cecelia's husband, and the whole family became fast friends and supporters of the ministry and its work. Fran Russi, Cathy's husband, with his Colchester Auto-Body Shop became the 'answer' for much of the ministry's vehicle rehabilitation problems! And the Cecelia Lambert story is just one of hundreds of such ways that 'the Lord did indeed provide for the new, growing ministry' in its early days. It became my conviction, and often repeated pet phrase, those early months and years, that as long as we were 'doing His work' He would pay for it.

The ministry had flourished well its first couple of years. In the fall of 1976, Bishop Reilly had offically appointed Father James Carini, Director of the Ministry to the Deaf, for the diocese. Father Jim had worked with the deaf for almost eleven years up to that point. The following summer, 1977, his work with the deaf became full time and he had moved into God's Gift House with us. That same summer Bishop Reilly had appointed Sister Claire Beaulieu, of the Daughters of the Holy Spirit, Director for the Mentally Retarded and she too had her office at God's Gift House. What a family we had already! How well I recall our monthly get-togethers for prayer/discussion and dinner. Gerry, my brother, always joined us for those absolutely *crazy* dinners. The laughter and teasing that went on at those dinners always led us to wonder if we'd be welcomed back to those respective restaurants a second time! In the summer of 1978, Gerry Lachance had joined the ministry staff as 'Administrator' to free me from the administrative nitty gritties of the work, with ordination to the priesthood. Gerry and his wife, Barbara, had donated the equity from the sale of their own home as the down payment for what was intended to be the first of several 'group homes' for the handicapped operated by the ministry! The house purchased was in Wauregan, Connecticut, the northeast corner of the diocese. The Lachance family moved in as 'host family' for the house when it was purchased in the summer of 1978, and my brother and I gave up the apartment in Norwich and moved to 'Ave Maria House', as the new facility was named, to help support it. In March of 1979, with the donation of a print shop full of equipment, and the generous trucking and moving help of another dear friend of the ministry, James DeVivo of Willimantic, Connecticut, a 'training print shop' was set up in one of Jim DeVivo's buildings which he leased to the ministry for the purpose *at no charge!* The print shop, it was dreamed, would take in handicapped trainees and prepare them with marketable skills while accomplishing the printing needs of the ministry and other offices and parishes of the diocese.

Then the gas hike came. The cost of commuting daily to Norwich and to Willimantic became prohibitive. State programs which had begun to support trainees at the print shop were withdrawn a few months later. Purchased supplemental equipment, supplies, and training materials now had to be paid for from the shop's production. Donations to the ministry which had held to several thousand dollars a month even long after the drive for *God's Gift House* had ended, now dropped to only 'hundreds' each month. The bare operating expenses of the various facilities were unable to be met. The situation became critical in the fall of 1979; the staff gathered to study the situation; it was suggested a 'begging letter' go out to all of the ministry's mail recipients outlining the costs of operating the ministry and asking for support. Some five thousand dollars came in as a result of the letter – the first of its kind that had ever gone out from the ministry other than the actual campaign for the center. These generous gifts helped momentarily but they were but a stop-gap...

Many a night those months I went to bed wondering. I had always believed and stated that 'if we're doing His work He'll pay for it.' 'He' wasn't paying for it now! Was 'He' trying to tell me something. Was something wrong with the way the ministry was going?

I think the answer to the first problem, finances, came really through the second problem... we as a ministry were having less and less contact with the handicapped who had once been so involved with the ministry and we had almost no volunteer support at that time. Our volunteer Christmas luncheon, that December of 1979, brought a dozen people to the center. In February, 1977, with the planned kick-off for the drive for God's Gift House we had also begun our 'First Saturday Club' in the diocese. Modeled on a similar organization founded in New Jersey some twenty years previous and in which I had participated while living and working in the New York area, the First Saturday Club in our diocese was the monthly grouping of handicapped persons, their families and friends for renewal and inspiration in their efforts to discover and be the gifts they are called to be. The group, which has no defined membership and no dues, each month travels to a different parish church or facility in the diocese. The group's coming is advertised during the previous month in the parish's bulletin, so that local handicapped persons, shut-ins, and interested persons can feel free to participate in the Mass and luncheon. The aim is to visit every parish in the entire diocese! The idea of the group here in the diocese grew out of the social/informational group that had first formed when the ministry had begun 'Brother Pat's FANTASTIC Club!' The group had wanted to do something for the Church, for the community! By traveling to each parish the members of the group would affect that parish with their own spirit, courage, beliefs, etc. and they would also be instrumental in bringing local broken persons out! The group had limped for almost a year and a half, a dozen or so persons showing up each month! How many times we had questioned, 'Should we forget it?' But no, we had decided quitting wasn't the answer; the few 'old faithfuls' stuck with it and finally after a year and a half or so it had suddenly 'caught fire.' Today as much as a hundred and fifty or two hundred show up for some of the 'First Saturdays' and the fewest is usually about fifty or seventy-five. For sixty-six months now the group has not canceled a First Saturday! Its motto has come to be 'Come sleet or tornado, rain or shine, we don't cancel!'

During that whole period, however, of 1979-80, the First Saturday Club was practically the only program attended by the handicapped. There was no ministry sponsored retreat weekend in the fall of 1979 or in the spring of 1980; programs, prayer meetings, etc. were sparsely − if at all − attended by the handicapped. My dream as a priest had been to celebrate Mass and the sacraments for those who could not come to the Church, but now, after the dream of the priesthood had come true, I was getting fewer and fewer calls from the handicapped. Was the ministry perhaps 'not needed' anymore? Is that why the giving had all but stopped?

In February, 1980, I went 'on the road' alone for about three weeks. I looked up people I hadn't seen in a long time, volunteer families who had once been deeply involved and had now withdrawn, and the handicapped persons themselves all over the diocese. I left the community that had become my home − the Lachance family, my brother Gerry, and others who stayed at the house, and went back to sleeping on living room floors and couches for those three weeks. It felt good, too!

To every person and family I visited, I put two questions during the course of our conversations: *What's wrong with the ministry?* and *Why aren't you involved anymore? Why don't I hear from you?* At the beginning of Lent that year, on Ash Wednesday, discouraged and deeply troubled by the whole ministry situation, I had knelt beside my bed and cried for a long time. "What's wrong? Please, tell me what's wrong?"

My sister Annette had told me the previous fall about the *Marian Movement of Priests,* an affiliation of priests devoted in a special way to Mary. I had toyed for months with the idea of making the special consecration of my priesthood to Mary and thereby joining the movement but had never done so until that night. At the end of my cry, I could not understand why, the consecration came to mind. I took up the printed text and very slowly made the prayer my own, consecrating myself and my priesthood and my work for the spread of God's kingdom and the salvation of all His people. A deep peace came over me that night and I was able to fall asleep, but little changed with the ministry situation. It was that Lent that I went 'on the road again' for three weeks and by mid-March it seemed that I had at least part of my answer. To my question: *what's wrong with the ministry?...* most were vague and unable to put their finger on anything specific. But to my second question, *why aren't you involved anymore?...* they responded, almost as a chorus though they were asked separately and without preparation, "We're not needed." They didn't all use those words but their answers melted down to the same. And to the second part of that question, *why don't I hear from you anymore?...* they responded "We don't want to bother you at meals, on weekends, etc., in case you're involved with the community. Some who had had problems had been afraid to come to see me... "in case others were there, they'd feel like they were taking me away..."

I had had a Vow of Chastity as a brother for some twelve years before leaving the community to go on for the priesthood. Before ordination to the diaconate, I had made an Oath of Celibacy. For most people these are simply translated 'I promise not to get married!' And, I must confess, for me, practically, they didn't mean much more than that either until this time in March, 1980. We had often discussed in the novitiate and scholasticate theology courses the theology of the vow and the beautiful gift of virginity and it had all impressed me very much; I had not questioned the vow's importance. But, I can say honestly that I never saw the beauty of that vow until I began to look at its positive side during these weeks and months of 1980. It not only entailed not getting married, the negative side of the vow; it also demanded that total availabity to those I am called to serve, its positive side. My life had to speak to my people that I was not 'a' brother but *their* brother, not 'a' priest, but *their* priest. I thought back much those days to Bishop Reilly's words on ordination day, "He belongs to you, you know!" when he had talked about calling me 'Brother Pat' or 'Father Pat.' Had I, by living in the community, perhaps spoken nonverbally "Don't bother me when I'm home'?" The rectory at St. Mary's in Norwich, where I had stayed when I first came to the diocese, had quickly become merely the place I went to empty the suitcase and refill it again.

In April of that year, 1980, I moved from the community

residence in Norwich, where it had moved the previous fall to conserve commuting gas. Ave Maria House had gone back to its original dream, a group home centered with a family. Six physically handicapped persons lived there with a host family, Robert and Irene Demers and their eight children. They had taken over the house that fall, recruited the residents and were operating the Wauregan property from the residents' contributions and donations from well-wishers. The barn on the Wauregan property was, as yet, unused. With the help of some of those long lost volunteers, I built a tiny apartment in front of the barn's main room, and retained that main room as a chapel/multi-purpose center as the bishop had dedicated it the previous spring. The fourteen by thirty foot apartment, that Ray and Simonne Laliberty constructed for me, was more than adequate space for me to hang my hat and change suitcases as I went back on the road again! Ray and Simonne had helped in the furnishing of my very first office, on Hickory Street, in Norwich, and now they and other long, lost volunteers, like the Beauregards, who had given that first gift for the drive, moved all my things for me to 'my barn.' Ray and Simonne threw a 'Welcome Back On the Road' birthday party on the very floor they used to vacuum as my bed!!! I cried with relief as I saw all the people who came to say their enthusiastic *yes* to my move! But that was only the beginning move...

In May and June the diocesan 'budget hearings' had taken place for each ministry office in the diocese. It was then that Bishop Reilly had come together with the entire staff of our ministry and it was after these discussions with the staff and observations of the ministry operations that we had come to the conclusion, maybe it's time to begin again! The print shop had already closed in March. May Lou DeVivo, Jim's wife, who had replaced Sister Claire with the ministry to the mentally retarded a year before when Sister Claire had left to work in Appalachia, gave in her resignation that spring because of family needs at home. The diocesan Office of Community Ministries, which served the needs of the poor as our ministry did those of the handicapped, had had a hard time finding and maintaining space for a soup kitchen and other facilities for the poor of the downtown Norwich area. God's Gift House's main floor, approximately three thousand square feet of space, had been used very little for programming or other needs for the last year or so. None of the agencies and organizations that had needed space in its planning days were now using it. The second floor of the center had been used by the Diocesan Charismatic Renewal Office almost from the day the building was first opened. It was decided at that late June, 1980, meeting to turn God's Gift House into somewhat of a diocesan 'services center' — a center not run by the ministry for the handicapped but a center whose services were all available and accessible to the handicapped. The ministry for the poor would move its soup kitchen onto that main floor and its clothing or other outlets could use space on the floor below. The Ministry to the Deaf, under the direction of Father Jim Carini, retained its office at God's Gift House. Eventually an 'Office of Prison Ministry' for the diocese also found office space in the new diocesan services center. The Daughters of Isabella Chapel in memory of Claire Little remained intact on the first floor and, with a full-time chaplain for the center, served the needs of the whole downtown area!

The ministry for the handicapped would move its office to the barn in Wauregan and become a primarily 'on the road' ministry as it had been in its earlier days. All of the efforts and resources that had gone into the staffing, maintaining, and operation of the centers would now simply go into programs and services. It was a time filled with many, many mixed emotions when we began dismantling shelves, packing equipment and supplies, and moving all of this, and furniture from the center in Norwich to the barn in Wauregan. Many of the emotions centered around the *relief* feeling, like an albatross had just been taken from around our necks! I recalled the bishop's cautioning to my board way back at the beginning of the drive for the center — we don't want to hang a noose around Pat's neck! Somehow, it felt like the noose had finally been cut. But there were also feelings of failure, discouragement... brokenness as a ministry!

Happily, the business of building the office space in the barn and setting up shelves, etc. kept me too busy to dwell on the negative aspects of the move that summer. It was interesting that the two programs that survived the clean up were the First Saturday Club and Ave Maria House, both programs run by the handicapped themselves with the aid of volunteers, and both programs under the patronage of Mary. It was Mary in her apparitions at Fatima who had called people to dedicate five First Saturdays to praying for peace in the world and the conversion of Russia. It was that call of our blessed Mother that had led Mary Varrick, a handicapped woman in New Jersey, some two dozen years ago now to attempt to make those five First Saturdays, attending Mass and praying her Rosary on each of them. She's been at it — with hundreds of other persons in her area and probably a dozen 'off shoots' of her group like our own, for more than two hundred First Saturdays! Our own First Saturday Club had been coordinated almost from its very beginning in 1977 by a young woman, Sandra Parkinson, who is herself now totally blind. She had learned Braille in a ministry-sponsored class and had then put her new skill to work for the ministry! She had set up a 'telephone tree' in the diocese involving other handicapped persons contacting groups of handicapped individuals in their respective areas. During that time of decision when the ministry's newsletter didn't come out for almost a year, it was Sandy's telephone tree that kept me somewhat in touch with the handicapped for announcements, etc.

Based on the survival and success of the First Saturday Club through all the turmoil and ultimate dissolution of the ministry, it was decided that in our 'new beginnings' we would model the ministry on the First Saturday Club somewhat, using the group as the 'core' of the office. The ministry, which had begun as the Office of Special Religious Education and had become the Office of Ministries *for* the Handicapped, now changed its name once more with its new birth. It became the Office of Ministry *of* the Handicapped — it would not be a ministry to serve them so much as a ministry whereby they can serve others! As many opportunities as possible would be provided within the diocese ministry for handicapped persons themelves to do the work of the ministry. The ministry office in Wauregan today is manned by the young lady whom I taught to type in New York as a girl of ten years! It was at the time of bitterness with Brother Francis, you will recall, when Patty Mount of the Xavier Society for the Blind, had brought me into contact with Justine Hopper. The Hopper family had truly become 'my family'; I had never dreamed those days, as Justine struggled with the typewriter with her *one hand* and almost *no* useable sight, of the work that she was being prepared to do with me in the Diocese of Norwich, Connecticut, ten years later! I didn't even know the Diocese of Norwich existed — but He did. Justine today answers the phone, takes all the messages, keeps up the mailing list, etc., keeping the office running and thereby freeing me to be on the road.

My brother, Gerry, who had come to Norwich as custodian/watchman for our center came with me to Wauregan as driver/assistant. It was one excited Gerry who had burst into the center in February, 1979, flashing his hard-earned, just-received *driver's license!* He had never learned to drive before because of difficulties with reading. Hearing about the 'Literacy Volunteers of America' on the Norwich radio station one day, he had gone to the local library and registered for tutorial instruction in reading and math. He had gone from there to register at a drivers' training school... and now he was 'behind the wheel' for me! He had bought a car from a priest which now served to get the two of us from Maine to Pennsylvania to Delaware to New York City and Long

Island and, of course, all over Connecticut. "If you know the way," he'd say, "I'll get you there!" With me not being able to see the signs as we sped along the highways and Gerry having a hard time reading them... we were quite a pair on the road! He drove me around to program after program for almost a year but finally got somewhat restless with sitting through programs and house visits, etc., and decided in February, 1981, to go back to work, as he put it. He applied on his own, for the first time in his life, for several jobs, went for the interviews, and – in these days of such high unemployment – got himself a job in a local hospital in Norwich where he is now in his second year! He now has his own apartment and is a FANFASTIC model of a handicapped person making a difference in his world! He's not totally separated from the ministry, though. In addition to participating in many of our First Saturdays and other special programs, he's also now training handicapped volunteers to make rosaries for our parish missions and *Persons are Gifts Weekends.*

With the ministry reorganization well underway, a pilgrimage to Canada that August was a real *gift,* a chance to forget everything and gain some peace! We went to the Shrine of Our Lady of the Cape in Three Rivers, Quebec. Some fifty handicapped persons from the diocese made this, our second pilgrimage to the shrines of Quebec. In 1978, we had made our first such pilgrimage. With the turmoil and actual moving just about completed this year's trip couldn't have come at a better time.

This was to be my first pilgrimage with our people since my ordination to the priesthood; I had been a deacon on the previous trip. With all the pain and strife of that winter and spring in the ministry's dissolution and rebirth, I decided I wanted to make a good confession before the privilege of celebrating Mass for the first time at Mary's altar at the shrine. "Mary," I prayed as we arrived late that night, "please help me find a priest for confession tomorrow before the evening Mass."

All day long the following day, I went around with our group of pilgrims and all day long I never met a priest for confessions. Mass was scheduled that evening for 7:30 so my brother, Gerry, and I went to the church at 6:45 to pray. I was sure I would see a priest come in to prepare the altar for Mass and I would ask him to hear my confession. A seminarian did the preparations!

At 7:20 no priest had appeared so with somewhat of a heavy heart I went in to prepare for Mass. "Mary," I said as I was dressing for the celebration, "I asked you to find me a priest today and I can't believe you didn't!" As I finished that simple prayer the sacristy door opened, in walked a priest and he walked right over to me!

Motioning with his index finger he beckoned me to follow him out onto the 'Rosary Walk' adjacent to the church. As we were alone on the walk he turned to me and said, "I have to preach about our Lady tonight and I'd like to go to confession first. Would you please hear my confession?" I cried without shame! "I'll hear yours if you'll hear mine!" I blurted out! Mary didn't let me down.

We began the Mass together that night with close to a thousand English speaking pilgrims in the Church. At the time for the sermon, I sat down as Father began his beautiful testimony of Mary in his life. As I followed him from point to point I suddenly sat straight up. He was talking to me! "Father," he said, "would you please come and tell the people about Mary in your life!" *He knew nothing about Mary in my life!* I walked over to the pulpit, somewhat shaken by the surprise and then told that beautiful gathering of Mary's children the story of *The Gift of Mary* in my life after I had rejected her for so long! I concluded with the story of that very day how Mary had found me a priest just before I celebrated Mass at her altar!

That night, as I lay in my bed, I pondered the gift I had been given, the privilege of speaking about Mary to all those pilgrims *after my life of rejecting her!* If I were the one who had been rejected I could not picture myself calling upon the one who had thus shut me out for so long now to speak tenderly about me! Mary did just that! How dear, how loving and forgiving a Mother she is! What peace that pilgrimage brought!

As exciting as it was watching the *Office of Ministry of the Handicapped* come alive and begin to grow again and even become financially stable again – operating in the black for the past two years with a total budget each year of more than $65,000.00!!! – all the moves and changes were not readily accepted by the handicapped and friends of the ministry who watched with sorrow and even anger as *their* center was let go of.

After only a couple of months operating from the barn and being back on the road again, I *knew* that the move was right, but I had no idea how to communicate that to the many who still stood on the sidelines and just watched. In October, 1980, the newsletter, *Caring & Sharing,* finally came out again after many months lying dormant. The 'Spirit of God's Gift House' who had written at the time of the center's dedication and had promised to write again had indeed written again and again – in almost every issue of the newsletter that had come out since the opening of the center he had placed his pen. His letters had stirred our readers to tears and brought them back to laughter; the Spirit had made the handicapped see themselves as he had come to see them; he had often applauded them and even scolded and challenged them at times through his letters. The ministry's newsletter goes out to dozens of states and several provinces of Canada, to more than twenty-five hundred readers today! Readers all over had often written or called asking for a compilation of the Spirit's letters. The Spirit was read — and even *listened to...* by many.

As that October newsletter went to press, I wondered if and/or what the Spirit would write now that we had left 'his center.' He wrote...

"The Spirit of God's Gift House Writes..." — *October, 1980.*

"Dear Brother,

In the years that have passed since first we met, I have experienced many feelings very alien to my spiritural nature. Yes, Patrick, association with you has taken me to the pinacles of exhilaration and to the deepest depths of despair! The dream that was yours, the dream that I adopted, certainly did not lead us down the glory road, did it? The path we followed was paved with stumbling blocks, pock-marked with potholes, and crosspatched with pitfalls! But, we have survived! That is glorious and FANTASTIC in itself, Patrick!

Recently I wallowed in the deepest chasm of despair. I had no thoughts of survival or even continuance of the dream we share. I had overheard many conversations, listened to the many rumors of your leaving, and then, on a dismal day, you and your brother and two young men had begun to clear your belongings from my rooms. I was ready to give up. I was in a state of total collapse. You were leaving God's Gift House. It was all true. Patrick, need I tell you that my world was in total chaos! I retreated to my desolate third floor and there, amid the dust and litter of the years, I firmly made up my mind to stay there until my building crumbled around me. Never again, I promised myself, would I become involved with humans! I cried because you were leaving but the tears were more for the apparent loss of my beloved handicapped. Without you there, there would be no handicapped, Patrick, for you know that I have always said that you drew them to you as a magnet draws a pin! Yes, Patrick, I cried, I moaned, I ranted and raved! I even cursed the beautiful day when you had entered my life! And then, when I was at my lowest, it began to happen...

I have described it to you many times, Patrick... the low, moaning wind that stirred the dusty floor to life. I knew immediately that I am was near! I shrank into a dark corner, hoping that He would not find me, although I knew that He would.

I waited what seemed like hours for Him to speak, but, Patrick, the noise grew louder, the low moaning wind became a shrieking gale. Dust billowed all around me and loose plaster fell heavily from the time-ravaged walls! I cowered in my corner, certain that all was ending. The dream I am in His Godly wrath was going to destroy everything! Surely this wind, stronger than the several hurricanes that I have witnessed, would tear my beloved building from its foundations!

Then, amid the howl of the wind I could hear voices, thousands of voices, as if a hoard of unseen beings were chanting at me. The voices chanted one word over and over, again and again... Choose! Choose! Choose! I had no idea what they meant, Patrick, Choose, but Choose what?

Suddenly it was quiet, as though every beating heart on earth had been stilled at the same instant. The silence was deafening. A ray of sunlight streamed in through a skylight window. The dust was still swirling but slowly settling back to its accustomed place. I closed my eyes and held my breath in utter awe of what had happened.

"Our Father is quite upset with you, Spirit!" It was a soft, musical voice, a voice filled with peace and good will. My eyes flew open, wider than they had ever opened before. A young man stood in the ray of sunlight, a beautiful young man, dressed in a garb that is very different from the dress that is affected today. His flowing white robe shimmered in the sunlight, or was the sunlight coming from His robe? I couldn't tell. His bearded face glowed with an inner light; sort of an aura surrounded His whole being. He repeated with emphasis: "Our Father is quite upset with you, Spirit!"

I was very confused. I stammered and finally said, "You said 'Our Father?' Then You are.." My voice failed me at the very thought of what I was going to say. He smiled a radiant smile and finished my thought in a soft voice" ...the Son." He said it so simply as though it was the least thing in all this universe. "Spirit," he continued, "you are very dense." He smiled as though to calm me. "I would say that you have a handicap of your own — borderline stupidity!" He laughed low, and very quietly. I didn't care if He called me stupid, Patrick, not at all.

"Are you chained to this building, Spirit?" He didn't wait for me to answer. "What is most important to you, this building or our people?" Before I could answer him, Patrick, he continued. "Our

190

Father gave you many gifts, Spirit. He gave you feelings and emotions. He made you so humanlike that you felt pain and sadness, joy and happiness. He let you laugh and cry. He gave you another gift, too, Spirit, one that you have used occasionally but seem to have forgotten in your present distraught state.

He paused as if to give me time to digest what he had said. Then He continued sternly, as an older brother lecturing a spoiled little boy. "You have the gift to choose what you want to do, what you want to be, where you want to go. Use your gift wisely, Spirit.!

As He finished the wind again began to moan and the dust began to swirl in eddies around Him. His form slowly began to fade from my sight. "Don't go!" I pleaded, "stay and tell me what to do!" His voice came back to me faintly through the moaning wind, "Choose ...choose..."

I stood there for a few minutes. Choose?... Choose between building and people... That had to be what he'd meant. My brain was in a whirl, Patrick. Without knowing that I had moved I found myself on the first floor of my building in the center of the main room. My eyes darted about the room, looking for what? I don't know, but taking in everything. One item stood out, a picture you had left behind. It was the one of the small crippled boy and with him was the young man who had just appeared to me, The young man was beckoning to the boy, 'Come, follow Me.'

I wandered into what had been your office. There in a corner, forgotten in your haste, was a small Bible. A slight breeze wafted through the room. The pages of the book fluttered and turned. I looked at the open page, Patrick, and the words seemed to jump off the page to my eyes, "LEAVE ALL OF YOUR WORLDLY POSSESSIONS, COME FOLLOW ME!"

My mind was racing back over the years, things that had happened, words that had been spoken... One phrase kept repeating itself to me. It was what your Bishop had said during a handicapped retreat at Camp Hemlock. Do you remember, Patrick? He said that wherever the handicapped, the Spirit of God's Gift House would be! He didn't speak of me as just the spirit of a building; he truly believed that I was the spirit of the handicapped themselves! Everything clicked into place at once, Patrick! I made my choice in that instant! I took one more look around the rooms, Patrick; you will note that I did not say 'my' rooms! They were still beautiful. They still rang with the sounds of my beloved handicapped. After that last look I walked slowly out the door, no backward glances, no tears over departure. I was embarking on a new adventure. I was picking up the same old dream. I had made my choice, wisely, I hope, to be with our people.

I will leave you now, Patrick, but I shall always be with you in your quest — no, OUR quest — to find the handicapped wherever they are and to minister to them.

With the Peace of the great I AM,
The Spirit... OF THE HANDICAPPED

With that one letter *The Spirit of the Handicapped* accomplished what my heart ached for but what I had never dreamed could be accomplished! He brought the magnet and the pins back together! In October of that year, just after the letter from the spirit appeared, I took a dare. I have never held my breath so fearfully as with that dare. I offered a 'renewal' *Persons are Gifts Weekend.* "Will they come?" I wondered. I didn't dare believe they would. I knew I couldn't condemn them if they didn't. But *they did.* They came in hesitantly Friday night but I just thanked our Daddy that *they were there!* Saturday afternoon's talk is called *"People Who Need People are the Luckiest People in the World."* When it came my turn to share in the talk, I scrapped what I had written, looked at those beautiful people whom I had missed so dearly without realizing it, and I shared with them how I had needed them to be there that weekend, how crushed I would have been had they, understandably, chosen not to get involved again, how I needed them to be a part of 'us... We floated to supper together on our tears that night!

In October, 1981, just a bit more than a year after the ministry reorganization, the Spirit who had done so much to mold and rejuvenate the ministry joined the ministry with his wife in a brand new way. Don James and his wife, Dotty, had been a part of the ministry with their whole family almost from its very beginning. Their son, Don — DJ as many know him — had been one of the ministry's first volunteers, running the mimeograph to print the first newsletter issues and helping out in a hundred other ways in the Hickory Street office and at the center. He and a couple of friends had made the sign for the new center. He started the center's first print shop in the vault and then in the basement and when the Willimantic print shop, God's Gift House Press had gone into operation he had gone on the staff in the art and layout department. When the print shop had quickly run into trouble he was one of the first to be let go. Don and Dotty and all their kids and countless families like the Smiths and the Beauregards for several years had collected, assembled, stapled, folded, addressed and mailed the ministry's newsletter from their living rooms and kitchens. Their fancy collating machines were their furniture — spreading out the various colored sheets on chairs, tables, and even the floors, one on top of each other, gathering up each bundle, stapling... *greater love than this...* They had been with the ministry for its picnics and First Saturdays... and they had stayed with it even through the turmoil. Dotty had been transportation coordinator for the ministry almost from its beginning, finding rides with volunteers for any and all of the handicapped for the various programs. How many times, late at night, my phone would ring and it would be Dotty — "Father Pat, do you know *anyone* in (this area or that) who can bring him/her down to the program? I don't want to see him/her not come." I'd think of a few names and she'd hang up and call them. *Always* I got a call back saying, "We've got 'em!"

As the new ministry began to grow and I was *free* to get back on the road more and more requests for programs, retreats, days of awareness, days of recollection, etc., began coming in not only from all over the diocese but from all over the country and a good deal of *Canada!* In September, 1980, the first 'Parish Mission on Brokenness in Our lives' was done for a small parish in central Pennsylvania. It was a magnificent way to reach out to the unbranded handicapped — the alcoholics, divorced, widowed and widowered, the emotionally and/or psychologically broken, the financially broken — as well as to the physically, visually, hearing, mentally impaired, etc., with the ministry's message of *'Giftedness in Suffering!'* Since that parish mission at least a dozen more have been done in Connecticut, Michigan, Ohio, and several dioceses in Ontario, not to mention *South Dakota! The Persons are Gifts Retreat Weekends* have spread to a dozen different dioceses!

As I looked at the heavy schedule of on-the-road work last fall something began eating me inside. *I need help!* Help to keep up the at-home work while the on-the-road work goes on. While we had greatly simplified the nitty gritty type of work by the ministry reorganization, that simplified work still had to be kept up and I had tried to manage on my own since June of 1980, when Gerry Lachance had gone back to the work he had before coming to the ministry. With my vision, reading and handwriting are quite a chore — as is reading anything. That makes mail handling quite a problem. *I needed help.* Again, I went to my bishop. What a gift! How does he hold up! I'm not the only one, I'm sure, who wets his shoulders with tears!!! I wanted someone to help; I wanted a handicapped person who would know and feel the life frustrations, challenges and joys of other handicapped persons. But I wanted someone also who would be able to carry on with and for me in challenging the handicapped of our diocese to *be our ministry, to be the church* in their world! Who could I find? It was obvious – 'our' Spirit and his wife! No wonder he knew 'us' so well and touched so deeply our inmost thoughts and struggles and joys in his letters. Don James himself had been laid up for a full year on his back with tuberculosis of the spine – lying on a hospital bed in his living room he had celebrated Christmas and New Years, Easter and birthdays with his family and friends. He had recovered, somewhat, from that and other surgeries but had been gifted with that keen understanding and sensitivity for *us,* the broken of the world, as we see it and taste it in his 'letters' as our Spirit! Dotty not only cared for her Don at home through that year but has served for years the needs of the homebound as a 'home care aide' with United Workers of Norwich. Bishop Reilly agreed at once that, if they would, they should be our 'Program Coordinators' for the diocesan ministry of the handicapped. And what a gift they have been as such since last November! Don retains his own regular job to support his family and the two of them work for the ministry *full time* besides – paying the bills, working on the mail, putting the newsletters together, arranging programs and all the nitty gritties that go with them. It is their main goal to involve the handicapped themselves in the day-to-day running of the ministry and especially in active participation in their world! And what a gift they are to me as I'm off doing a program here at home or in North Bay, Ontario, just to know that 'things are well at home!'

"Don't you see what God is doing?" Jeanne of Ellington, Connecticut, said as we went over the outline for this chapter of this book. We had gone over the materials for this book in total detail, chapter by chapter and from all her questioning and taping she had prepared the outline for the preparation of this book. "What has He done *every time* you've gotten yourself trapped in some organization that caged you in away from your people? He's stepped in, broken the cage and set you free!" she said, pleading for me to see it as she seemed to see it so clearly! I had cried all the while I had shared with her the story of the dissolution of the ministry, the 'going back to the beginning.' "Your bishop saw it," she said. "You've got to be free, free to go to your people wherever and whenever you find them – and you keep getting yourself trapped in structures. But 'He' has always come through and set you free. And now He's done it again!"

Christmas of 1979 was right in the middle of the ministry struggles. The financial problems were beginning to emerge and the handicapped were being heard less and less from. For Christmas I received a book from dear friends in Ontario, Daniel and Mary Dauvin, devoted followers of Francis, the Saint of Assisi. The book they sent me was *"Francis: The Journey and The Dream.* * Inside the book was a note, "Dear Father Pat," it read. "Read the Chapter called 'A Wild Canary' first, p. 117. Francis had a dream. You too have a dream given to you by our Daddy. Some will dream with us; others won't, but we can only live and die for our dreams' God Bless!" The chapter cited spoke of Francis watching his brothers, who once had been totally free and unattached, free to roam wherever needed, wherever God called them, with no neat and ordered life to cling to, now settling down into more comfortable routines of life and homes. He had anguished over the scene, and tried to prevent the loss of 'the dream' but had been frustrated in his efforts. Now as he prayed for light as to what his brothers should be like, he had seen a wild canary alight on the ledge of his mud hermitage; the bird had sung and carried on with wild abandon with no apparent regard for Francis — but it had totally distracted Francis from his worries for the brothers. Then the bird winged away as quickly and unannounced as it had come! And as it left, Francis knew he had been given a parable of his brothers. They too should be wild canaries, free to carry on and sing and praise the Lord so that all who saw them might be distracted for some time at least from their own worries and pains and ills and might turn to their God and to each other. For Francis it meant his brothers should be as available and free as a bird on everyone's window sill! What a calling!

As I look back with you over these past twenty nine years since that day when I first saw that jack-o-lantern in the hands of that thoughtful minister, I goosebump with awe at what God has done with one of his little birds. He's loved that little bird so much in every joy and in every pain of his short life and He's given that little wild canary a song to sing on everybody's window sill!

> *He loves me. He loves me!*
> *He loves me as I am, oh yes, He loves me!*
> *Yes, He loved me yesterday and yes, He'll love me still tomorrow!*
> *For He loves me just today the way I am!*
>
> *He loves me. He loves me!*
> *And all He asks is that I let Him love me!*
> *Let Him love me as He chooses with no thoughts for wins or losses,*
> *Let Him love me as I am is all He asks!*

* *Francis: The Journey and The Dream, by Murray Bodo, St. Anthony Messenger Press, 1972, A Wild Canary, page 117.*

He knows me. He knows me!
Better than I know myself, oh yes, He knows me!
Who I was the other day and who I will become tomorrow!
But He loves me just the same the way I am!

He calls me. He calls me!
He calls me as I am to spread His love!
Knowing well who I have been, who I will be, who I am,
Yet, He calls me just the same to spread His love!

He frees me. He frees me!
He frees me to say yes whenever He calls me!
Showing me His own compassion, love, and care and understanding,
He frees me to say my "yes" when He calls me!

He loves me! He loves me!
He loves me as I am, oh yes, He loves me!
Finding me wherever I am He gently guides me by the hand,
For He loves me as I am, oh He loves me!
For He loves me as I am, oh He loves me!

Dear Brother,

Well, Patrick, I finished it. I really couldn't put your manuscript down once I reached the part where you came to Norwich, Connecticut. After all, you were now telling about a part of your life that I was very aware of. I thought I knew all about those years... the start of your ministry... the campaign to establish a center for the handicapped... the roadblocks on the way to your ordination, but there were many things that I didn't know or maybe didn't remember.

I was thrilled to see that my poor literary efforts had been placed in your book. That first letter, my friend surely remembers the night at God's Gift House when I made myself known to Him... I imagine that many times He has wished that He had paid no attention to my whisperings, that He had just walked away thinking that it was just the wind blowing in through a half opened window. I don't know what I would have done if He had ignored me... how would I have ever made my plight known to you, how would I have ever come to know I AM?

For me, the chapters toward the end of the book, from the opening of God's Gift House until the present time, were like a review of my own history. It was wonderful to remember all of the good times, the fun and the laughter that echoed all around me in those rooms on Main Street. I cried a little as I read of the poor times, the mistakes that were made and the struggle that took place to keep the ministry from dying.

As I read the part, where you so kindly included my ramblings about leaving 'my building,' I had the feeling that I AM was very near me... He didn't make His usual noisy approach, not even a whisper... but He was there. And I could almost hear Him saying to me, "You made the right choice, you have grown much wiser over the years. Patrick and you are a part of each other. Continue to grow in your love and understanding of the handicapped with him."

I never thought in the beginning, Patrick, that some day I would read about you... get all of the answers to my questions about you... and find that you considered me so much a part of you. I adopted your dream... you made me an integral part of it.

Your story is FANTASTIC, Patrick... it should make whoever reads it stop in their tracks. It should make them want to share in the dream... make them want to be a part of that wonderful, wacky group that follows along with that very FANTASTIC priest, who just happens to be 'my brother.'

Enough, Patrick, I am going to read your story again. I may have missed something... some part where my eyes were blurred with tears of remembrance, or where I was chuckling about some glorious time we shared together. I can't foretell the future of your story, Patrick. I hope that it will be a great success, a million-seller if you want. I do know that your life and your ministry have weathered the storms and trials... and that both your life and 'our' ministry will be a smashing success. How do I know that, you are wondering. I know because I AM has told me it would happen the way He wants it to happen... His will is our future... Patrick, my brother, we can not fail.

With the peace and love of the great I AM
The Spirit of the Handicapped